OpenACC™ for Programmers

Concepts and Strategies

Edited by

Sunita Chandrasekaran
Guido Juckeland

Addison-Wesley

Boston • Columbus • Indianapolis • New York • San Francisco • Amsterdam • Cape Town
Dubai • London • Madrid • Milan • Munich • Paris • Montreal • Toronto • Delhi • Mexico City
São Paulo • Sydney • Hong Kong • Seoul • Singapore • Taipei • Tokyo

Library of Congress Control Number: 2017945500

ISBN-13: 978-0-13-469428-3
ISBN-10: 0-13-469428-7

1 17

OpenACC™ for Programmers

*To all students, programmers, and computational scientists
hungry for knowledge and discoveries—
may their work make this world a more open, tolerant,
peaceful, livable, and lovable place for all of us,
regardless of gender, origin, race, or belief!*

Contents

Chapter 12: Innovative Research Ideas Using OpenACC, Part II 237

Foreword

In the previous century, most computers used for scientific and technical programming consisted of one or more general-purpose processors, often called CPUs, each capable of carrying out a diversity of tasks from payroll processing through engineering and scientific calculations. These processors were able to perform arithmetic operations, move data in memory, and branch from one operation to another, all with high efficiency. They served as the computational motor for desktop and personal computers, as well as laptops. Their ability to handle a wide variety of workloads made them equally suitable for word processing, computing an approximation of the value of pi, searching and accessing documents on the web, playing back an audio file, and maintaining many different kinds of data. The evolution of computer processors is a tale of the need for speed: In a drive to build systems that are able to perform more operations on data in any given time, the computer hardware manufacturers have designed increasingly complex processors. The components of a typical CPU include the arithmetic logic unit (ALU), which performs simple arithmetic and logical operations, the control unit (CU), which manages the various components of the computer and gives instructions to the ALU, and cache, the high-speed memory that is used to store a program's instructions and data on which it operates. Most computers today have several levels of cache, from a small amount of very fast memory to larger amounts of slower memory.

Application developers and users are continuously demanding more compute power, whether their goal is to be able to model objects more realistically, analyze more data in a shorter time, or for faster high-resolution displays. The growth in compute power has enabled, for example, significant advances in the ability of weather forecasters to predict our weather for days, even weeks, in the future and for auto manufacturers to produce fuel-efficient vehicles. In order to meet that demand, the computer vendors were able to shrink the size of the different features of a processor in order to configure more transistors, the tiny devices that are actually responsible for performing calculations. But as they got smaller and more densely packed, they also got hotter and hotter. At some point, it became clear that a new approach was needed if faster processing speeds were to be obtained.

Thus multicore processing systems were born. In such a system, the actual compute logic, or core, of a processor is replicated. Each core will typically have its own ALU and CU but may share one or more levels of cache and other memory with other cores. The cores may be connected in a variety of different ways and will typically share some hardware resources, especially memory. Virtually all of our laptops, desktops, and clusters today are built from multicore processors.

Each of the multiple cores in a processor is capable of independently executing all of the instructions (such as add, multiply, and branch) that are routinely carried out by a traditional, single-core processor. Hence the individual cores may be used to run different programs simultaneously, or they can be used collaboratively to speed up a single application. The actual gain in performance that is observed by an application running on multiple cores in parallel will depend on how well it has exploited the capabilities of the individual cores and how efficiently their interactions have been managed. Challenges abound for the application developer who creates a multicore program. Ideally, each core contributes to the overall outcome continuously. For this to (approximately) happen, the workload needs to be evenly distributed among cores and organized to minimize the time that any core is waiting, possibly because it needs data that is produced on another core. Above all, the programmer must try to avoid nontrivial amounts of sequential code, or regions where only one core is active. This insight is captured in Amdahl's law, which makes the point that, no matter how fast the parallel parts of a program are, the speedup of the overall computation is bounded by the fraction of code that is sequential. To accomplish this, an application may in some cases need to be redesigned from scratch.

Many other computers are embedded in telephone systems, toys, printers, and other electronic appliances, and increasingly in household objects from washing machines to refrigerators. These are typically special-purpose computing chips that are designed to carry out a certain function or set of functions and have precisely the hardware needed for the job. Oftentimes, those tasks are all that they are able to perform. As the demands for more complex actions grow, some of these appliances today are also based on specialized multicore processors, something that increases the available compute power and the range of applications for which they are well suited.

Although the concept of computer gaming has been around since sometime in the 1960s, game consoles for home use were first introduced a decade later and didn't take off until the 1980s. Special-purpose chips were designed specifically for them, too. There was, and is, a very large market for gaming devices, and considerable effort has therefore been expended on the creation of processors that are very efficient at rapidly constructing images for display on a screen or other output device. In the meantime, the graphics processing units (GPUs) created for this marketplace have become very powerful computing devices. Designed to meet a specific purpose, namely to enable computer gaming, they are both specialized and yet capable of running a great variety of games with potentially widely differing content. In other words, they are not general-purpose computers, but neither are they highly tuned for one very specific sequence of instructions. GPUs were designed to support, in particular, the rendering of sequences of images as smoothly and realistically as possible. When a game scene is created in response to player input—a series of images are produced and displayed at high speed—there is a good deal of physics involved. For instance, the motion of grass can be simulated in order to determine how the individual stalks will sway in the (virtual) wind, and shadow effects can be calculated and used to provide a realistic experience. Thus it is not too surprising that hardware designed for games might be suitable for some kinds of technical computing. As we shall shortly see, that is indeed the case.

Very large-scale applications such as those in weather forecasting, chemistry and pharmaceuticals, economics and financing, aeronautics, and digital movies, require significant amounts of compute power. New uses of computing that require exceptional hardware speed are constantly being discovered. The systems that are constructed to enable them are known as high-performance computing (HPC) clusters. They are built from a collection of computers, known as nodes, connected by a high-speed network. The nodes of many, although not all, such systems are built using essentially the same technology as our desktop systems. When multicore processors entered the desktop and PC markets, they were also configured as nodes of HPC platforms. Virtually all HPC platforms today have multicore nodes.

The developers and operators of HPC systems have been at the forefront of hardware innovation for many decades, and advances made in this area form the backdrop and motivation for the topic of this book. IBM's Roadrunner (installed at the Department of Energy's Los Alamos National Laboratory [LANL] in 2008) was the first computing system to achieve 1 petaflop/s (1,000 trillion floating-point calculations per second) sustained performance on a benchmark (the Linpack TOP500) that is widely used to assess a system's speed on scientific application code. Its nodes were an example of what is often called a hybrid architecture: They not only introduced dual-core processors into the node but also attached Cell processors to the multicores. The idea was that the Cell processor could execute certain portions of the code much faster than the multicore. However, the code for execution on the Cell had to be specifically crafted for it; data had to be transferred from the multicore's memory to Cell memory and the results then returned. This proved to be difficult to accomplish as a result of the tiny amount of memory available on the Cell.

People at large data centers in industry as well as at public institutions had become concerned about the rising cost of providing computing services, especially the cost of the computers' electricity consumption. Specialized cores such as the Cell were expected to offer higher computational efficiency on suitable application code at a very reasonable operating cost. Cores with these characteristics were increasingly referred to as accelerators. At LANL they encountered a major challenges with respect to the deployment of accelerators in hybrid nodes. The application code had to be nontrivially modified in order to exploit the Cell technology. Additionally, the cost of transferring data and code had to be amortized by the code speedup.

Titan (installed at the Department of Energy's Oak Ridge National Laboratory in 2013) was a landmark computing system. At 20 pflop/s (20,000 trillion calculations per second, peak) and with more than 18,000 nodes, it was significantly more powerful than Roadrunner. Its hybrid nodes, each a powerful computing system in its own right, were configured with 16-core AMD processors and an NVIDIA Tesla K20 GPU. Thus graphics processing units had entered the realm of high-performance computing in particular, and of scientific and technical computing in general. The device market had always been concerned with the power consumption of its products, and GPUs promised to deliver particularly high levels of performance with comparatively low power consumption. As with the Cell processor, however, the application programs required modification in order to be able to benefit from the GPUs. Thus the provision of a suitable programming model to facilitate the necessary adaptation was of paramount importance. The programming model that was developed to support Titan's users is the subject of this book.

Today, we are in an era of innovation with respect to the design of nodes for HPC systems. Many of the fastest machines on the planet have adopted the ideas pioneered by Titan, and hence GPUs are the most common hardware accelerators. Systems are emerging that will employ multiple GPUs in each node, sometimes with very fast data transfer capabilities between them. In other developments, technology has been under construction to enable multicore CPUs to share memory—and hence data—directly with GPUs without data transfers. Although there will still be many challenges related to the efficient use of memory, this advancement will alleviate some of the greatest programming difficulties. Perhaps more importantly, many smaller HPC systems, as well as desktop and laptop systems, now come equipped with GPUs, and their users are successfully exploiting them for scientific and technical computing. GPUs were, of course, designed to serve the gaming industry, and this successful adaptation would have been unthinkable without the success stories that resulted from the Titan installation. They, in turn, would not have been possible without an approachable programming model that meets the needs of the scientific application development community.

Other kinds of node architecture have recently been designed that similarly promise performance, programmability, and power efficiency. In particular, the idea of manycore processing has gained significant traction. A manycore processor is one that is inherently designed for parallel computing. In other words, and in contrast to multicore platforms, it is not designed to support general-purpose, sequential computing needs. As a result, each core may not provide particularly high levels of performance: The overall computational power that they offer is the result of aggregating a large number of the cores and deploying them collaboratively to solve a problem. To accomplish this, some of the architectural complexities of multicore hardware are jettisoned; this frees up space that can be used to add more, simpler cores. By this definition, the GPU actually has a manycore design, although it is usually characterized by its original purpose. Other hardware developers are taking the essential idea behind its design—a large number of cores that are intended to work together and are not expected to support the entire generality of application programs—and using it to create other kinds of manycore hardware, based on a different kind of core and potentially employing different mechanisms to aggregate the many cores. Many such systems have emerged in HPC, and innovations in this area continue.

The biggest problem facing the users of Titan, its successor platforms, and other manycore systems is related to the memory. GPUs, and other manycores, have relatively small amounts of memory per core, and, in most existing platforms, data and code that are stored on the multicore host platform must be copied to the GPU via a relatively slow communications network. Worse, data movement expends high levels of electricity, so it needs to be kept to the minimum necessary. As mentioned, recent innovations take on this problem in order to reduce the complexity of creating code that is efficient in terms of execution speed as well as power consumption. Current trends toward ever more powerful compute nodes in HPC, and thus potentially more powerful parallel desktops and laptops, involve even greater amounts of heterogeneity in the kinds of cores configured, new kinds of memory and memory organization, and new strategies for integrating the components. Although these advances will not lead to greater transparency in the hardware, they are expected to reduce the difficulty of creating efficient code employing accelerators. They will also increase the range of systems for which OpenACC is suitable.

—Dr. Barbara Chapman

Professor of Applied Mathematics and Statistics,
and of Computer Science, Stony Brook University

Director of Mathematics and Computer Science,
Brookhaven National Laboratory

Preface

Welcome to *OpenACC™ for Programmers*. This book reflects a collaborative effort from 19 highly established authors, from academia and public research as well as industry. It was the common goal of the authors to assemble a collection of chapters that can be used as a systematic introduction to parallel programming using OpenACC. We designed the chapters to build on one another so that they would be useful in a classroom setting. Hence, it is highly likely that you, dear reader, are a student who signed up for this potentially daunting parallel programming class. Please rest assured that you made the right choice with this class. Compute devices no longer come in nonparallel types, and parallel programming is more important than ever.

How This Book Is Organized

It was our goal to introduce OpenACC as one way to express parallelism in small incremental steps to not overwhelm you. Here is how the book is organized.

- The first three chapters serve as an introduction to the concepts behind OpenACC and the tools for OpenACC development.

- Chapters 4–7 take you through your first real-world OpenACC programs and reveal the magic behind compiling OpenACC programs, thereby introducing additional concepts.

- Chapter 8–10 cover advanced topics, such as alternatives to OpenACC, low-level device interaction, multidevice programming, and task parallelism.

- Chapters 11 and 12 serve as a look into the diverse field of research in OpenACC implementation of potential new language features.

Most chapters contain a few exercises at the end to review the chapter contents. The solutions as well as the code examples used in the chapters are available online at https://github.com/OpenACCUserGroup/openacc_concept_strategies_ book. This URL also presents a slide deck for each chapter to help teachers kick-start their classes.

Join OpenACC User Group and Register on Informit.com

Because it has been our pleasure to work with so many friends from the (extended) OpenACC family on this book, we also want to extend an invitation to you to join the OpenACC User Group and become a family member as well. You can find access to all OpenACC resources at https://www.openacc.org.

Register your copy of *OpenACC™ for Programmers* at informit.com/register for convenient access to downloads, updates, and/or corrections as they become available (you must log in or create a new account). Enter the product ISBN (9780134694283) and click Submit. Once the process is complete, you will find any available bonus content under "Registered Products." If you would like to be notified of exclusive offers on new editions and updates, please check the box to receive email from us.

Acknowledgments

This book would not have been possible without a multitude of people who are not listed as contributors. The idea of the book was originated by Duncan Poole, the longtime OpenACC president. He wanted to offer not only online material but also really old-fashioned printed material so that students and interested readers can use this book to uncover the magic of parallel programming with OpenACC. When Duncan could not pursue this idea any further, he passed the torch to Sunita and Guido, and the result is now finally in all our hands.

We are eternally grateful to our helpers in keeping the flame going:

- Pat Brooks and Julia Levites from NVIDIA, for bringing us in contact with publishers and answering questions that require inside knowledge

- Laura Lewin and Sheri Replin—our editors—and production manager Rachel Paul and copy editor Betsy Hardinger for guiding us safely through the maze of actually generating a book

- Our chapter reviewers: Mat Colgrove, Rob Faber, Kyle Friedline, Roberto Gomperts, Mark Govett, Andreas Herten, Maxime Hugues, Max Katz, John Larson, Junjie Li, Sanhu Li, Meifeng Lin, Georgios Markomanolis, James Norris, Sergio Pino, Ludwig Schneider, Thomas Schwinge, Anne Severt, and Peter Steinbach

Some chapters would not have been possible without assistants to the contributors. Many thanks to Lingda Li, Masahiro Nakao, Hitoshi Murai, Mitsuhisa Sato, Akihiro Tabuchi, and Taisuke Boku!

Have we already thanked our contributors who went with us on this crazy journey, never let us down, and kept delivering content on time?

THANK YOU all.

—*Sunita Chandrasekaran and Guido Juckeland*

About the Contributors

Randy Allen is director of advanced research in the Embedded Systems Division of Mentor Graphics. His career has spanned research, advanced development, and start-up efforts centered around optimizing application performance. Dr. Allen has consulted on or directly contributed to the development of most HPC compiler efforts. He was the founder of Catalytic, Inc. (focused on compilation of MATLAB for DSPs), as well as a cofounder of Forte Design Systems (high-level synthesis). He has authored or coauthored more than 30 papers on compilers for high-performance computing, simulation, high-level synthesis, and compiler optimization, and he coauthored the book *Optimizing Compilers for Modern Architectures*. Dr. Allen earned his AB summa cum laude in chemistry from Harvard University, and his PhD in mathematical sciences from Rice University.

James Beyer is a software engineer in the NVIDIA GPU software organization. He is currently a cochair of the OpenMP accelerator subcommittee as well as a member of both the OpenMP language committee and the OpenACC technical committee. Prior to joining NVIDIA, James was a member of the Cray compiler optimization team. While at Cray he helped write the original OpenACC specification. He was also a member of the Cray OpenMP and OpenACC runtime teams. He received his PhD in CS/CE from the University of Minnesota.

Sunita Chandrasekaran is an assistant professor and an affiliated faculty with the Center for Bioinformatics & Computational Biology (CBCB) at the University of Delaware. She has coauthored chapters in the books *Programming Models for Parallel Computing*, published by MIT Press, and *Parallel Programming with OpenACC*, published by Elsevier, 2016. Her research areas include exploring high-level programming models and its language extensions, building compiler and runtime implementations and validating and verifying implementations and their conformance to standard specifications. She is a member of the OpenMP, OpenACC, and SPEC HPG communities. Dr. Chandrasekaran earned her PhD in computer science engineering from Nanyang Technological University (NTU), Singapore, for creating a high-level software stack for FPGAs.

Barbara Chapman is a professor of applied mathematics and statistics, and of computer science, at Stony Brook University, where she is also affiliated with the Institute for Advanced Computational Science. She also directs Computer Science and Mathematics Research at the Brookhaven National Laboratory. She has performed research on parallel programming interfaces and the related implementation technology for more than 20 years and has been involved in several efforts to develop community standards for parallel programming, including OpenMP, OpenACC, and OpenSHMEM. Her group created the OpenUH compiler that enabled practical experimentation with proposed extensions and implementation techniques. Dr. Chapman has coauthored more than 200 papers and two books. She obtained a BSc with 1st Class Honours in mathematics from the University of Canterbury, and a PhD in computer science from Queen's University of Belfast.

Robert Dietrich studied information systems technology at the TU Dresden and graduated in 2009. His focus as a junior researcher and his diploma thesis were about programming of FPGAs in the context of high-performance computing. After graduation, he worked as research associate on the support of hardware accelerators and coprocessors in known performance tools such as Score-P and Vampir. His research interests revolve around programming and analysis of scalable heterogeneous applications.

Lin Gan is a postdoctoral research fellow in the Department of Computer Science and Technology at Tsinghua University, and the assistant director of the National Supercomputing Center in Wuxi. His research interests include HPC solutions to geo-science applications based on hybrid platforms such as CPUs, FPGAs, and GPUs. Gan has a PhD in computer science from Tsinghua University and has been awarded the ACM Gordon Bell Prize (2016), the Tsinghua-Inspur Computational Geosciences Youth Talent Award (2016), and the most significant paper award by FPL 2015.

David Gutzwiller is a software engineer and head of high-performance computing at NUMECA-USA, based in San Francisco, CA. David joined NUMECA in 2009 after completion of a graduate degree in aerospace engineering from the University of Cincinnati. His graduate research was focused on the automated structural design and optimization of turbomachinery components. Since joining NUMECA, David has worked on the adaptation of the FINE/Turbo and FINE/Open CFD solvers for use in a massively parallel, heterogeneous environment. In collaboration with industry users, David has constructed frameworks for intelligently driven design and optimization leveraging leadership supercomputers at scale.

Oscar Hernandez is a staff member of the Computer Science and Mathematics Division at Oak Ridge National Laboratory. He works on the programming environment for the next-generation leadership class machines for NCCS and OLCF. His research focuses on programming languages and compilers, static analysis tools, performance tools integration, and optimization techniques for parallel languages, especially OpenMP and accelerator directives. He represents ORNL at the OpenACC and OpenMP ARB standard organizations and collaborates with the SPEC/HPG effort.

Adrian Jackson is a research architect at EPCC, The University of Edinburgh. He leads the Intel Parallel Computing Centre at EPCC and specializes in optimizing applications on very large resources and novel computing hardware. He is also active in support and training for high-performance computing, leading the HPC Architectures course in EPCC's MSc program in HPC and running a range of training courses on all aspects of parallel computing around the United Kingdom.

Guido Juckeland just founded the Computational Science Group at Helmholtz-Zentrum Dresden-Rossendorf (HZDR), Germany. He is responsible for designing and implementing end-to-end research IT-workflows together with scientists and IT experts at HZDR. His research focuses on better usability and programmability for hardware accelerators and application performance monitoring as well as optimization. He is the vice-chair of the SPEC High Performance Group (HPG), an active member of the OpenACC technical and marketing committees, and also contributes to the OpenMP tools working group. Guido earned his PhD in computer science from Technische Universität Dresden, Germany, for his work on trace-based performance analysis for hardware accelerators.

Jiri Kraus has more than eight years' experience in HPC and scientific computing. As a senior developer technology engineer with NVIDIA, he works as a performance expert for GPU HPC applications. At the NVIDIA Julich Applications Lab and the Power Acceleration and Design Center (PADC), Jiri collaborates with developers and scientists from the Julich Supercomputing Centre, the Forschungszentrum Julich, and other institutions in Europe. A primary focus of his work is multi-GPU programming models. Before joining NVIDIA, Jiri worked on the parallelization and optimization of scientific and technical applications for clusters of multicore CPUs and GPUs at Fraunhofer SCAI in St. Augustin. He holds a Diploma in mathematics (minor in computer science) from the University of Cologne, Germany.

Jeff Larkin is a software engineer in NVIDIA's Developer Technology group, where he specializes in porting and optimizing HPC applications to accelerated computing platforms. Additionally, Jeff is involved in the development and adoption of the OpenMP and OpenACC specifications and has authored many book chapters, blog posts, videos, and seminars to advocate use of directive-based parallel programming. Jeff lives in Knoxville, TN, with his wife and son. Prior to joining NVIDIA, he was a member of the Cray Supercomputing Center of Excellence at Oak Ridge National Laboratory, where he worked with many application development teams including two Gordon Bell prize-winning teams. He has a Master's degree in computer science from the University of Tennessee, and a Bachelor's degree in computer science from Furman University.

Jinpil Lee received his master's and PhD degree in computer science from University of Tsukuba in 2013, under the supervision of Prof. Mitsuhisa Sato. From 2013 to 2015, he was working at KISTI, the national supercomputing center in Korea, as a member of the user support department. Since 2015, he has worked at Riken AICS in Japan as a member of the programming environment research team. He has been doing research on parallel programming models and compilers for modern cluster architectures such as manycore clusters. Currently he is working on developing a programming environment for the next flagship Japanese supercomputer.

Seyong Lee is a computer scientist in the Computer Science and Mathematics Division at Oak Ridge National Laboratory. His research interests include parallel programming and performance optimization in heterogeneous computing environments, program analysis, and optimizing compilers. He received his PhD in electrical and computer engineering from Purdue University, West Lafayette, Indiana. He is a member of the OpenACC Technical Forum, and he has served as a program committee/guest editor/external reviewer for various conferences, journals, and research proposals.

Graham Lopez is a researcher in the Computer Science and Mathematics Division at Oak Ridge National Laboratory, where he works on programming environments preparation with the application readiness teams for the DOE CORAL and Exascale computing projects. Graham has published research in the areas of computational materials science, application acceleration and benchmarking on heterogeneous systems, low-level communication APIs, and programming models. He earned his MS in computer science and PhD in physics from Wake Forest University. Prior to joining ORNL, he was a research scientist at Georgia Institute of Technology, where he worked on application and numerical algorithm optimizations for accelerators.

Sameer Shende serves as the director of the Performance Research Laboratory at the University of Oregon and the president and director of Para-Tools, Inc. He has helped develop the TAU Performance System, the Program Database Toolkit (PDT), and the HPCLinux distribution. His research interests include performance instrumentation, measurement and analysis tools, compiler optimizations, and runtime systems for high-performance computing systems.

Xiaonan (Daniel) Tian is a GPU compiler engineer at the PGI Compilers and Tools group at NVIDIA, where he specializes in designing and implementing languages, programming models, and compilers for high-performance computing. Prior to joining NVIDIA, Daniel worked with Dr. Barbara Chapman in her compiler research group at the University of Houston, where he received a PhD degree in computer science. Prior to his work at the University of Houston, Daniel worked on GNU tool-chain porting for a semiconductor company. His research includes computer architectures, directive-based parallel programming models including OpenACC and OpenMP, compiler optimization, and application parallelization and optimization.

Christian Trott is a high-performance computing expert with extensive experience in designing and implementing software for GPU and MIC compute clusters. He earned a Dr. rer. nat. from the University of Technology Ilmenau in theoretical physics focused on computational material research. As of 2015 Christian is a senior member of the technical staff at the Sandia National Laboratories. He is a core developer of the Kokkos programming model, with a large role in advising applications on adopting Kokkos to achieve performance portability for next-generation supercomputers. Additionally, Christian is a regular contributor to numerous scientific software projects including LAMMPS and Trilinos.

John Urbanic is a parallel computing scientist at the Pittsburgh Supercomputing Center, where he spends as much time as possible implementing extremely scalable code on interesting machines. These days that means a lot of MPI, OpenMP, and OpenACC. He now leads the Big Data efforts, which involve such things as graph analytics, machine learning, and interesting file systems. John frequently teaches workshops and classes on all of the above and is most visible as the lead for the NSF XSEDE Monthly Workshop Series, the Summer Boot Camp, and the International HPC Summer School on HPC Challenges in Computational Sciences. John graduated with physics degrees from Carnegie Mellon University (BS) and Pennsylvania State University (MS) and still appreciates working on applications that simulate real physical phenomena. He is an honored recipient of the Gordon Bell Prize but still enjoys working on small embedded systems and real-time applications for various ventures. Away from the keyboard he swaps into a very different alter ego.

Chapter 1

OpenACC in a Nutshell

James Beyer, NVIDIA
Sunita Chandrasekaran, University of Delaware
Guido Juckeland, Helmholtz-Zentrum Dresden-Rossendorf

OpenACC[1] is a high-level, directive-based programming model for C/C++ and Fortran. It is designed to require significantly less programming effort than using a low-level model to program heterogeneous high-performance computing (HPC) hardware architectures.

The OpenACC programming model is based on programmers inserting hints into their C/C++ or Fortran programs on how the code can be parallelized. The compiler runs the code on the hardware platform that is specified at the time of compilation. In this way, the compiler handles most of the complex details of the translations without burdening the application scientist or programmer. This allows scientists to focus on their science rather than the intricate details of the architecture that is being targeted.

Because OpenACC is a directive-based model that augments a given code base with hints, the code can be compiled simply in a serial manner, ignoring the directives and still producing correct results. Thus you can maintain or preserve a single code base while offering portability across more than one platform.

---

1. http://www.openacc.org/.

Currently, OpenACC production compilers can target hardware platforms including traditional X86; multicore platforms; accelerators such as graphics processing units (GPUs); OpenPOWER processors; and Knights Landing (KNL) and Advanced RISC Machines (ARM) processors. OpenACC research compilers can also target field-programmable gate arrays (FPGAs). Development efforts targeting the Intel Xeon Phi and ARM processors have been reported publicly.[2,3]

The heterogeneous computing trend will continue. Pre-exascale machines are setting the architectural stage for what to expect in an exascale system (time frame 2020–2023).[4] Most of these machines feature heterogeneous nodes composed of a mixture of processing element types. This trend is likely to continue with exascale architectures featuring one million nodes, each with up to one thousand cores, resulting in a capability of roughly one billion cores. With energy-efficient accelerators, these machines seem to be one of the leading types of devices that could address the most critical challenges of exascale computing, which is power consumption. With such innovation in hardware, software has to evolve that can exploit massive on-node concurrency and handle multiple generations of future HPC hardware.

This chapter introduces the OpenACC programming model. We explain some of its fundamental features irrespective of the target platform:

- How the OpenACC directive syntax is structured

- How to use parallel and kernel constructs to accelerate compute-intensive portions of a program

- How to exploit loop constructs to express loop-level parallelism

- How to move data between traditional cores and accelerators using data environment clauses

---

2. http://www.pgroup.com/about/news.htm#55.
3. https://www.hpcwire.com/2015/10/29/pgi-accelerator-compilers-add-openacc
   -support-for-x86-multicore-cpus-2/.
4. https://exascaleproject.org/wp-content/uploads/2017/04/Messina-ECP-Presentation
   -HPC-User-Forum-2017-04-18.pdf.

1.1 OpenACC Syntax

Is OpenACC a language? By itself, no. According to the OpenACC specification[5] OpenACC is a collection of compiler directives, library routines, and environment variables. However, when the application programming interface (API) is combined with one of the supported base languages (C, C++, or Fortran), a new programming language is born. This new language allows you to express parallelism inherent in your code so that a compiler can translate it to a form that suits various parallel architectures.

OpenACC uses so-called directives to annotate the source code of a program. An OpenACC-capable compiler interprets these directives and generates parallel executable code as specified through the directives. If the code is compiled using a non-OpenACC-capable compiler or with OpenACC interpretation disabled, the compiler ignores the directives and generates a serial program without any parallelism.

OpenACC directives are always set up in the following fashion (for C/C++):

```
#pragma acc <directive> [clause [[,] clause] . . .] new-line
```

Here it is in Fortran:

```
!$acc <directive> [clause [[,] clause]. . .]
```

The keyword for a compiler directive (which is #pragma for C/C++, or !$ for Fortran) is followed by the directive type, which is acc for OpenACC directives. Next comes the actual directive to tell the compiler what to do, followed by one or more optional clauses to provide further information. A line with directives can be continued on the following line by putting a **backslash** (\) at the end of the preceding line. Such an OpenACC directive is applied to the immediately following statement, loop, or structured code block. Together they form a so-called **OpenACC construct.**

1.1.1 DIRECTIVES

The first word following the acc label is called the directive. A **directive** is an "instruction" to the compiler to do something about the code block that follows it. OpenACC distinguishes three directive types.

---

5. https://www.openacc.org/sites/default/files/inline-files/OpenACC_2pt5.pdf.

1. **Compute directives.** They mark a block of code that you can accelerate by exploiting the inherent data parallelism and distribute work to multiple threads. The OpenACC compute directives are `parallel`, `kernels`, `routine`, and `loop`.

2. **Data management directives.** A key optimization of OpenACC programs is to avoid unnecessary data movement between memory locations. Using only compute directives can lead to such movement of data, because the compiler has to be conservative and ensure a state that would be equal to a serial execution. You can override these defaults by specifying data lifetimes on the accelerator that extend beyond compute constructs. Furthermore, it is possible to specify a certain type of data access treatment. The OpenACC data directives are `data`, `update`, `cache`, `atomic`, `declare`, `enter data`, and `exit data`.

Note

Enter `data` and `exit data` are currently the only OpenACC directives that consist of two words.

---

3. **Synchronization directives.** OpenACC also supports some task parallelism, which allows multiple constructs to be executed concurrently. To explicitly wait for one or all concurrent tasks, you use the `wait` directive.

1.1.2 CLAUSES

Each OpenACC directive can be augmented by one or more clauses. A **clause** adds additional information to what the compiler needs to do with an OpenACC construct. Not all clauses can be combined with all directives, as is explained in detail in the remainder of this book. Most clauses accept additional arguments in parentheses. In general, clauses fall into three categories.

1. **Data handling.** These clauses override the compiler analysis for the specified variables by assigning a certain behavior for them. Example clauses are `default`, `private`, `firstprivate`, `copy`, `copyin`, `copyout`, `create`, `delete`, and `deviceptr`.

2. **Work distribution.** These clauses override the compiler-selected values for the work distribution among generated threads. The clauses are `seq`, `auto`, `gang`, `worker`, `vector`, `tile`, `num_gangs`, `num_workers`, and `vector_length`.

3. **Control flow.** These clauses allow for steering of the parallel execution during program runtime. Execution can be marked as conditional (`if` or `if_present`), dependencies overridden (`independent` and `reduction`), and task parallelism specified (`async` and `wait`).

1.1.3 API ROUTINES AND ENVIRONMENT VARIABLES

OpenACC also offers more fine-grained, low-level control of program execution. For this purpose you have an API into the OpenACC runtime, which is also used by the compiler when translating the directives. To make the API usable you include the OpenACC header file via this code (for C/C++):

```
#include "openacc.h"
```

Here it is in Fortran:

```
use openacc
```

> **Note**
>
> Using the OpenACC API routines leads to a dependency on an OpenACC runtime environment. If the program is now compiled with a non-OpenACC-capable compiler, the compilation and linking fail because of the lack of the runtime environment within that compiler.

Now the program can use a number of functions directly from the OpenACC runtime. The routines are used for the following.

- **Device management:** Querying and setting the used compute device types and numbers. This can also be set by the environment variables `ACC_DEVICE_TYPE` and `ACC_DEVICE_NUM`.

- **Initialization and shutdown** of the OpenACC runtime.

- **Task parallelism:** Testing and waiting for asynchronously launched work.

- **Memory management:** Manually allocating, mapping, and freeing memory on the compute device and manual data transfers.

1.2 Compute Constructs

The bread and butter of every OpenACC program are the compute constructs, because they distribute work among the parallel threads in the hunt for better performance and reduced program execution time. OpenACC distributes loops over threads with the goal of assigning one loop iteration to one thread. To do so it distinguishes two general distribution directives: `kernels` and `parallel`. Both can be augmented with the `loop` directive to mark individual loops for certain types of work distribution or assign additional clauses to those loops.

1.2.1 KERNELS

The `kernels` directive is the first of two compute constructs provided by OpenACC. Both constructs are used to offload code to the compute device; however, the philosophy of the two directives is different. The kernels construct merely acts as a sentinel to tell the compiler that this region of code should be placed on the accelerator if possible. However, when loops are present inside of a kernels construct, things become interesting.

```
int a[n][m], b[n][m], c[n][m];
init(a,b,n,m);
#pragma acc kernels
for(int j = 0; j < n; ++j) {
  for(int k = 0; k < m; ++k) {
    c[j][k] = a[j][k];
    a[j][k] = c[j][k] + b[j][k];
  }
}
```

Because the kernels construct tells the compiler to do the heavy lifting of parallelizing the code, the compiler is expected either to run this code sequentially or to parallelize the loop nest to exploit the parallelism. No matter what the compiler chooses to do, it must ensure that correct, sequentially consistent results are computed.

You can use several clauses to modify the kernels construct, but because it is intended to be a compiler-driven mechanism, we discuss these clauses in the next section. There is, however, one situation that merits examining: multiple loop nests inside a kernels construct.

```
int a[n][m], b[n][m], c[n][m];
init(a,b,n,m);
#pragma acc kernels
{
```

```
for(int j = 0; j < n; ++j) {
  for(int k = 0; k < m; ++k) {
    c[j][k] = a[j][k];
    a[j][k] = c[j][k] + b[j][k];
  }
}
for(int j = 0; j < n; ++j) {
  for(int k = 0; k < m; ++k) {
    d[j][k] = a[j][k] - 5;
  }
}
}
```

In this code, the compiler is free to choose to do at least two things. First, it can decide to fuse the two loop nests into one loop nest:

```
int a[n][m], b[n][m], c[n][m];
init(a,b,n,m);
#pragma acc kernels
for(int j = 0; j < n; ++j) {
  for(int k = 0; k < m; ++k) {
    c[j][k] = a[j][k];
    a[j][k] = c[j][k] + b[j][k];
    d[j][k] = a[j][k] - 5;
  }
}
```

This fusion will likely allow for more efficient usage of the available resources, because it will not incur the overhead of launching two kernels.

Or, second, the compiler can choose to generate two kernels that could be also coded as two parallel regions.

```
int a[n][m], b[n][m], c[n][m];
init(a,b,n,m);
#pragma acc parallel loop
for(int j = 0; j < n; ++j) {
  for(int k = 0; k < m; ++k) {
    c[j][k] = a[j][k];
    a[j][k] = c[j][k] + b[j][k];
  }
}
#pragma acc parallel loop
for(int j = 0; j < n; ++j) {
  for(int k = 0; k < m; ++k) {
    d[j][k] = a[j][k] - 5;
  }
}
```

1.2.2 PARALLEL

The `parallel` directive is the second compute construct provided by OpenACC. Whereas the `kernels` directive places the onus on the compiler to generate correct code, the `parallel` directive put the onus on the user to spell out what to parallelize and to ensure that correct code was generated. The `parallel` directive takes the position that users are much smarter about the parallel nature of the code that is being written and thus puts you on the spot to correctly express all the parallelism in the region.

Now look at the example from the preceding section, naively changed to use only the parallel construct.

```
int a[n][m], b[n][m], c[n][m];
init(a,b,n,m);
#pragma acc parallel
for(int j = 0; j < n; ++j) {
  for(int k = 0; k < m; ++k) {
    c[j][k] = a[j][k];
    a[j][k] = c[j][k] + b[j][k];
  }
}
```

What is wrong with this code? It is running the loop nest with some parallelism, but redundantly. We will fix the redundant execution later, but it is important to note that the compiler is free to choose the number of threads to execute this loop with. This means that the code may run slowly and give correct results, or it might not give correct results.

Also note that the compiler will detect that the objects a and b are used inside the parallel region and generate any data movements that may be needed to move the objects to the device. Because the compiler is free to run this code with any number of parallel threads, it is not portable, because some implementations will choose one thread and give the correct answer, whereas others may choose something else and give the wrong answer.

1.2.3 LOOP

The loop construct can be used inside both the parallel construct and the kernels construct. Inside the parallel construct, the loop construct tells the compiler that the iterations of this loop are independent. No iteration of the loop modifies data that is used by another iteration, and hence all iterations can be executed in a parallel manner. Inside the kernels construct, the loop construct can be used to tell the compiler that a loop is independent when the compiler cannot determine this at compile time. Inside both compute constructs, you can use the `seq` clause to tell the compiler to execute the loop in a sequential manner.

```
void foo( int *a, int *b, n ) {
#pragma acc parallel
#pragma acc loop
  for(int j = 0; j < n; ++j) {
    a[j] += b[j];
  }
}
void bar( int *a; int *b, n) {
#pragma acc parallel
#pragma acc loop gang worker vector
  for(int j = 0; j < n; ++j) {
    a[j] += b[j];
  }
}
```

The code in `foo` and `bar` are two different ways of saying similar things in OpenACC. The reason is that the compiler is always free to use more levels of parallelism on a loop if it sees no better uses elsewhere. The code in `foo()` allows the compiler to choose the levels of parallelism it wishes to exploit. The code in `bar()` tells the compiler it should exploit all thread levels of parallelism as discussed in Chapter 2.

1.2.4 ROUTINE

Throughout this section, with one exception, a function or subroutine has only occurred outside a compute construct. This is deliberate, because making calls inside compute constructs is more complex than just calling a simple function. Because the function can be called from within a compute construct having any arbitrary parallelism, it must be compiled for such a situation as well. Hence we use the `routine` directive to mark the function as potentially parallel.

The `routine` directive is used in two places: in procedure definitions and in procedure declarations.

```
#pragma acc routine
extern void foo(int *a, int *b, int n);

#pragma acc routine(foo)

#pragma acc routine
void foo(int *a, int *b, int n) {
#pragma acc loop gang
  for(int j = 0; j < n; ++j) {
    a[j] += b[j];
  }
}
```

This code example shows the three ways that the function foo can be modified with the routine directive. The first approach places the directive on the declaration of the function and tells the compiler that any calls to this function inside compute constructs will exploit parallelism. The second uses a named form of the directive to declare a function that has already been prototyped to have a device version of the code, as with the first example. The third use of the routine directive tells the compiler to generate a device version of the function so that compute constructs can call the procedure.

Note

There are more intricacies about combining the routine directive with the three levels of parallelism (gang, worker, vector), which are introduced in Chapter 2. For simplicity it can be said that no level of parallelism can be requested more than once, especially for nested routines and loops.

The routine directive takes three other clauses that are covered here.

```
#pragma acc routine vector device_type(nvidia) gang bind(foo_nvidia)
void foo(int *a, int *b, int n);

#pragma acc routine nohost
void foo_nvidia(int *a, int *b, int n) {
#pragma acc loop gang
  for(int j = 0; j < n; ++j) {
     a[j] += b[j];
  }
}
```

The first directive in this code tells the compiler that whenever it sees a call to foo() inside a compute construct while compiling for NVIDIA targets, it should replace the call name with foo_nvidia.[6] The directive also tells the compiler that for all targets other than NVIDIA, the function foo() will exploit only vector parallelism; however, on NVIDIA targets the function foo_nvidia will use both gang and vector parallelism, leaving no parallelism available outside the function.

The second directive tells the compiler to generate code for the device but not for the host. This is useful for at least two reasons. First, it reduces the text size of the

---

6. NVIDIA, founded in 1993, is a vendor of GPUs, notably for gaming platforms. See http://www.nvidia.com/object/about-nvidia.html.

generated code. Second, it ensures that code that could not be compiled for the host—that is, a device-specific intrinsic—is not given to the host compiler.

Now while this looks extremely complicated, rest assured that this is also about the maximum level of complexity of very advanced OpenACC programs and in many cases not necessary.

1.3 The Data Environment

OpenACC is designed to handle environments where the compute constructs are executed on a device that has a disjoint memory space from the main program and thus requires data movement between the host and the device. In this section, we discuss the complete set of directives and clauses provided by OpenACC to control memory placement and motion. But first we look at what the specification says will be done automatically for you.

The following variables are predetermined to be `private`, meaning that one copy per execution element will be created, depending on the type of parallelism being exploited:

1. Loop control variables associated with a loop construct

2. Fortran `do` loop index variables contained in a parallel or kernels region

3. Variables declared inside a C block

4. Variables declare inside procedures

Scalar variables used in parallel regions but not listed in data clauses are predetermined as `firstprivate` (a private variable that is initialized with the value from before the construct) or `private`, depending on whether the object is read or written first in the region.

The specification defines two important concepts related to data objects: data regions and data lifetimes. A **data region** is the dynamic scope of a structured block associated with an implicit or explicit data construct. A **data lifetime** starts when an object is first made available to a device, and ends when the object is no longer available on the device. Four types of data regions are defined: the data construct, the compute construct, a procedure, and the whole program.

1.3.1 DATA DIRECTIVES

There are two types of data directives: structured and unstructured. A **structured data region** defines in a single lexical scope when a data lifetime both begins and ends.

```
#pragma acc data copy(a)
{
  <use a>
}
```

The data lifetime for a begins at the opening curly brace (or curly bracket) and ends at the closing curly brace. Here is the Fortran equivalent.

```
!$acc data copy(a)
  <use a>
!$acc end data
```

An **unstructured data region** is delimited with a begin-end pair that need not be in the same lexical scope.

```
void foo(int *array, int n) {
#pragma acc enter data copyin(array[0:n])
}

void bar(int *array, int n) {
#pragma acc exit data copyout(array[0:n])
}
```

The proper placement of data directives can greatly increase the performance of a program. However, placing data directives should be considered an optimization, because you can handle all data motion at parallel and kernels constructs by adding the same data clauses that are available to the structured data construct.

1.3.2 DATA CLAUSES

Six data clauses can be used on compute constructs as well as data constructs, along with one data clause that is unique to the exit data construct. **Data clauses** specify a certain data handling for the named variables and arrays.

The foundation of all the clauses that allocate data is the create clause. This clause creates a data lifetime for the objects listed in the clause on the device. This means that on a nonshared memory device, memory for the object is to be available during the associated construct. "Available" means that if the object has already had memory created for it on the device, then the runtime need only update the reference count it uses to track when an object's memory is no longer needed on the device. If the object does not already have memory assigned to it, then the runtime will allocate memory for the object and update the reference count as in use.

So we know that data on the device is tracked by the runtime, but why even expose this to users? Enter the `present` clause. It is the first part of every data clause, but it is more of a bookkeeping clause than a data clause. Rather than ensure an object is made available on the device, it ensures that the object is available on the device. Why is this useful? A library writer may want to ensure that the objects are already on the device so that a computation—one that would normally not be beneficial if data motion were required—can be sent to the device.

The next three clauses are related, both in name and in function. We start with the most complex clause: `copy`. This clause starts with a `present` clause. Then if the data is not present, the `create` clause is performed. Once the object is on the device, the `copy` clause copies the data from the host to the device at the beginning of the region. When the region ends, if an object's reference count—the number of data constructs associated with the object—is about to go to zero, then the data is copied back to the host and the memory is freed.

The `copyin` clause does everything the `copy` clause does on the way into a data region, but at the end of the region the data is not copied back to the host. Data storage is released only if the reference count goes to zero.

The `copyout` clause does everything the `copy` clause does, except `copyout` does not copy the data to the device on entry to the data region.

The `delete` clause is powerful. However, as with many other powerful things, it is also dangerous. The `delete` clause does two things. First it determines whether the object is present, and if not it does nothing; second, it removes the object from the device's data environment by forcing the reference count to zero and releasing the memory.

The `deviceptr` clause was added to improve support for native libraries and calls that use the device. It tells the OpenACC system that the pointer in the clause contains an address that is resident on the device. This allows you to take control of data placement outside OpenACC but still use the data inside via the API.

1.3.3 THE CACHE DIRECTIVE

The `cache` directive provides a mechanism for describing data that should be moved to a faster memory, if possible.

```
#pragma acc loop
for(int j = 0; j < m; ++j) {
#pragma acc cache(b[j])
  b[j] = b[j]*c;
}
```

In this example, cache tells the compiler that each iteration of the for loop uses only one element of the array b. This is sufficient information for the compiler to determine that if the loop is going to be run by n threads, the compiler should move n elements of the array into faster memory and work from this faster memory copy. This movement does not come without a cost, but if the body of the loop contains sufficient reuses of the objects that are moved to fast memory, the overhead can be well worth the cost. If the object that is in the cache directive is read-only, the cost is greatly reduced. However, the compiler must do the data analysis to determine whether the object is live on entry or exit from the loop.

1.3.4 PARTIAL DATA TRANSFERS

There are two cases when a programmer has to be more specific with data clauses: when the array is dynamically allocated or when the programmer only wants to transfer a part of the array. (Note: The compiler cannot always determine size of arrays.) In the first case when the user only declares a pointer and then uses a malloc to attach memory to it, the compiler cannot determine the size of the array at compile time and thus cannot generate a data transfer size. In the latter case the programmer wants to override the conservative compiler approach, transferring the whole array by manually selecting which part(s) of the array to copy.

OpenACC offers the capability for partial data transfers on all data constructs and clauses, which is often termed **array shaping**. The syntax of this feature is for C/C++:

```
#pragma acc data copy(a[0:n])
```

Here it is in Fortan:

```
!$acc data copy(a(1:n))
```

The array boundary notation differs for C and Fortran. In C you specify the start index and after the colon the number of elements, whereas in Fortran you specify the range by listing the starting and ending index.

A typical use case, like the example provided, is when you use dynamically allocated arrays of n elements. The provided code snippet will copy the whole array a to the device memory at the start of the data construct and transfer its contents back to the host at the end. Additionally, this notation is very helpful when dealing with arrays that are larger than the available device memory or when only part of the array is needed on the device. With array shaping one can build a software pipeline to stage processing of array parts, as discussed later in Chapter 10.

It should also be noted that when you transfer/update only parts of your array, you as the programmer are responsible that your code only accesses the transferred parts in your compute regions. Otherwise you risk unspecified behavior of your application and potentially a very time-consuming error search.

1.4 Summary

OpenACC programmers can target various types of processors and program to an abstract machine model. You also have available a range of fundamental directives for developing a functioning program. You can run code on an accelerator, and you can use various mechanisms to reduce the amount of data traffic that is required for distributed memory machines. With the knowledge of these tools, you are now ready to begin writing parallel programs using OpenACC.

1.5 Exercises

1. Turn one of the following "hello world" codes into an actual program, and run it to see what happens.

```
Simple hello world in C
#pragma acc parallel
printf("hello world!");
```

```
Simple hello world in C++
#pragma acc parallel
std::cout << "Hello, world!\n";
```

```
Simple Hello world in Fortran
!$acc parallel
print *, 'hello world!'
!$acc end parallel
```

2. Is the following code guaranteed to behave the same on both a shared-memory and a distinct-memory machine? Why or why not?

```
int a[n];
for ( int i = 0; i < n; i++ ) {
```

```
    a[i] = 0;
  }
#pragma acc parallel loop
for ( int i = 0; i < n; i++ ) {
  a[i] = i;
}
for ( int i = 0; i < n; i++ ) {
  if ( a[i] == 0 ) {
    a[i] = i;
  }
  else {
    a[i] = (a[i] + i) * i;
  }
}
myPrint(a, i);
```

3. Write a program that puts two separate loop nests inside a kernels construct. If the compiler does not already generate two kernels, modify the code to force the compiler to generate two kernels.

4. Write a program that calls this function, `foo`, on the device.

```
void foo(int *a, int *b, int n) {
  for(int j = 0; j < n; ++j) {
    a[j] += b[j];
  }
}
```

Chapter 2

Loop-Level Parallelism

Adrian Jackson, EPCC

Loops are at the heart of the key computational kernels of many applications, especially in computational simulations. Because of the nature of the data that applications or algorithms operate on, data is stored in arrays, often multidimensional in scope. This means that the majority of work in the application is in iterating over those arrays and updating them using the algorithm being employed.

The simplest method for iterating over a multidimensional array in programming languages like C, C++, and Fortran is by using nested loops. Here's an example in C:

```
double particles[N][M][P];
. . .
for(int i=0; i<N; i++){
    for(int j=0; j<M; j++){
        for(int k=0; k<P; k++){
            particles[i][j][k] = particles[i][j][k] * 2;
            . . .              }
    }
}
```

Here is one in Fortran:

```
float, dimension(P,M,N) :: particles
. . .
do i=1,N
    do j=1,M
        do k=1,P
            particles(k,j,i) = particles(k,j,i) * 2
            . . .
        end do
    end do
end do
```

When you are looking for a way to use the large range of computational resources that are available in parallel computing hardware, it is therefore natural to alight on the idea of distributing the iterations of these nests of loops to different processing elements in a computational resource; in this way, you distribute work across available hardware and reduce the overall runtime of the application. Indeed, this is a core feature of parallel programming constructs, such as OpenMP[1] and OpenCL.[2]

OpenACC, as discussed in Chapter 1, also provides for mapping loops to computational hardware by annotating loops to be parallelized with the `kernels` directive (`#pragma acc kernels` for C/C++, and `!$acc kernels` for Fortran) or `parallel loop` directive (`#pragma parallel loop` for C/C++, and `!$acc parallel loop` for Fortran).

However, recognizing that accelerators or manycore (more than 12–18 cores) hardware may have several levels of parallelism—that is, cores, threads, and vector units—OpenACC allows you to specify a more detailed description of the way loops are mapped to the hardware being exploited by a given execution of an application.

This chapter explores in detail how to parallelize loops using OpenACC, discussing the various levels of parallelism provided and the clauses that can be added to the parallelization directives to ensure that the resulting parallelism still produces correct results, or to improve performance.

2.1 Kernels Versus Parallel Loops

Before we discuss the details of the loop-level parallelism available in OpenACC, it is worth spending a little time exploring the differences between the two main types of OpenACC directives you can use to parallelize loops (`kernels` and `parallel`) using a real code example.

As mentioned in Chapter 1, both directives can be used to distribute one or more loops on parallel hardware, but each achieves parallelization in a slightly different way. The `kernels` directive specifies a region of code that the compiler should analyze and decides what to parallelize and how to distribute it to the computing hardware. The `parallel` directive, on the other hand, specifies which code in the parallel region is safe to parallelize and will run all the code within that parallel region on all the available threads in the hardware being used.

---

1. http://www.openmp.org.
2. https://www.khronos.org/opencl/.

For instance, if you were to use the `kernels` directive to parallelize the loops outlined in this chapter, it could look like this, for C:

```c
#pragma acc kernels
{
    for(int i=0; i<N; i++){
        for(int j=0; j<M; j++){
            for(int k=0; k<P; k++){
                particles[i][j][k] = particles[i][j][k] * 2;
            }
        }
    }
}
```

Here it is in Fortran:

```fortran
!$acc kernels
do i=1,N
    do j=1,M
        do k=1,P
            particles(k,j,i) = particles(k,j,i) * 2
        end do
    end do
end do
!$acc end kernels
```

If you were to use the `parallel` directive to parallelize the same code, it would look like this, for C:

```c
#pragma acc parallel
{
    for(int i=0; i<N; i++){
        for(int j=0; j<M; j++){
            for(int k=0; k<P; k++){
                particles[i][j][k] = particles[i][j][k] * 2;
            }
        }
    }
}
```

Here it is in Fortran:

```fortran
!$acc parallel
do i=1,N
    do j=1,M
        do k=1,P
            particles(k,j,i) = particles(k,j,i) * 2
        end do
    end do
end do
!$acc end parallel
```

However, remember that the `parallel` directive, by itself, is relatively useless. Indeed, the preceding code, when parallelized using the `parallel` directive on its own, will not actually achieve any splitting or sharing of work; rather, it will simply run the same code on many threads at once, and will therefore neither speed up the code nor produce the correct result.

To achieve correct and efficient parallelization when using the `parallel` directive, you must combine it with one, or more, `loop` directives to specify where to apply work sharing. Therefore, the example should have been parallelized as follows, in C:

```
#pragma acc parallel loop
for(int i=0; i<N; i++){
    for(int j=0; j<M; j++){
        for(int k=0; k<P; k++){
            particles[i][j][k] = particles[i][j][k] * 2;
        }
    }
}
```

And this way in Fortran:

```
!$acc parallel loop
do i=1,N
    do j=1,M
        do k=1,P
            particles(k,j,i) = particles(k,j,i) * 2
        end do
    end do
end do
!$acc end parallel
```

Both `kernels` and `parallel` allow you to include multiple loops inside them; however, the way they treat those loops differs. If there are multiple loops inside a `kernel` region, each loop (that the compiler decides it can parallelize) will generate a separate kernel to be executed, and these will run sequentially, one after the other. In contrast, if there are multiple loops inside a single `parallel` region, then these may run at the same time, or at least there is no guarantee that the first loop will have finished before the second one starts. Consider this example, in Fortran:

```
!$acc parallel
!$acc loop
do i=1,1000
    a(i) = b(i)
end do
!$acc loop
do i=1,1000
    b(i) = b(i)*2
    c(i) = b(i)+a(i)
end do
!$acc end parallel
```

Here it is in C:

```
#pragma acc parallel{
    #pragma acc loop
    for(int i=0; i<1000; i++){
        a[i] = b[i];
    }
    #pragma acc loop
    for(int i=0; i<1000; i++){
        b[i] = b[i]*2;
        c[i] = b[i]+a[i];
    }
}
```

This code is not guaranteed to be correct, because the second loop could start executing before the first loop has finished, depending on how the loops have been mapped to the hardware by the compiler. If `kernels` had been used instead, this would have generated code that was guaranteed to be correct.

2.2 Three Levels of Parallelism

Because parallel hardware has different places where parallelism can occur—across processors, cores, threads, hyperthreads, vector units, and so on—OpenACC provides functionality for you to specify how to split work across different hardware units. This functionality is implemented in `gang`, `worker`, and `vector`.

These clauses, which can be applied to the `loop` directive, affect how loops and loop iterations are distributed to hardware components on the targeted processors or accelerator. This may affect both the performance and the functionality of an application, because the types of synchronization that are available between loop iterations are dependent on the hardware where the iterations are executed.

We discuss these clauses in this section, but note that what they actually translate to depends on the hardware your application is running and the compiler you are using. Most hardware that OpenACC programs run on supports at least two levels of parallelism (across cores and across vector units), but some hardware may support more or fewer levels. However, you can make some general assumptions: `gang` is the most coarse-grained, mapping to chunks of work assigned to various gangs of workers to perform independently; `worker` defines how work is distributed inside a `gang`; and `vector` maps to the hardware's instruction-level parallelism (i.e., vector operations).

The use of gang, worker, and vector allows the complexity of different hardware to be abstracted by programmers, providing a generalized level of mapping between the program's functionality and the hardware the program is running on. However, it is possible to specify in more detail exactly how to map loops to hardware—for instance specifying the vector length along with specifying the number of workers, or gangs, to use. This construct may provide optimized performance for specific hardware, albeit at the expense of how well the application's performance stands up when the application is ported, often termed as **performance portability** to other hardware.

Finally, note that OpenACC does not require programmers to specify this mapping between program functionality and parallel hardware. If you choose not to specify gang, worker, or vector clauses on your loop directive, then the compiler will attempt a mapping based on what it knows about the compiled code and hardware being used.

2.2.1 GANG, WORKER, AND VECTOR CLAUSES

Gangs can best be thought about as groups of workers, wherein different groups (gangs) can work independently, possibly at the same time, possibly at different times. Gangs do not allow for synchronization between different gangs but can allow workers in the same gang to synchronize (pause and wait for all workers or a subset of workers to be in the same place in the code, or protect the update to a shared variable between the gang workers).

Workers are threads within a gang, and they allow users or developers to specify how threads can be mapped to the hardware being used. As such, they are an intermediate level between the group of threads (the gang) and the low-level parallelism implemented in vector (which specifies how instructions are mapped to the hardware available to an individual thread).

Vector parallelism has the finest granularity, with an individual instruction operating on multiple pieces of data (much like single-instruction, multiple-data (or SIMD) parallelism on a modern CPU, or warps on NVIDA GPUs). These operations are performed with reference to a vector length, which specifies how many units of data will be operated on for a given instruction.

In general, a gang consists of one or more workers, each of which operates on a vector of some length. Within a gang the OpenACC model exposes a cache memory, which can be used by all workers and vectors within that gang and allows synchronization within the gang, although not as a programmer-specifiable feature (i.e., you cannot add clauses or directives to manually control this synchronization).

These three levels of parallelism layout enable a mapping to all current hardware platforms, as shown in Table 2.1.

Table 2.1 Potential mapping of gang, worker, and vector to various hardware platforms

PLATFORM	MAPPING OF		
	GANG	WORKER	VECTOR
Multicore CPU	Whole CPU (NUMA domain)	Core	SIMD vector
Manycore CPU (e.g., Xeon Phi)	NUMA domain (whole chip or quadrant)	Core	SIMD vector
NVIDIA GPU (CUDA)	Thread block	Warp	Thread
AMD GPU (OpenCL)	Workgroup	Wavefront	Thread

Note: The mapping actually used is up to the compiler and its runtime environment, and this table is not guaranteed for an actual OpenACC implementation. The programmer can guide the compiler only by specifying a number of each element to use.

2.2.2 MAPPING PARALLELISM TO HARDWARE

As discussed earlier, you do not have to specify mapping to hardware via these clauses in order to write a correct OpenACC program. Therefore, it is good practice not to include them until your developed or ported program has been validated and you are ready to start optimizing it.

At this point it is crucial to understand both the hardware you are targeting and your algorithm or application. If you know the sizes of your loops (or at least roughly the range of sizes they may be) and the synchronization you need between loop iterations, then you should be able to make sensible choices about what hardware mapping directives you can use on which loops.

For NVIDIA GPU hardware, it is likely that gangs map to thread blocks, workers to warps, and vector to threads. Alternatively, you could simply use a gang to map to thread blocks and workers to map to threads in those thread blocks. Likewise, different loops in a parallel or kernel region could map to different thread blocks.

On multicore or manycore processors you can imagine gangs mapping to a processor or NUMA region of a processor, workers to cores or hyperthreads on the processor, and vectors to the vector units in the cores.[3] Alternatively, you could imagine gangs and workers mapping to cores, vectors to the vector units, and the

3. NUMA stands for non-uniform memory access. If you have multiple processors in a node it is likely all of them can access the memory of the node, but it's quicker to access memory directly attached to a processor than it is to access memory attached to another processor in the node. Each processor would be a **NUMA region**: a region where local memory accesses are faster than remote memory accesses.

NUMA characteristics of the node being ignored when mapping OpenACC directives to hardware.

For `parallel` and `kernels` regions, in addition to manually specifying these mapping clauses on individual loops, you can specify the sizes of gangs, workers, and vectorization to use at the higher level (i.e., on the `parallel` or `kernels` directive itself). This is done using the clauses `num_gangs()`, `num_workers()`, and `vector_length()`.

These clauses take an integer value that specifies, respectively, the number of gangs to be used for each kernel or gang loop in the region, the number of workers per gang, and the vector length to use in vector operations. Note that these are optional clauses, and you can use any combination of them required. Here's an example:

```
!$acc parallel loop num_gangs(32) vector_length(128)
do i=1,N
    do j=1,M
        do k=1,P
            particles(k,j,i) = particles(k,j,i) * 2
        end do
    end do
end do
!$acc end parallel
```

If the value you specify is not supported or implementable on the hardware being used, the actual implementation may use a lower value than what you specify in these clauses.

2.3 Other Loop Constructs

This section discusses the loop constructs available in OpenACC.

2.3.1 LOOP COLLAPSE

When you manually specify how loop iterations should be mapped to the available parallel hardware, the loops you are parallelizing must have enough iterations to map to the various hardware levels. You must also specify loop clauses on all loops inside a parallel region, something that can be tedious and can impact the readability of the code.

As an alternative, you can treat a whole nest of loops as a single loop space to be distributed to the parallel hardware, specify the parallelism at a single loop level, and allow the compiler to sort out the mapping of those loops to specific hardware. This approach also can have the benefit of providing a larger loop iteration space to be distributed across hardware threads or vector hardware, and this is useful if some loops in the loop nest have small iteration counts, as demonstrated in the following code:

```
for(int i=0; i<8; i++){
    for(int j=0; j<8; j++){
        for(int k=0; k<8; k++){
. . .

        }
    }
}
```

To tell the compiler to treat a whole loop nest as a single loop, you can use the collapse keyword for the loop directive. This directive takes a single positive number as an argument and uses this number to determine how many loops within the loop nest to collapse into a single loop. Here's an example:

```
!$acc parallel
!$acc loop collapse(3)
do i=1,8
    do j=1,8
        do k=1,8
            ...
        end do
    end do
end do
!$acc end parallel
```

For collapse to work, the loops need to be tightly nested—that is, there is no code between loops—and the size of the loops must be computable and must not change during the loop.

2.3.2 INDEPENDENT CLAUSE

A large fraction of OpenACC's functionality is based on the compiler's ability to analyze code and work out whether it can be safely parallelized or not (i.e., kernel regions), but compilers do not always have enough information to make this decision safely.

Therefore, compilers often err on the side of caution when deciding which loops can be parallelized, and this may mean performance is lost in code because the functionality that could be run across many threads is being run sequentially. Here's an example of such code:

```
!$acc kernels
!$acc loop
do i = 1, 512
    do j = 1, 1024
        local_index = (((i-1)*1024)+j
        halo_data(local_index) = particle_data(j,i)
    enddo
enddo
!$acc end kernels
```

The code in the innermost loop depends on the outer loop counter (to calculate `local_index`), and therefore the compiler may decide this is a loop dependency (i.e., one iteration of the loop depends on the result of the previous iteration); as a result, the compiler produces a sequential kernel rather than parallelize the loops. You can address this problem by adding the `independent` clause to the loop directive to tell the compiler you guarantee that the loop iterations are independent and therefore it can safely parallelize the loops.

Note that this issue is not restricted to OpenACC or accelerator applications; compilers have similar issues trying to vectorize code, and many compilers or parallel programming approaches will give you methods for giving the compiler a bit more information about loops to help it in distributing iterations to parallel hardware.

The `independent` clause is applicable only to loops in kernels regions, because the `parallel` directive already informs the compiler that all loops inside the parallel region are independent unless they explicitly include a `seq` clause.

In general, it is not necessary to add `independent` to all your loops in kernels regions. This is primarily an optimization step after you have parallelized your code with OpenACC.

You can usually be guided by compiler reports on the parallelism that it has implemented, or by profiling data on your application, regarding loops that don't seem to be parallelizing. Then you can decide whether they truly are independent and therefore whether you can apply this clause.

For instance, the PGI compiler, when compiling code using the `-Minfo=accel` flag, may produce output like this:

```
. . . Parallelization would require privatization of
    array 'halo_data(:)'
  Accelerator kernel generated
  !$acc loop seq
```

Such output indicates that the associated code loop needs further investigation.

2.3.3 SEQ AND AUTO CLAUSES

At times a loop may appear parallelizable but contains some data dependency or calculations that the compiler does not recognize as restricting the parallelism. In these cases, when using the `kernels` directive, the compiler may erroneously parallelize a loop when it should not.

Furthermore, the `parallel` directive instructs the compiler to parallelize all the code contained within the parallel region, whether or not it is correct to do so.

Also, loop nests to be parallelized with OpenACC directives may have more loops available than the various types of parallelism you are targeting (i.e., more than three loops, which you could map to `gang`, `worker`, or `vector`). In this scenario it is often possible to collapse loops to reduce the loops to be distributed to hardware, but in some situations loop collapsing is not possible (e.g., loops that are not perfectly nested).

Therefore, OpenACC provides a clause, `seq`, that you can add to a loop to stop the compiler from parallelizing or vectorizing that loop, or to control where parallelism happens in the loop nest. You can add `seq` to any loop directive, but it is mutually exclusive with the `gang`, `worker`, and `vector` clauses (because they specify parallelism, and `seq` disables parallelism). Here's an example:

```
#pragma acc parallel
#pragma acc loop gang
for (f=0; f<A; f++){
    #pragma acc loop worker
    for (g=0; g<B; g++){
        #pragma acc loop seq
        for (h=0; h<X; h++){
            #pragma acc loop vector
            for (i=0; i<Q; i++){
                ...
            }
        }
    }
}
```

You can use `auto`, on the other hand, to instruct the compiler to define the various levels of parallelism that loops should be mapped to. This clause is automatically applied to loops inside a kernel region that have not had a parallelism clause (`worker`, `vector`, `gang`, or `seq`) applied to them.

However, note that `auto` does not instruct the compiler that loops are independent. Therefore, `auto` may need to be combined with the `independent` clause for loops the compiler is struggling to automatically parallelize.

You can also use `auto` to enable compiler checking on loops inside a `parallel` region. As previously discussed, these loops are assumed to be independent and parallelizable by default.

2.3.4 REDUCTION CLAUSE

A number of code or algorithm features can cause compilers not to be able to automatically parallelize loops. One occurs when a single variable, or an array of variables, is updated during each loop iteration. Here's an example, in C:

```
total = 0;
for(i=0;i<100;i++){
    total += data[i];
}
```

Here it is in Fortran:

```
total = 0
do i=1,100
    total = total + data(i)
end do
```

Because the variable `total` at iteration i depends on iteration $i-1$, the compiler will not be able to automatically parallelize the loop. However, you can fix this issue by using a `reduction` clause.

The `reduction` clause, which can be added to a `kernels`, `parallel`, or `loop` directive, specifies that a variable will be operated on locally for each thread that is working on it, and then there will be a final operation to bring together all the local versions of the final variable. It does something like the following.

Convert this loop:

```
total = 0
do i=1,100
    total = total + data(i)
end do
```

To this set of loops:

```
!declare an array of local_totals with an entry for each thread
    !running the code
total = 0
local_totals(thread_number) = 0
```

```
!parallelize this loop
do i=1,100
   local_totals(thread_number) =
&        local_totals(thread_number) + data(i)
end do
!do this loop in serial
do i=1,number_of_threads
   total = total + local_totals(i)
end do
```

The `reduction` clause enables you to maintain your original loop in your source code and automatically convert it into a set of parallel and sequential loops when compilation happens. In this way, the compiler parallelizes as much as possible while producing the correct result.

In OpenACC, a `reduction` clause can specify the operators on scalar variables, as shown in Table 2.2. (Reductions are currently not allowed for arrays or array elements, C structure members, C++ class or structure members, or parts of a derived type in Fortran.)

Table 2.2 Supported reduction operations

C AND C++	FORTRAN
+	+
*	*
Max	max
Min	min
&	iand
|	ior
&&	ieor
||	.and.
	.or.
	.eqv.
	.neqv.

When using a `reduction` clause, you do not need to initialize your variable; it will be automatically initialized correctly for you.

Here's an example of applying a reduction to the loop outlined earlier:

```
total = 0
!$acc parallel loop reduction(+:total)
do i=1,100
    total = total + data(i)
end do
!$acc end parallel loop
```

Here it is for C:

```
total = 0;
#pragma acc parallel loop reduction(+:total)
for(i=0; i<100; i++){
    total = total + data[i];
}
```

With parallel regions, you can use the `reduction` clause either for the whole parallel region (as a clause on the `parallel` directive itself) or on a `loop` directive.

If you are using the `kernels` directive, the `reduction` clause can be applied only at the `loop` directive level.

Within a parallel region, if you apply reduction on a loop by using the `vector` or `worker` clause (and no `gang` clause) and if the reduction variable is listed as a `private` variable, then the value of the private copy of the scalar will be updated at the exit of the loop. If the reduction variable is not specified as `private`, or if you apply the reduction to a loop by using the `gang` clause, the value of the variable will not be updated until execution reaches the end of the parallel region.

2.4 Summary

Loop parallelization functionality is at the heart of the ability of OpenACC to exploit multicore, manycore, and GPU hardware. Efficiently and correctly parallelizing loops across hardware is key to ensuring good performance.

The `parallel` and `kernels` directives differ; `kernels` gives the compiler more responsibility for identifying parallelism, and `parallel` mandates that the compiler parallelize the code within that region.

OpenACC provides extra functionality, additional clauses that can be added to parallelization directives, to enable you to help the compiler efficiently parallelize your code and then to sensibly map it to the hardware you are using.

Judicious use of `independent`, `collapse`, and `reduction` clauses, where required and safe, will enable the compiler to parallelize your code as much as possible. Specifying how to map loops to hardware features (threads, cores, vector hardware, etc.)—based on the hardware you are exploiting and your knowledge of your code—can lead to further performance improvements.

Hopefully, with this information and some experimenting, you will be able to build correct OpenACC code and make it fly. Just remember that correctness should come before performance, so having well-tested and validated OpenACC code should be your first target before you start optimizing the loops and exploiting the hardware you are using to its full potential.

2.5 Exercises

1. If you run the following fragment of OpenACC on a GPU using all 1,536 threads that the GPU has, how many times as fast would you expect it to run, compared with using a single thread on the GPU?

```
#pragma acc parallel
for(i=0;i<2359296;i++){
    answer[i] = part1[i] + part2[i] * 4;
}
```

2. The following fragment of code produces an incorrect answer. Can you fix it?

```
passing_count = 0
!$acc parallel loop
do i=1,10000
    moving(i) = (left(i) - right(i)) * 2
    left(i) = left(i) + 0.6
    right(i) = right(i) - 3
    passing_count = passing_count + 1
end do
!$acc end parallel loop
```

3. The following code does not efficiently utilize the hardware available on a GPU. Can you suggest a way of optimizing it to improve the utilization of the GPU?

```
#pragma acc parallel loop
for(i=0;i<8;i++){
    for(j=0;j<320;j++){
        for(k=0;k<320;k++){
            new_data[i][j][k] = (old_data[i][j][k] * 2) + 4.3;
        }
    }
}
```

Chapter 3

Programming Tools for OpenACC

Robert Dietrich, Technische Universität Dresden
Sameer Shende, ParaTools/University of Oregon

Software tools can significantly improve the application development process. With the spread of GPU-accelerated systems and OpenACC programs, a variety of development tools are now available, including code editors, compilers, debuggers, and performance analysis tools.

A proper code editor with syntax highlighting or an integrated development environment (IDE) helps spot syntax errors. Compilers print error messages in case of nonconforming or erroneous source code. Typically, they also provide the option to print additional information on the compilation process, such as the implementation of OpenACC directives. However, several types of errors occur during the execution of the binary. Debuggers provide the means to dynamically track errors in the program at run time. When programming models, such as OpenACC, are used to accelerate an application, the performance of the program should be investigated and tuned with the help of performance analysis tools.

3.1 Common Characteristics of Architectures

The OpenACC programming model has been developed for many core devices, such as GPUs. It targets host-directed execution using an attached or integrated accelerator. This means that the host is executing the main program and controls the activity of the accelerator. To benefit from OpenACC directives, the executing devices should provide parallel computing capabilities that can be addressed with at least one of the three levels of parallelism: gang, worker, or vector.

OpenACC accelerator devices typically provide capabilities for efficient vector processing, such as warps for CUDA devices, wavefronts on AMD GPUs, and 512-bit SIMD (single-instruction, multiple-data) units on Intel Xeon Phi. The architecture of Intel MIC (Many Integrated Core) devices works well with multithreading and thus worker parallelism. GPUs are typically split into clusters of ALUs (arithmetic logic units), such as NVIDIA SMs (streaming multiprocessors), which maps to gang parallelism. Thus, the device capabilities should match the values of the OpenACC vector, worker, and gang size. Performance tools that use the OpenACC 2.5 profiling interface can acquire this information for a compute kernel in the respective `enqueue` operation, because these values are fixed per compute kernel.

OpenACC uses the concept of **computation offloading.** This allows you to execute computationally intensive work, or workloads that simply fit to the architecture of an accelerator, on an offloading device. This means that OpenACC devices are most often host-controlled and not self-hosted. Nevertheless, some OpenACC compilers (e.g., PGI's multicore back end) generate code for multicore CPUs from OpenACC directives.

In terms of performance analysis, computation offloading requires that you capture information on the host and device execution, and a correlation must be established between host and device data. Performance measurement on host processors can provide fine-grained data, whereas accelerator data typically are not more detailed than up to the task level, such as start and end of compute kernels and data transfers. Transfer times can determine the bandwidth of a data movement.

In general, acquisition of device-side performance data depends on the accelerator and respective APIs to access them. For example, a device-specific API may provide access to hardware counters, such as cache accesses or IPCs (instructions per cycle).

3.2 Compiling OpenACC Code

OpenACC builds on top of the programming languages C, C++, and Fortran. Therefore, OpenACC programs are compiled similarly to other programs written in
one of these three languages. Because of the nature of compiler directives, every
compiler for these languages can compile a program that contains OpenACC directives. Compilers can simply ignore directives, as it does comments. A compiler
with OpenACC support is needed when OpenACC runtime library routines are used.
Keep this in mind if you intend to also run the code without OpenACC.

Compilers with support for the OpenACC API typically provide a **switch** that
enables the interpretation of OpenACC directives (for example, `-acc` for the PGI
compiler, and `-fopenacc` for the GNU compiler). This usually includes the header
`openacc.h` automatically, as well as a link to the compiler's OpenACC runtime
library. Because OpenACC has been developed for performance portable programming, there is typically a compiler option to specify the target architecture.
The default target might fit a variety of devices, but most often it does not provide
the best performance. Table 3.1 shows an overview of OpenACC compiler flags for
several known OpenACC compilers.

Table 3.1 Compiler flags for various OpenACC compilers

COMPILER	COMPILER FLAGS	ADDITIONAL FLAGS
PGI	`-acc`	`-ta=`target architecture
		`-Minfo=accel`
GCC	`-fopenacc`	`-foffload=`offload target
OpenUH	Compile: `-fopenacc`	`-Wb,-accarch:`target architecture
	Link: `-lopenacc`	
Cray	C/C++: `-h pragma=acc`	`-h msgs`
	Fortran: `-h acc,noomp`	

An example of a complete compile command and the compiler output are given in
Listing 3.1 for the PGI C compiler. It generates an executable `prog` for the OpenACC
program `prog.c`. The switch `-ta=tesla:kepler` optimizes the device code
for NVIDIA's Kepler architecture. The flag `-Minfo=accel` prints additional information on the implementation of OpenACC directives and clauses.

Listing 3.1 Exemplary PGI compiler output with -Minfo=accel for a simple OpenACC reduction

```
pgcc -acc -ta=nvidia:kepler -Minfo=accel prog.c -o prog
reduceAddOpenACC_kernel:
  40, Generating implicit copyin(data[1:size-1])
  41, Loop is parallelizable
      Accelerator kernel generated
      Generating Tesla code
      41, #pragma acc loop gang, vector(128)
                /* blockIdx.x threadIdx.x */
      42, Generating implicit reduction(+:sum)
```

The number of compilers with OpenACC support[1] has grown over time. PGI and Cray are commercial compilers. PGI also provides a community edition without license costs. Among the open source compilers are the GCC[2] and several OpenACC research compilers, such as Omni from the University of Tsukuba,[3] OpenARC from Oak Ridge National Laboratory,[4] and OpenUH from the University of Houston.[5]

3.3 Performance Analysis of OpenACC Applications

OpenACC is about performance. It provides the means to describe parallelism in your code. However, the compiler and the OpenACC runtime implement this parallelism. Furthermore, many execution details are implicitly hidden in the programming model. Performance analysis tools can expose those implicit operations and let you investigate the runtime behavior of OpenACC programs. You can gain insight into execution details, such as IO (input/output) and memory operations as well as host and device activities.

There is a variety of performance-relevant information that helps you understand the runtime behavior of an application. For small OpenACC programs that run on a single node, it might be enough to use simple profiling options, such as the PGI_ ACC_TIME environment variable. Setting it to 1 prints profiling output to the console. However, this variable is available only with the PGI OpenACC implementation. Other compilers provide similar options.

---

1. http://www.openacc.org/content/tools.
2. https://gcc.gnu.org/wiki/OpenACC.
3. http://omni-compiler.org.
4. http://ft.ornl.gov/research/openarc.
5. https://you.stonybrook.edu/exascallab/downloads/openuh-compiler/..

To analyze complex programs, a performance tool should support all paradigms and programming models used in the application, because inefficiency might arise from their interaction. Depending on the tool, three levels of parallelism can be covered: process parallelization, multithreading, and offloading. OpenACC refers to the latter, but offloading is often used in combination with Message Passing Interface (MPI) for interprocess communication, and with OpenMP for multithreading. When a specific region has been exposed for optimization, hardware counters might help identify more fine-grained performance issues.

Performance analysis is obviously useful for tuning programs and should be a part of a reasonable application development cycle. It starts with the measurement preparation, followed by the measurement run and the analysis of the performance data, and concludes with code optimization. In the following, we focus on the first three steps.

During measurement preparation you select and configure data sources, which will provide information on program execution. It does not require changing the application code in every case (see the following section). The measurement itself is an execution run while performance data are recorded. The measurement data are then analyzed, often with the help of performance tools. Based on the performance analysis results you try to optimize the code, and then you repeat the whole process.

Optimizations or code changes might not always result in better performance. Comparing different execution runs helps you understand the impact of code changes or evaluate the application's performance on different platforms and target devices. Several tools are available that enable such performance comparisons (for example, TAU[6] and Vampir[7]).

3.3.1 PERFORMANCE ANALYSIS LAYERS AND TERMINOLOGY

The goal of performance analysis is the detection of bottlenecks and inefficiencies in the execution of a program to support application developers in tuning. As depicted in Figure 3.1, there are three analysis layers: data acquisition, data recording, and data presentation. Performance tools typically implement all layers and try to hide the complexity of the analysis process from the user. For a better understanding of the analysis results and a clarification of terminology, analysis layers and techniques are discussed next.

6. Sameer Shende and Allen D. Malony, "The TAU Parallel Performance System," *International Journal of High Performance Computing Applications*, 20(2) (2006): 287–311. http://tau.uoregon.edu.
7. Andreas Knüpfer et al., "The Vampir Performance Analysis Tool-Set," *Tools for High Performance Computing* (2008): 139–155.

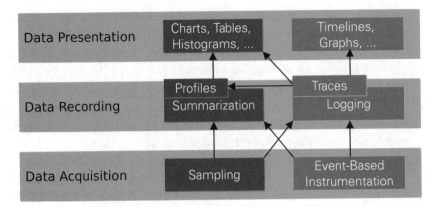

Figure 3.1 Performance analysis layers and terminology
Note: Compare to Thomas Ilsche, Joseph Schuchart, Robert Schöne, and Daniel Hackenberg, "Combining Instrumentation and Sampling for Trace-Based Application Performance Analysis," Tools for High Performance Computing *(2014): 123–136.*

3.3.2 PERFORMANCE DATA ACQUISITION

There are two fundamental approaches to acquire data during the program run.

- **Sampling** is a "pull" mechanism, which queries information on what the application is doing. The rate of such queries (samples) can be set to a fixed value, resulting in a constant and predictable runtime perturbation. However, the measurement accuracy depends on the sampling frequency. A low sampling frequency might miss valuable information; a high sampling frequency might introduce too much overhead. Also, timer-based interrupts generate a constant sampling rate, whereas other interrupt generators, such as counter overflow, might not provide samples at regular intervals.

- **Event-based instrumentation** typically modifies the application to "push" information about its activity to the performance measurement infrastructure. Instrumentation can be placed anywhere in the code to mark, for instance, begin and end of program functions, library calls, and code regions. All instrumented events must be executed to be observed and thus will reflect how the program behaved. Because the event rate is unknown at compile time, the runtime perturbation cannot be predicted and can be of several orders of magnitude in a worst-case scenario. Advantages and drawbacks of both approaches have been discussed in literature—for example, by Ilsche et al.[8]

---

8. Thomas Ilsche, Joseph Schuchart, Robert Schöne, and Daniel Hackenberg, "Combining Instrumentation and Sampling for Trace-Based Application Performance Analysis," *Tools for High Performance Computing* (2014): 123–136.

Since OpenACC 2.5, the specification describes a profiling interface that enables you to record OpenACC events during the execution of an OpenACC program. It is described in Section 3.3.4. Interfaces can be used for data acquisition for many other programming models, such as CUPTI for CUDA,[9] OMPT for OpenMP,[10] the MPI tool information interface, PMPI for MPI,[11] and MPI_T tools for MPI 3.0.[12]

3.3.3 PERFORMANCE DATA RECORDING AND PRESENTATION

Data recording can either immediately summarize all data (**profiling**) or fully log all activity (**tracing**). There are several types of profiles (e.g., flat, call-path profiles, or call-graph profiles), which differ in preserving caller-callee relationships. In a simple **flat** function profile, only the accumulated runtime and the invocation count of functions are stored. A **trace** stores each event or sample that occurs during the program execution. It can be presented as a timeline or converted into a profile for any arbitrary time interval. A **profile** represents summarized data of the whole application run without the temporal context of the recorded activity. Immediate summarization maintains a low memory footprint for the performance monitor. Profiles immediately show activities per their impact on the application (typically runtime distribution over the functions). **Timelines** show the temporal evolution of a program while making it harder to isolate the most time-consuming activity right away.

3.3.4 THE OPENACC PROFILING INTERFACE

Version 2.5 of the OpenACC specification introduces a profiling interface that is intended for use by instrumentation-based performance tools such as Score-P[13] and TAU.[14] The rest of this chapter discusses these tools. The interface defines runtime events that might occur during the execution of an OpenACC program. A tool library can register callbacks for individual event types, which are dispatched by the OpenACC runtime, when the respective event occurs. Table 3.2 lists all events that are specified in the OpenACC 2.5 profiling interface, with a short description of their occurrence.

---

9. docs.nvidia.com/cuda/cupti/.
10. www.openmp.org/wp-content/uploads/ompt-tr2.pdf.
11. http://mpi-forum.org/docs/mpi-3.0/mpi30-report.pdf.
12. https://computation.llnl.gov/projects/mpi_t.
13. Dieter an Mey et al., "Score-P: A Unified Performance Measurement System for Petascale Applications," *Competence in High Performance Computing 2010* (2012): 85–97. http://www.score-p.org.
14. https://www.cs.uoregon.edu/research/tau/home.php.

Table 3.2 Runtime events specified in the OpenACC 2.5 profiling interface for use in instrumentation-based performance tools

EVENT acc_ev_	OCCURRENCE
KERNEL LAUNCH EVENTS	
enqueue_launch_[start|end]	Before or after a kernel launch operation
DATA EVENTS	
enqueue_upload_[start|end]	Before or after a data transfer to the device
enqueue_download_[start|end]	Before or after a data transfer from the device
create/delete	When the OpenACC runtime associates or disassociates device memory with host memory
alloc/free	When the OpenACC runtime allocates or frees memory from the device memory pool
OTHER EVENTS	
device_init_[start|end]	Before or after the initialization of an OpenACC device
device_shutdown_[start|end]	Before or after the finalization of an OpenACC device
runtime_shutdown	When the OpenACC runtime finalizes.
wait_[start|end]	Before or after an explicit OpenACC wait operation
compute_construct_[start|end]	Before or after the execution of a compute construct
update_construct_[start|end]	Before or after the execution of an update construct
enter_data_[start|end]	Before or after the execution of an enter data directive, before or after entering a data region
exit_data_[start|end]	Before or after the execution of an exit data directive, before or after leaving a data region

Events are categorized into three groups: kernel launch, data, and other events. Independent of the group, all events provide information on the event type and the parent construct, as well as whether the event is triggered by an implicit or explicit directive or runtime API call. For example, implicit wait events are triggered for waiting at synchronous data and compute constructs. Event-specific information for kernel launch events is the kernel name as well as gang, worker, and vector size. Data events provide additional information on the name of the variable and the number of bytes, as well as a host and a device pointer to the corresponding data. For a complete list of all information that is provided in OpenACC event callbacks, consult the OpenACC specification.

Event callbacks also provide an interface to low-level APIs such as CUDA, OpenCL, and Intel's COI (Coprocessor Offload Infrastructure).[15] This interface allows access to additional information that is not available with the OpenACC profiling interface or access to hooks into the execution of the low-level programming model. Tools

---

15. https://software.intel.com/en-us/articles/offload-runtime-for-the-intelr-xeon-phitm-coprocessor.

might use this capability to gather runtime information of device activities—for example, by inserting CUDA events at an enqueue start and enqueue end event.

Portable collection of device data and sampling are not part of the OpenACC 2.5 profiling interface. However, the runtime of device tasks generated from OpenACC directives can be estimated based on enqueue and wait events.

3.3.5 PERFORMANCE TOOLS WITH OPENACC SUPPORT

Tool support for OpenACC has two sides: the host side and the device side. You've learned that OpenACC is a host-directed programming model, where device activity is triggered by a host thread. Hence, a reasonable OpenACC performance analysis gathers information on the implementation of OpenACC directives on the host and the execution of device kernels as well as data transfers between host and device. Many performance tools support CUDA and OpenCL, but only a small number also provide information on the execution of OpenACC directives on the host. The latter enable a correlation with the program source code and give insight into the program execution even if the target, which is most often CUDA or OpenCL, is not tracked or is unknown.

This section introduces three powerful performance tools that support the combined analysis of OpenACC host and device activities. First, the NVIDIA profiler, as part of the CUDA toolkit, focuses specifically on performance measurement and analysis of OpenACC offloading to CUDA target devices. Second, the Score-P environment supports many paradigms, including message passing (e.g., with MPI) and multithreading as well as offloading with CUDA, OpenCL, and OpenACC. The CUDA toolkit is one of the most capable tool sets when additional paradigms and programming models are used next to OpenACC. Last, the TAU Performance System provides comprehensive performance measurement (instrumentation and sampling) and analysis of hybrid parallel programs, including OpenACC.

3.3.6 THE NVIDIA PROFILER

The NVIDIA command-line profiler (nvprof) and the corresponding front end NVIDIA Visual Profiler (nvvp)[16] have supported the OpenACC profiling interface since CUDA 8.0. Both are available on all systems where a recent CUDA toolkit is installed. You can use nvprof (and nvvp) to profile and trace both host and device activities. For CUDA-capable target devices, this tool can gather information from

---

16. NVIDIA, "Profiler User's Guide," http://docs.nvidia.com/cuda/profiler-users-guide.

CUDA kernels, such as their runtime, call parameters, and hardware counters. The profiler can also capture calls into the CUDA runtime and CUDA driver API. A dependency analysis exposes execution dependencies and enables highlighting of the critical path between host and device. `nvprof` (and `nvvp`) also support CPU sampling for host-side activities.

Because the GUI (`nvvp`) is not always available, `nvprof` can export the analysis results in a file to be imported by `nvvp`, or it can directly print text output to `stdout` or a specified file. Listing 3.2 shows an example analysis for a C program with OpenACC directives, which solves the 2D Laplace equation with the Jacobi iterative method.[17] It shows the most runtime-consuming GPU tasks (kernels and memory copies), CUDA API calls, and OpenACC activities. Optimization efforts should focus on these hot spots. Note that `nvprof` is simply prepended to the executable program. When no options are used, the output for an OpenACC program with a CUDA target has three sections: global profile, CUDA API calls, and OpenACC activities. The list in each section is sorted by exclusive execution time.

Figure 3.2 shows the `nvvp` visualization for the same example as mentioned earlier. The main display shows a timeline that visualizes the execution of OpenACC activities, CUDA driver API calls, and CUDA kernels that have been generated by the PGI 16.10 (community edition)[18] compiler for a Tesla K80 GPU. The properties of the selected region are shown on the upper right of the figure. The region is an OpenACC enter data region with duration of about 33ms followed by a compute region. The respective CUDA API calls and CUDA kernels are shown in the underlying timeline bars. This illustrates the implementation of OpenACC constructs in the CUDA programming model in a timeline view. The `nvvp` profiler also provides summary profile tables, chart views, and a guided analysis (see the bottom half of Figure 3.2), information that supports programmers in identifying performance issues and optimization opportunities. You can use `nvvp` directly to analyze an application binary. It also allows loading a performance report that has been generated with `nvprof` or `nvvp`.

---

17. https://devblogs.nvidia.com/parallelforall/getting-started-openacc/.
18. As of July 2017, PGI 17.4 is the most recent community edition; see https://www.pgroup .com/products/community.htm.

Listing 3.2 Exemplary nvprof usage and output for an iterative Jacobi solver

```
nvprof ./laplace2d_oacc
. . .
==50330== Profiling result:
Time(%)      Time   Calls      Avg       Min       Max  Name
 58.25%  1.30766s    1000  1.3077ms  1.3022ms  1.3212ms  main_92_gpu
 40.12%  900.64ms    1000  900.64us  887.69us  915.98us  main_102_gpu
  0.55%  12.291ms    1000  12.290us  12.128us  12.640us  main_92_gpu_red
  0.54%  12.109ms    1004  12.060us    864ns   2.7994ms  [CUDA memcpy HtoD]
. . .
==50330== API calls:
Time(%)      Time   Calls      Avg       Min       Max  Name
 45.24%  1.31922s    1005  1.3127ms  9.2480us  1.3473ms  cuMemcpyDtoHAsync
 31.28%  912.13ms    3002  303.84us  2.7820us  2.4866ms  cuStreamSynchroni
  9.86%  287.63ms       1  287.63ms  287.63ms  287.63ms  cuDeviceCtxRetain
  9.55%  278.42ms       1  278.42ms  278.42ms  278.42ms  cuDeviceCtxRelease
  1.55%  45.202ms    3000  15.067us  12.214us  566.93us  cuLaunchKernel
. . .
==50330== OpenACC (excl):
Time(%)      Time   Calls      Avg       Min       Max  Name
 54.73%  1.32130s    1000  1.3213ms  1.2882ms  1.3498ms  acc_enqueue_download@laplace2d_oacc.c:92
 37.49%  905.04ms    1000  905.04us  347.17us  1.0006ms  acc_wait@laplace2d_oacc.c:102
  2.52%  60.780ms       1  60.780ms  60.780ms  60.780ms  acc_enter_data@laplace2d_oacc.c:86
  1.05%  25.246ms       1  25.246ms  25.246ms  25.246ms  acc_exit_data@laplace2d_oacc.c:86
. . .
```

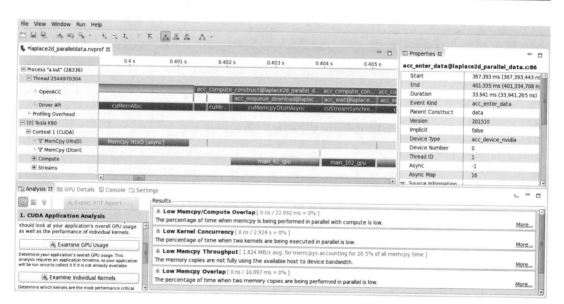

Figure 3.2 Exemplary nvvp visualization of OpenACC activities of a 2D Jacobi solver

3.3.7 THE SCORE-P TOOLS INFRASTRUCTURE FOR HYBRID APPLICATIONS

Score-P is an open source performance measurement infrastructure for several analysis tools, such as Vampir and CUBE (Cube Uniform Behavioral Encoding).[19] Score-P has a large user community and supports programming models, such as MPI, OpenMP, SHMEM,[20] CUDA, OpenCL, and OpenACC, as well as hardware counter and IO information.[21] Score-P can generate profiles in the CUBE4 format and OTF2[22] traces.

In comparison to the NVIDIA profiling tools, the focus is more on global optimizations of the program parallelization on all parallel layers. Hence, the Score-P tools scale to hundreds of thousands of processes, threads, and accelerator streams. The VI-HPS workshop material[23] and the Score-P documentation[24] provide detailed information on the Score-P analysis workflow, which can be summarized by the following steps.

1. Prepare the measurement.

2. Generate a profile.

    a. Visualize the profile with CUBE.

    b. Estimate the trace file size.

    c. Create a filtering file.

3. Generate a trace.

    a. (Optionally) Automatically analyze trace file.

    b. Visualize the trace with Vampir.

Before the measurement starts, the executable must be prepared. For OpenACC programs, the simplest way is to prepend `scorep --cuda --openacc` before

---

19. Pavel Saviankou, Michael Knobloch, Anke Visser, and Bernd Mohr, "Cube v4: From Performance Report Explorer to Performance Analysis Tool," *Procedia Computer Science* 51 (2015): 1343–1352.

20. http://www.openshmem.org/site/.

21. docs.cray.com/books/004-2178-002/06chap3.pdf.

22. Dominic Eschweiler et al., "Open Trace Format 2: The Next Generation of Scalable Trace Formats and Support Libraries," *Applications, Tools and Techniques on the Road to Exascale Computing* 22 (2012): 481–490.

23. http://www.vi-hps.org/training/material/.

24. https://silc.zih.tu-dresden.de/scorep-current/html/.

the compiler command and recompile the application. The options `cuda` and `openacc` link the respective measurement components for CUDA and OpenACC into the binary. Typing `scorep --help` prints a summary of all available options.

The measurement itself is influenced by several environment variables. The variable `scorep-info config-vars` shows a list of all measurement configuration variables with a short description. Dedicated to OpenACC is the variable `SCOREP_OPENACC_ENABLE`, which accepts a comma-separated list of features.

- `regions`: Record OpenACC regions or directives.

- `wait`: Record OpenACC wait operations.

- `enqueue`: Record OpenACC enqueue kernel, upload, and download operations.

- `device_alloc`: Record OpenACC device memory deallocation or deallocation as a counter.

- `kernel_properties`: Record kernel name as well as the gang, worker, and vector size for kernel launch operations.

- `variable_names`: Record variable names for OpenACC data allocation and enqueue upload or download.

As defined in the OpenACC 2.5 specification, you must statically link the profiling library into the application, or you must specify the path to the shared library by setting `ACC_PROFLIB=/path/to/shared/library` or `LD_PRELOAD=/path/to/shared/library`. Score-P's OpenACC profiling library is located in Score-P's `lib` directory and is called `libscorep_adapter_openacc_events.so`.

To record additional information for CUDA targets, the environment variable `SCOREP_CUDA_ENABLE` can be specified. Relevant options are as follows.

- `driver`: Record the run time of calls to CUDA driver API.

- `kernel`: Record CUDA kernels.

- `memcpy`: Record CUDA memory copies.

- `gpumemusage`: Record CUDA memory allocations or deallocations as counter.

- `flushatexit`: Flush the CUDA activity buffer at program exit.

The amount of device memory to store device activities can be set with the environment variable `SCOREP_CUDA_BUFFER` (value in bytes), if needed.

You should carefully select the events to record to avoid unnecessary measurement overhead. For example, OpenACC `enqueue` operations are typically very short regions, and the CUDA `driver` feature includes similar information by tracking API functions such as `cuLaunchKernel`. There is an option to track the device memory allocations and deallocations in both the OpenACC and the CUDA features. A recommended low-overhead setup would use `regions` and `wait` from the OpenACC features, and `kernel` and `memcpy` from the CUDA features, an approach that supplies enough information to correlate OpenACC directives with CUDA device activities.

Figure 3.3 shows the profile visualization with the CUBE GUI for a hybrid MPI/OpenMP/OpenACC program (molecular dynamics code from Indiana University[25]). Selecting the exclusive runtime in the Metric tree box on the left of the figure, the CUDA kernel `accel_296_gpu` is dominating the runtime on the GPU (with 73.63 sec) as shown in the Flat view in the center. Immediately after the kernel launch, the host starts waiting for its completion (code location is `int_ion_mix_acc.f` in line 296). The System tree on the right shows the distribution of the execution time over processes, threads, and GPU streams.

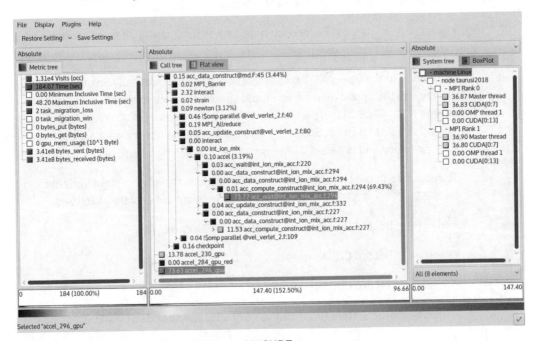

Figure 3.3 Exemplary profile visualization with CUBE
Note: Color coding (if you're viewing this electronically) or shading (if you're reading the paper version) highlights high values of a metric.

25. http://hgpu.org/?p=11116.

Figure 3.4 shows the Vampir visualization of an OTF2 trace that has been generated from the SPEC ACCEL[26] 363.swim benchmark. The selected time interval illustrates the level of detail that can be investigated using tracing. The timeline at the top of the figure shows a host stream (captioned Master thread) that triggers activities on the CUDA device stream (captioned CUDA[0:13]). Data transfers are visualized as black lines between two execution streams. Details on the selected data transfer are shown on the lower right in the Context View box. Each region in the timelines can be selected to get additional information. The Function Summary box on the upper right provides profile information of the selected time interval in the program execution. The runtime-dominating regions are an OpenACC launch in line 92 of file `swim.f`, and an OpenACC wait operation in line 124 of the same file. The CUDA stream shows some CUDA kernels (in orange if you're viewing this electronically), but most of the time the GPU is idle. The lower timeline highlights regions on the critical path, which is the longest path in the program execution that does not contain any wait states. Optimizing regions that are not on the critical path has no effect on the total program run time.

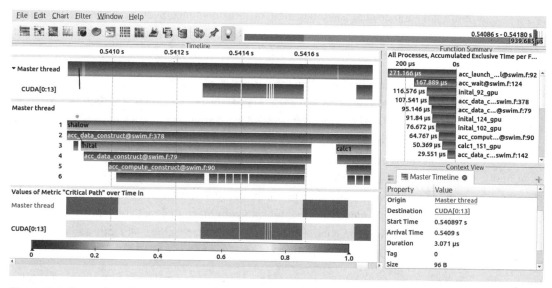

Figure 3.4 Exemplary Vampir trace visualization of the SPEC ACCEL 363.swim benchmark
Note: The GUI provides several timeline views and statistical displays. All CUDA kernels are on the critical path (lower timeline), making them reasonable optimization targets.

26. Guido Juckeland et al., "SPEC ACCEL: A Standard Application Suite for Measuring Hardware Accelerator Performance," *5th International Workshop on Performance Modeling, Benchmarking and Simulation of High Performance Computer Systems* (2014): 46–67.

OTF2 traces can provide additional OpenACC runtime information that is not available in CUBE profiles. If the feature `kernel_properties` has been set, kernel launch parameters such as gang, worker, and vector size are added to the trace. The feature `variable_names` includes the name of variables for OpenACC data allocation and OpenACC data movement. Furthermore, implicit OpenACC operations are annotated. Vampir visualizes this information in the Context View box or by generating metrics from these attributes as counters in the Counter Data Timeline or Performance Radar box. All Vampir views can be opened using the chart menu or the icons that are shown on the bar at the top of Figure 3.4.

3.3.8 TAU PERFORMANCE SYSTEM

TAU is a versatile performance analysis tool suite that supports all parallel programming paradigms and parallel execution platforms. It enables performance measurement (profiling and tracing) of hybrid parallel applications and can capture the inner workings of OpenACC programs to identify performance problems for both host and device. The integrated TAU Performance System is open source and includes tools for source analysis (PDT), parallel profile analysis (ParaProf), profile data mining (PerfExplorer), and performance data management (TAUdb).

TAU provides both probe-based instrumentation and event-based sampling to observe parallel execution and generate performance data at the routine and statement levels. Although probe-based instrumentation relies on a pair of bracketed begin and end interval events, event-based sampling relies on generating a periodic interrupt when the program's state is examined. Instrumentation in TAU is implemented by powerful mechanisms that expose code regions, such as routines and loops, at multiple levels: source, library, compiler, and binary. These features work consistently together and integrate with mechanisms to observe parallel performance events in runtime libraries. The latter include MPI, pthreads, OpenMP (via OMPT), CUDA (via CUPTI), and OpenACC.

The OpenACC 2.5 profiling interface is fully supported in TAU. Instrumentation-based performance measurement in TAU can use libraries such as PAPI to measure hardware performance counts, as well as Score-P, VampirTrace, and OTF2 to generate profiles and traces. In addition, TAU offers special measurement options that can capture performance of user-defined events, context events, calling parameters, execution phases, and so on.

TAU also supports event-based sampling (EBS) to capture performance data when the program's execution is interrupted, either periodically by an interval timer or after a hardware counter overflow occurs. With sampling, fine-grained performance measurement at the statement level is possible, as is aggregation of all statement-level performance within a routine. TAU is one of very few systems that support both probe-based instrumentation and event-based sampling. It is the only tool that integrates the performance data at run time into a hybrid profile.[27]

To automatically activate a parallel performance measurement with TAU, the command `tau_exec` was developed. The command-line options to `tau_exec` determine the instrumentation functionality that is enabled. For example, to obtain a parallel performance profile for an MPI application that uses OpenACC, you can launch the application using this line:

```
% mpirun --np <ranks> tau_exec --openacc -ebs ./a.out
```

This command will collect performance data from the OpenACC profiling interface (`-openacc`) using instrumentation, as well as data from event-based sampling (`-ebs`). A separate profile will be generated for every MPI process in this case. Note that if OpenACC is offloaded to a CPU "device" that uses multithreading, every thread of execution will have its own profile.

TAU's parallel profile browser, ParaProf, analyzes the profile generated when the application is launched by `tau_exec`. Figure 3.5 shows a view of ParaProf's thread statistics window that gives the breakdown of performance data for the Cactus BenchADM benchmark[28] from the PGI tutorial on OpenACC. Because event-based sampling was enabled for this performance experiment, ParaProf presents a hybrid performance view, where [SAMPLE] highlights an EBS sample measurement and [SUMMARY] shows the total contribution of events from that routine; "[CONTEXT]" highlights the "context" for EBS sample aggregation of the parent node. All other identifiers are instrumentation-based measurements.

In Figure 3.5, you see low-level routines that are called by the `openacc_enter_data` event for the `bench_staggeredleapfrog2` routine (in green on electronic versions), which can be found in the `StaggeredLeapfrog2_acc2.F` file.

---

27. Alan Morris, Allen D. Malony, Sameer Shende, and Kevin Huck, "Design and Implementation of a Hybrid Parallel Performance Measurement System," *Proc. International Conference on Parallel Processing (ICPP '10)* (2010).

28. PGI, "Building Cactus BenchADM with PGI Accelerator Compilers," *PGI Insider,* 2017, http://www.pgroup.com/lit/articles/insider/v1n2a4.htm.

Note that the routine calls the `openacc_enqueue_upload` event at line 369 in this file (just below the enter data event). This operation takes 5.725 seconds, as shown in the columns for exclusive and inclusive time. You also see samples generated in a routine `__c_mcopy8` (also in green), a low-level routine from `libpgc.so` that presumably copies data. This routine executes for 6.03 seconds, as reported by the EBS measurement.[29]

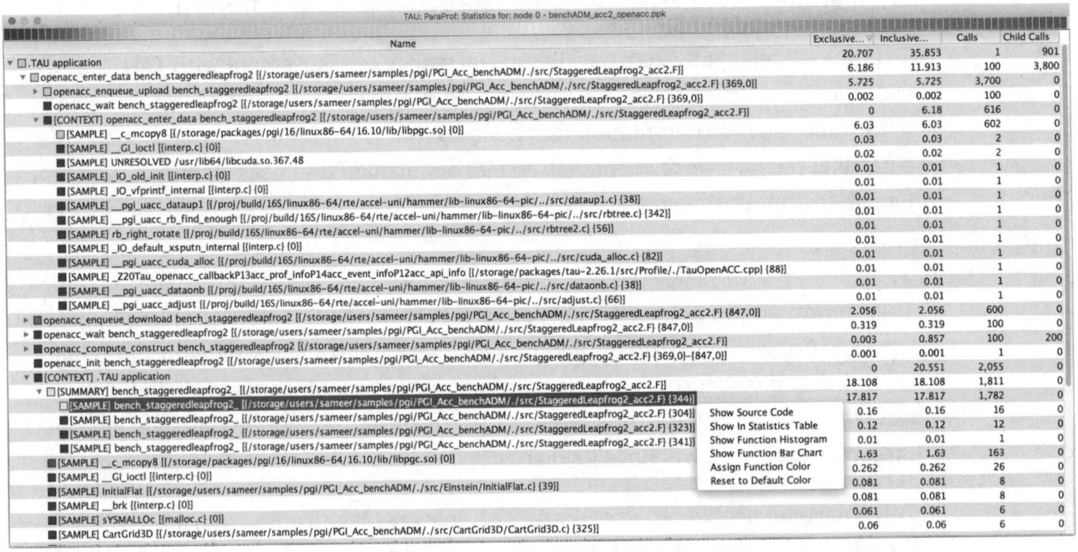

Name	Exclusive...	Inclusive...	Calls	Child Calls
.TAU application	20.707	35.853	1	901
openacc_enter_data bench_staggeredleapfrog2 [{/storage/users/sameer/samples/pgi/PGI_Acc_benchADM/./src/StaggeredLeapfrog2_acc2.F}]	6.186	11.913	100	3,800
openacc_enqueue_upload bench_staggeredleapfrog2 [{/storage/users/sameer/samples/pgi/PGI_Acc_benchADM/./src/StaggeredLeapfrog2_acc2.F} {369,0}]	5.725	5.725	3,700	0
openacc_wait bench_staggeredleapfrog2 [{/storage/users/sameer/samples/pgi/PGI_Acc_benchADM/./src/StaggeredLeapfrog2_acc2.F} {369,0}]	0.002	0.002	100	0
[CONTEXT] openacc_enter_data bench_staggeredleapfrog2 [{/storage/users/sameer/samples/pgi/PGI_Acc_benchADM/./src/StaggeredLeapfrog2_acc2.F}]	0	6.18	616	0
[SAMPLE] __c_mcopy8 [{/storage/packages/pgi/16/linux86-64/16.10/lib/libpgc.so} {0}]	6.03	6.03	602	0
[SAMPLE] __GI_ioctl [{interp.c} {0}]	0.03	0.03	2	0
[SAMPLE] UNRESOLVED /usr/lib64/libcuda.so.367.48	0.02	0.02	2	0
[SAMPLE] _IO_old_init [{interp.c} {0}]	0.01	0.01	1	0
[SAMPLE] _IO_vfprintf_internal [{interp.c} {0}]	0.01	0.01	1	0
[SAMPLE] __pgi_uacc_dataup1 [{/proj/build/16S/linux86-64/rte/accel-uni/hammer/lib-linux86-64-pic/../src/dataup1.c} {38}]	0.01	0.01	1	0
[SAMPLE] __pgi_uacc_rb_find_enough [{/proj/build/16S/linux86-64/rte/accel-uni/hammer/lib-linux86-64-pic/../src/rbtree.c} {342}]	0.01	0.01	1	0
[SAMPLE] rb_right_rotate [{/proj/build/16S/linux86-64/rte/accel-uni/hammer/lib-linux86-64-pic/../src/rbtree2.c} {56}]	0.01	0.01	1	0
[SAMPLE] _IO_default_xsputn_internal [{interp.c} {0}]	0.01	0.01	1	0
[SAMPLE] __pgi_uacc_cuda_alloc [{/proj/build/16S/linux86-64/rte/accel-uni/hammer/lib-linux86-64-pic/../src/cuda_alloc.c} {82}]	0.01	0.01	1	0
[SAMPLE] _Z20Tau_openacc_callbackP13acc_prof_infoP14acc_event_infoP12acc_api_info [{/storage/packages/tau-2.26.1/src/Profile/./TauOpenACC.cpp} {88}]	0.01	0.01	1	0
[SAMPLE] __pgi_uacc_dataonb [{/proj/build/16S/linux86-64/rte/accel-uni/hammer/lib-linux86-64-pic/../src/dataonb.c} {38}]	0.01	0.01	1	0
[SAMPLE] __pgi_uacc_adjust [{/proj/build/16S/linux86-64/rte/accel-uni/hammer/lib-linux86-64-pic/../src/adjust.c} {66}]	0.01	0.01	1	0
openacc_enqueue_download bench_staggeredleapfrog2 [{/storage/users/sameer/samples/pgi/PGI_Acc_benchADM/./src/StaggeredLeapfrog2_acc2.F} {847,0}]	2.056	2.056	600	0
openacc_wait bench_staggeredleapfrog2 [{/storage/users/sameer/samples/pgi/PGI_Acc_benchADM/./src/StaggeredLeapfrog2_acc2.F} {847,0}]	0.319	0.319	100	0
openacc_compute_construct bench_staggeredleapfrog2 [{/storage/users/sameer/samples/pgi/PGI_Acc_benchADM/./src/StaggeredLeapfrog2_acc2.F}]	0.003	0.857	100	200
openacc_init bench_staggeredleapfrog2 [{/storage/users/sameer/samples/pgi/PGI_Acc_benchADM/./src/StaggeredLeapfrog2_acc2.F} {369,0}-{847,0}]	0.001	0.001	1	0
[CONTEXT] .TAU application	0	20.551	2,055	0
[SUMMARY] bench_staggeredleapfrog2_ [{/storage/users/sameer/samples/pgi/PGI_Acc_benchADM/./src/StaggeredLeapfrog2_acc2.F}]	18.108	18.108	1,811	0
[SAMPLE] bench_staggeredleapfrog2_ [{/storage/users/sameer/samples/pgi/PGI_Acc_benchADM/./src/StaggeredLeapfrog2_acc2.F} {344}]	17.817	17.817	1,782	0
[SAMPLE] bench_staggeredleapfrog2_ [{/storage/users/sameer/samples/pgi/PGI_Acc_benchADM/./src/StaggeredLeapfrog2_acc2.F} {304}]	0.16	0.16	16	0
[SAMPLE] bench_staggeredleapfrog2_ [{/storage/users/sameer/samples/pgi/PGI_Acc_benchADM/./src/StaggeredLeapfrog2_acc2.F} {323}]	0.12	0.12	12	0
[SAMPLE] bench_staggeredleapfrog2_ [{/storage/users/sameer/samples/pgi/PGI_Acc_benchADM/./src/StaggeredLeapfrog2_acc2.F} {341}]	0.01	0.01	1	0
[SAMPLE] __c_mcopy8 [{/storage/packages/pgi/16/linux86-64/16.10/lib/libpgc.so} {0}]	1.63	1.63	163	0
[SAMPLE] __GI_ioctl [{interp.c} {0}]	0.262	0.262	26	0
[SAMPLE] InitialFlat [{/storage/users/sameer/samples/pgi/PGI_Acc_benchADM/./src/Einstein/InitialFlat.c} {39}]	0.081	0.081	8	0
[SAMPLE] __brk [{interp.c} {0}]	0.081	0.081	8	0
[SAMPLE] sYSMALLOc [{malloc.c} {0}]	0.061	0.061	6	0
[SAMPLE] CartGrid3D [{/storage/users/sameer/samples/pgi/PGI_Acc_benchADM/./src/CartGrid3D/CartGrid3D.c} {325}]	0.06	0.06	6	0

Figure 3.5 Exemplary TAU ParaProf thread statistics window showing the time spent in OpenACC and host code segments in a tree display

The color coding (or shading, if you're reading the paper edition) indicates performance intensity. For instance, the `bench_staggeredleapfrog2_` routine at sample line 344 takes as much as 17.817 seconds of the total inclusive time of 35.853 seconds for the top level (identified as the TAU Application routine). As you see in Figure 3.5, by right-clicking and selecting a line of code, you can select the Show Source Code option to launch the source browser. The result is shown in Figure 3.6. It appears that this is a highly intensive computational loop that can be moved to the GPU using OpenACC constructs. You could easily turn on additional measurement, such as hardware counters, to investigate the performance behavior further.

---

29. Note that TAU can generate call-path profiles showing the nesting of events up to a certain call-path depth. A pair of environment variables is used to enable call-path profiling (`TAU_CALLPATH`) and to set the depth (`TAU_CALLPATH_DEPTH`). In this example, these variables were set to `1` and `1000`, respectively.

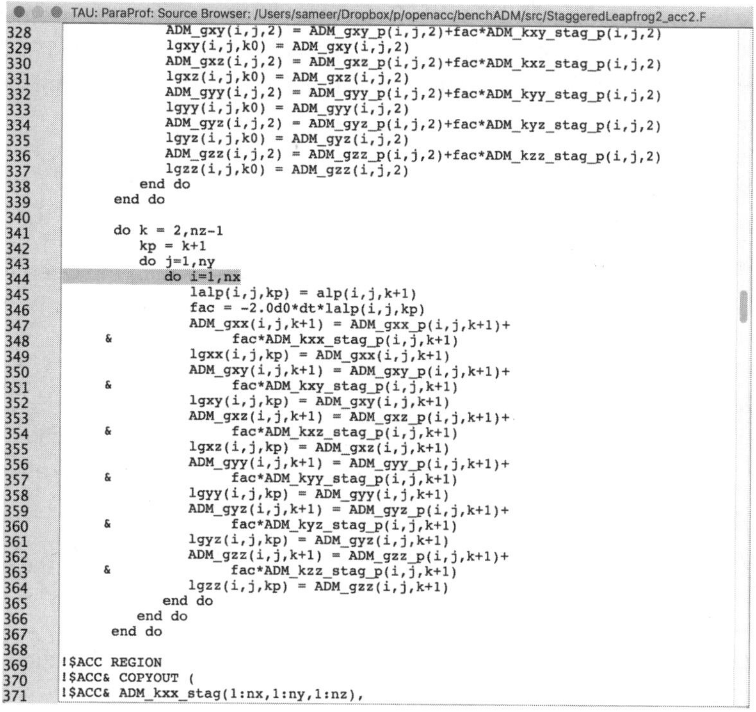

TAU: ParaProf: Source Browser: /Users/sameer/Dropbox/p/openacc/benchADM/src/StaggeredLeapfrog2_acc2.F

```
328                 ADM_gxy(i,j,2) = ADM_gxy_p(i,j,2)+fac*ADM_kxy_stag_p(i,j,2)
329                 lgxy(i,j,k0) = ADM_gxy(i,j,2)
330                 ADM_gxz(i,j,2) = ADM_gxz_p(i,j,2)+fac*ADM_kxz_stag_p(i,j,2)
331                 lgxz(i,j,k0) = ADM_gxz(i,j,2)
332                 ADM_gyy(i,j,2) = ADM_gyy_p(i,j,2)+fac*ADM_kyy_stag_p(i,j,2)
333                 lgyy(i,j,k0) = ADM_gyy(i,j,2)
334                 ADM_gyz(i,j,2) = ADM_gyz_p(i,j,2)+fac*ADM_kyz_stag_p(i,j,2)
335                 lgyz(i,j,k0) = ADM_gyz(i,j,2)
336                 ADM_gzz(i,j,2) = ADM_gzz_p(i,j,2)+fac*ADM_kzz_stag_p(i,j,2)
337                 lgzz(i,j,k0) = ADM_gzz(i,j,2)
338             end do
339         end do
340
341         do k = 2,nz-1
342             kp = k+1
343             do j=1,ny
344                 do i=1,nx
345                     lalp(i,j,kp) = alp(i,j,k+1)
346                     fac = -2.0d0*dt*lalp(i,j,kp)
347                     ADM_gxx(i,j,k+1) = ADM_gxx_p(i,j,k+1)+
348      &                  fac*ADM_kxx_stag_p(i,j,k+1)
349                     lgxx(i,j,kp) = ADM_gxx(i,j,k+1)
350                     ADM_gxy(i,j,k+1) = ADM_gxy_p(i,j,k+1)+
351      &                  fac*ADM_kxy_stag_p(i,j,k+1)
352                     lgxy(i,j,kp) = ADM_gxy(i,j,k+1)
353                     ADM_gxz(i,j,k+1) = ADM_gxz_p(i,j,k+1)+
354      &                  fac*ADM_kxz_stag_p(i,j,k+1)
355                     lgxz(i,j,kp) = ADM_gxz(i,j,k+1)
356                     ADM_gyy(i,j,k+1) = ADM_gyy_p(i,j,k+1)+
357      &                  fac*ADM_kyy_stag_p(i,j,k+1)
358                     lgyy(i,j,kp) = ADM_gyy(i,j,k+1)
359                     ADM_gyz(i,j,k+1) = ADM_gyz_p(i,j,k+1)+
360      &                  fac*ADM_kyz_stag_p(i,j,k+1)
361                     lgyz(i,j,kp) = ADM_gyz(i,j,k+1)
362                     ADM_gzz(i,j,k+1) = ADM_gzz_p(i,j,k+1)+
363      &                  fac*ADM_kzz_stag_p(i,j,k+1)
364                     lgzz(i,j,kp) = ADM_gzz(i,j,k+1)
365                 end do
366             end do
367         end do
368
369 !$ACC REGION
370 !$ACC& COPYOUT (
371 !$ACC& ADM_kxx_stag(1:nx,1:ny,1:nz),
```

Figure 3.6 Exemplary TAU ParaProf source browser window showing the innermost loop on line 344, where the application spends 17.817 seconds

3.4 Identifying Bugs in OpenACC Programs

Program bugs typically cause unexpected or incorrect results, or errors that occur during the run time of the program. In general, a **bug** is a mistake made in the logic of a solution to a problem or in programming of that solution. **Debugging** is the process of finding and fixing a bug. It is a major part in the application development process and requires tools to help expose the bugs. Because OpenACC programs are executed on host and device, debugging is complicated. Additionally, the compiler has some leeway in interpreting several OpenACC directives, which might lead to "false bugs."

The OpenACC specification does not define a debugging interface up to version 2.5. However, individual OpenACC compilers and runtimes provide environment variables to enable debugging output. You should consider this option before starting with tedious `printf` debugging, because the source code does not need to be changed. The GNU OpenACC runtime prints debug output if you set `GOMP_DEBUG=1`. The PGI compiler enables debug output with `ACC_NOTIFY=1`. Unfortunately, such debugging output can become lengthy, or the relevant information is not provided.

Thus, the following steps should help you systematically identify bugs in OpenACC programs.

1. Compile and execute the program without interpreting the OpenACC directives (without the `-acc` flag) to ensure that the bug arises in the context of the OpenACC implementation.

2. Use additional compiler output on OpenACC directives (e.g., `-Minfo=accel`) with the PGI compiler. This action typically provides information on the parallelization of loops and the implementation of data copy operations. Check whether the compiler does what it is supposed to do.

3. Check which version of the OpenACC specification is used by the compiler. Review the respective specification in uncertain cases.

4. Isolate the bug by, for example, moving code from OpenACC compute regions back to the host.

5. Use debuggers such as TotalView[30] and Allinea DDT,[31] which can be used for debugging at runtime in both host and device code.

Parallel debuggers, such as DDT and TotalView, allow debugging of host and device code. This includes viewing variables and intrinsic values such as the `threadIdx` in CUDA kernels. Similarly, it is possible to set breakpoints in host and device code. Debugging of the device code is restricted to CUDA targets in the current version of both debuggers. Figure 3.7 shows exemplary debugging output of DDT for a CUDA program with a memory access error.[32] Here, CUDA thread 254 tries to access an "illegal lane address" and causes a signal to occur. At this point, the respective pointer can be investigated, and the issue can be traced.

---

30. http://www.roguewave.com/products-services/totalview.
31. https://www.allinea.com/products/ddt.
32. https://www.allinea.com/blog/debugging-cuda-dynamic-parallelism.

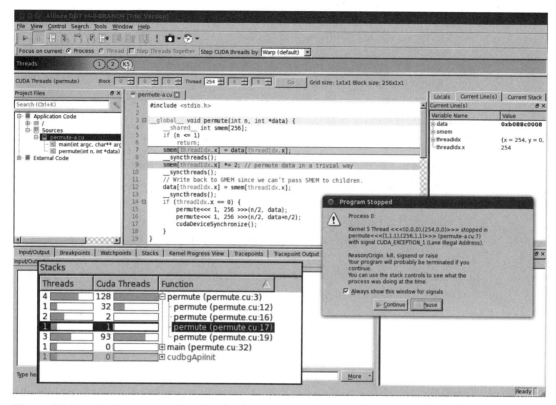

Figure 3.7 Parallel debugging with Allinea DDT supporting OpenACC with CUDA target devices
Image courtesy of Allinea.

3.5 Summary

Several tools are available to help developers analyze their OpenACC code to get correct and high-performing OpenACC applications. Programming tools for OpenACC must cope with the concept of computation offloading, and this means that performance analysis and debugging must be performed on the host and the accelerator.

OpenACC 2.5 provides a profiling interface to gather events from an OpenACC runtime. Information on the accelerator performance must be acquired based on the target APIs used for the respective accelerator. Tools such as Score-P and TAU measure those performance data on both the host and the accelerator.

Furthermore, they let you investigate programs that additionally use interprocess communication and multithreading.

Because the OpenACC compiler generates the device code, you would think you would not need to debug OpenACC compute kernels. But it is still possible to have logic and coding errors. Also, there are several other sources of errors that can be detected based on compiler or runtime debugging output. Tools such as TotalView and DDT support the debugging of OpenACC programs on host and CUDA devices.

Debugging and performance analysis are not one-time events. Because the compiler has some leeway in implementing the specification and because there are many different accelerators, optimizations can differ for each combination of compiler and accelerator. The same thing applies to bugs, which may occur only for a specific combination of compiler and accelerator. Software tools simplify the process of debugging and performance analysis. Because OpenACC is about performance, profile-driven program development is recommended. With the available tools, you can avoid do-it-yourself solutions.

3.6 Exercises

For a better understanding of compiling, analyzing, and debugging of OpenACC programs, we accelerate the Game of Life (GoL) with OpenACC. The C code appears in Listing 3.3.

The Game of Life is a cellular automaton that has been developed by mathematician John Horton Conway. The system is based on an infinite two-dimensional orthogonal grid. Each cell has eight neighbors and can have one of two possible states: dead or alive. Based on an initial pattern, further generations are determined with the following rules.

- Any dead cell with exactly three living neighbors becomes a living cell.

- Any living cell with two or three living neighbors lives on to the next generation.

- Any living cell with more than three or fewer than two living neighbors dies.

The program uses a two-dimensional stencil that sums up the eight closest neighbors and applies the game rules. The initial state can be randomly generated. Ghost cells are used to implement periodic boundary conditions. Cells are not updated until the end of the iteration.

Listing 3.3 Game of Life: CPU code

```c
#include <stdio.h>
#include <stdlib.h>
void gol(int *grid, int *newGrid, cons tint dim) {
  int i,j;
  // copy ghost rows
  for (i = 1; i <= dim; i++) {
    grid[(dim+2)*(dim+1)+i] = grid[(dim+2)+i];
    grid[i] = grid[(dim+2)*dim + i];
  }
  // copy ghost columns
  for (i = 0; i <= dim+1; i++) {
    grid[i*(dim+2)+dim+1] = grid[i*(dim+2)+1];
    grid[i*(dim+2)] = grid[i*(dim+2) + dim];
  }
  // iterate over the grid
  for (i = 1; i <= dim; i++) {
    for (j = 1; j <= dim; j++) {
      int id = i*(dim+2) + j;
      int numNeighbors =
          grid[id+(dim+2)] + grid[id-(dim+2)]   // lower + upper
          + grid[id+1] + grid[id-1]             // right + left
          + grid[id+(dim+3)] + grid[id-(dim+3)] // diagonal right
          + grid[id-(dim+1)] + grid[id+(dim+1)];// diagonal left
      // the game rules (0=dead, 1=alive)
      if (grid[id] == 1 && numNeighbors < 2)
        newGrid[id] = 0;
      else if (grid[id] == 1
               && (numNeighbors == 2 || numNeighbors == 3))
        newGrid[id] = 1;
      else if (grid[id] == 1 && numNeighbors > 3)
        newGrid[id] = 0;
      else if (grid[id] == 0 && numNeighbors == 3)
        newGrid[id] = 1;
      else
        newGrid[id] = grid[id];
    }
  }
  // copy new grid over, as pointers cannot be switched on the
  // device (the CPU code could switch pointers only)
  for (i = 1; i <= dim; i++) {
    for (j = 1; j <= dim; j++) {
      int id = i*(dim+2) + j;
      grid[id] = newGrid[id];
    }
  }
}
int main(int argc, char* argv[])
{
  int i, j, it, total;
  // grid dimension (without ghost cells)
  int dim = 1024;
  if (argc > 1) dim = atoi(argv[1]);
  // number of game steps
  int itEnd = 1 << 11;
```

Listing 3.3 Game of Life: CPU code (*continued*)

```
if (argc > 2) itEnd = atoi(argv[2]);
// grid array with dimension dim + ghost columns and rows
int arraySize = (dim+2) * (dim+2);

// current grid
int    *grid  = (int*)malloc(arraySize * sizeof(int));     // result grid
int *newGrid  = (int*) malloc(arraySize * sizeof(int));
// assign initial population randomly
srand(1985); // pseudo random with a fixed seed
for(i = 1; i <= dim; i++) {
  for(j = 1; j <= dim; j++) {
    int id = i*(dim+2) + j;
    grid[id] = rand() % 2;
  }
}
for (it = 0; it < itEnd; it++){
  gol( grid, newGrid, dim );
}
// sum up alive cells
total = 0; // total number of alive cells
for (i = 1; i <= dim; i++) {
  for (j = 1; j <= dim; j++) {
    int id = i*(dim+2) + j;
    total += grid[id];
  }
}
printf("Total Alive: %d\n", total);
return 0;
}
```

The following tasks demonstrate the tools presented in this chapter. Use a profile-driven approach to accelerate GoL with OpenACC.

1. Measure the runtime of the sequential CPU code that implements the game of life per Listing 3.3. Use 1024 as grid dimension and 2048 steps. What is dominating the runtime of the CPU code? The runtime can be easily measured by prepending `time` before the executable.

2. Add OpenACC compute directives to execute one game step (iteration) on the device.

   a. Compile the code using, for example, `pgcc -acc gol_acc.c -o gol_acc`.

   b. Use `-Minfo=accel` with the PGI compiler to spot potential issues.

   c. If necessary, use `ACC_NOTIFY=1` to identify when an error occurs or alternatively (and if available), use DDT or TotalView to find bugs.

d. Make sure that the `grid` and `newGrid` arrays are available on the device. Add a respective clause to the compute construct, if necessary.

e. Identify loops without dependencies between iterations, and add respective loop constructs (`#pragma acc loop independent`).

f. Measure the runtime of the OpenACC program.

3. Use `nvprof` to profile the program. What is dominating the device runtime or is preventing the device from computing?

4. Use the data construct (or data enter or exit constructs) to avoid unnecessary host-device data movement between game iterations. Verify the result using `nvprof` or `nvvp`.

5. Count all living cells in parallel on the device using the OpenACC parallel construct.

6. Use Score-P to analyze the final OpenACC program.

a. Instrument the program using Score-P.

b. Set all required environment variables to capture OpenACC events and eventually CUDA or OpenCL device activity.

c. Generate a profile, and visualize it with the CUBE GUI.

d. What is dominating the runtime on the host? Which kernels are dominating the device runtime?

e. Measure the effect of gang, worker, and vector clauses on loop constructs. Try different values. The performance might depend on the grid size.

   i. Add `kernel_properties` to `SCOREP_OPENACC_ENABLE`.

   ii. Generate a trace file and visualize it with Vampir.

   iii. Select the OpenACC kernel launch regions to get details on the launch properties.

   iv. Which OpenACC runtime operations have been implicitly generated?

Chapter 4

Using OpenACC for Your First Program

John Urbanic, Pittsburgh Supercomputing Center

In this chapter, you'll parallelize real code. You will start with code that does something useful. Then you'll consider how you might use OpenACC to speed it up. You will see that reducing data movement is key to achieving significant speedup, and that OpenACC gives you the tools to do so. By the end of the chapter you will be able to call yourself an OpenACC programmer—a fledgling one, perhaps, but on your way. Let's jump right into it.

4.1 Case Study

You are reading a book about OpenACC programming, so it's a safe bet the authors are fans of this approach to parallel programming. Although that's a perfectly sensible thing, it has its dangers. It is tempting for enthusiasts to cherry-pick examples that make it seem as if their favored technology is perfect for everything. Anyone with experience in parallel programming has seen this before. We are determined not to do that here.

Our example is so generically useful that it has many applications, and it is often used to demonstrate programming with other parallel techniques as well, such as the somewhat related OpenMP and the very different MPI. So, rest assured, we haven't rigged the game.

Another reason we prefer this example is that both the "science" and the numerical method are intuitive. Although we will solve the Laplace equation for steady-state temperature distribution using Jacobi iteration, we don't expect that you immediately know what that means.

Let's look at the physical problem. You have a square metal plate. It is initially at zero degrees. This is termed, unsurprisingly, the **initial conditions.** You will heat two of the edges in an interesting pattern where you heat the lower-right corner (as pictured in Figure 4.1A) to 100 degrees. You control the two heating elements that lead from this corner such that they go steadily to zero degrees at their farthest edge. The other two edges you will hold at zero degrees. These four edges constitute the **boundary conditions.**

For the metal plate, you would probably guess the ultimate solution should look something like Figure 4.1B.

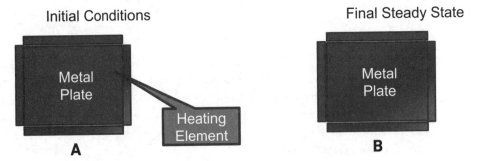

Figure 4.1 A heated metal plate

You have a very hot corner, a very cold corner, and some kind of gradient in between. This is what the ultimate, numerically solved solution should look like.

If you are wondering whether this is degrees centigrade or Fahrenheit, or maybe Kelvin, you are overthinking the problem. If you have a mathematical method or numerical background, you should be interested to know that the equation that governs heat distribution is the Laplace equation:

$$\nabla^2 T = 0$$

Although this equation has many interesting applications, including electrostatics and fluid flow, and many fascinating mathematical properties, it also has a straightforward and intuitive meaning in this context. It simply means that the value of interest (in our case, temperature) at any point is the average of the neighbor's values. This makes sense for temperature; if you have a pebble and you put a cold stone on one side and a hot stone on the other, you'd probably guess that the pebble would come to the average of the two. And in general, you would be right.

4.1.1 SERIAL CODE

Let's represent the metal plate using a grid, which becomes a typical two-dimensional array in code. The Laplace equation says that every point in the grid should be the average of the neighbors. This is the state you will solve for.

The simulation starting point—the set of initial conditions—is far from this. You have zero everywhere except some big jumps along the edges where the heating elements are. You want to end up with something that resembles the desired solution.

There are many ways you can find this solution, but let's pick a particularly straightforward one: Jacobi iteration. This method simply says that if you go over your grid and set each element equal to the average of the neighbors, and keep doing this, you will eventually converge on the correct answer. You will know when you have reached the right answer because when you make your averaging pass, the values will already be averaged (the Laplace condition) and so nothing will happen. Of course, these are floating-point numbers, so you will pick some small error, which defines "nothing happening." In this case, we will say that when no element changes more than one-hundredth of a degree, we are done. If that isn't good enough for you, you can easily change it and continue to a smaller error.

Your serial algorithm looks like this at the core.

```
for(i = 1; i <= HEIGHT; i++) {
    for(j = 1; j <= WIDTH; j++) {
        Temperature[i][j] = 0.25 * (Temperature_previous[i+1][j]
                                 + Temperature_previous[i-1][j]
                                 + Temperature_previous[i][j+1]
                                 + Temperature_previous[i][j-1]);
    }
}
```

Here it is in Fortran:

```
do j=1,width
   do i=1,height
        temperature(i,j) =0.25*(temperature_previous(i+1,j)&
                             + temperature_previous(i-1,j)&
                             + temperature_previous(i,j+1)&
                             + temperature_previous(i,j-1))
   enddo
enddo
```

Note that the C and Fortran code snippets are virtually identical in construction. This will remain true for the entire program.

This nested loop is the guts of the method and in some sense contains all the science of the simulation. You are iterating over your metal plate in both dimensions and setting every interior point equal to the average of the neighbors (i.e., adding together and dividing by 4). You don't change the very outside elements; those are the heating elements (or boundary conditions). There are a few other items in the main iteration loop as it repeats until convergence. Listing 4.1 shows the C code, and Listing 4.2 shows the Fortran code.

Listing 4.1 C Laplace code main loop

```
while ( worst_dt > TEMP_TOLERANCE ) {

    for(i = 1; i <= HEIGHT; i++) {
        for(j = 1; j <= WIDTH; j++) {
            Temperature[i][j] = 0.25 * (Temperature_previous[i+1][j]
                                + Temperature_previous[i-1][j]
                                + Temperature_previous[i][j+1]
                                + Temperature_previous[i][j-1]);
        }
    }

    worst_dt = 0.0;

    for(i = 1; i <= HEIGHT; i++){
        for(j = 1; j <= WIDTH; j++){
            worst_dt = fmax( fabs(Temperature[i][j]-
                                Temperature_previous[i][j]),
                        worst_dt);
            Temperature_previous[i][j] = Temperature[i][j];
        }
    }

    if((iteration % 100) == 0) {
        track_progress(iteration);
    }

    iteration++;
}
```

Listing 4.2 Fortran Laplace code main loop

```fortran
do while ( worst_dt > temp_tolerance )

    do j=1,width
        do i=1,height
            temperature(i,j) =0.25*(temperature_previous(i+1,j)&
                                + temperature_previous(i-1,j)&
                                + temperature_previous(i,j+1)&
                                + temperature_previous(i,j-1))
        enddo
    enddo

    worst_dt=0.0

    do j=1,width
        do i=1,height
            worst_dt = max( abs(temperature(i,j) - &
                            temperature_previous(i,j)),&
                        worst_dt )
            temperature_previous(i,j) = temperature(i,j)
        enddo
    enddo

    if( mod(iteration,100).eq.0 ) then
        call track_progress(temperature, iteration)
    endif

    iteration = iteration+1

enddo
```

The important addition is that you have a second array that keeps the temperature data from the last iteration. If you tried to use one array, you would find yourself using some updated neighboring elements and some old neighboring elements from the previous iteration as you were updating points in the grid. You need to make sure you use only elements from the last iteration.

While you are doing this nested loop copy to your backup array (and moving all this data around in memory), it's a good time to look for the worst (most changing) element in the simulation. When the worst element changes only by 0.01 degree, you know you are finished.

It might also be nice to track your progress as you go; it's much better than star-ing at a blank screen for the duration. So, every 100 iterations, let's call a modest output routine.

That is all there is to it for your serial Laplace Solver. Even with the initialization and output code, the full program clocks in at fewer than 100 lines. (See Listing 4.3 for the C code, and Listing 4.4 for Fortran.)

Listing 4.3 Serial Laplace Solver in C

```c
#include <stdlib.h>
#include <stdio.h>
#include <math.h>
#include <sys/time.h>

#define WIDTH       1000
#define HEIGHT      1000
#define TEMP_TOLERANCE 0.01

double Temperature[HEIGHT+2][WIDTH+2];
double Temperature_previous[HEIGHT+2][WIDTH+2];

void initialize();
void track_progress(int iter);

int main(int argc, char *argv[]) {

  int i, j;
  int iteration=1;
  double worst_dt=100;
  struct timeval start_time, stop_time, elapsed_time;

  gettimeofday(&start_time,NULL);

  initialize();

  while ( worst_dt > TEMP_TOLERANCE ) {

    for(i = 1; i <= HEIGHT; i++) {
      for(j = 1; j <= WIDTH; j++) {
        Temperature[i][j] = 0.25 * (Temperature_previous[i+1][j]
                                  + Temperature_previous[i-1][j]
                                  + Temperature_previous[i][j+1]
                                  + Temperature_previous[i][j-1]);
      }
    }

    worst_dt = 0.0;

    for(i = 1; i <= HEIGHT; i++){
      for(j = 1; j <= WIDTH; j++){
        worst_dt = fmax( fabs(Temperature[i][j]-
                              Temperature_previous[i][j]),
```

```
                               worst_dt);
            Temperature_previous[i][j] = Temperature[i][j];
       }
     }

     if((iteration % 100) == 0) {
       track_progress(iteration);
     }

     iteration++;
   }

   gettimeofday(&stop_time,NULL);
   timersub(&stop_time, &start_time, &elapsed_time);

   printf("\nMax error at iteration %d was %f\n",
           iteration-1, worst_dt);
   printf("Total time was %f seconds.\n",
           elapsed_time.tv_sec+elapsed_time.tv_usec/1000000.0);
}

void initialize(){

  int i,j;

  for(i = 0; i <= HEIGHT+1; i++){
    for (j = 0; j <= WIDTH+1; j++){
      Temperature_previous[i][j] = 0.0;
    }
  }

  for(i = 0; i <= HEIGHT+1; i++) {
    Temperature_previous[i][0] = 0.0;
    Temperature_previous[i][WIDTH+1] = (100.0/HEIGHT)*i;
  }

  for(j = 0; j <= WIDTH+1; j++) {
    Temperature_previous[0][j] = 0.0;
    Temperature_previous[HEIGHT+1][j] = (100.0/WIDTH)*j;
  }
}

void track_progress(int iteration) {

  int i;

  printf("---------- Iteration number: %d ------------\n",
          iteration);
  for(i = HEIGHT-5; i <= HEIGHT; i++) {
    printf("[%d,%d]: %5.2f  ", i, i, Temperature[i][i]);
  }
  printf("\n");
}
```

Listing 4.4 Fortran version of serial Laplace Solver

```fortran
program serial
  implicit none

  integer, parameter              :: width=1000
  integer, parameter              :: height=1000
  double precision, parameter     :: temp_tolerance=0.01

  integer                         :: i, j, iteration=1
  double precision                :: worst_dt=100.0
  real                            :: start_time, stop_time

  double precision, dimension(0:height+1,0:width+1) :: &
                          temperature, temperature_previous

  call cpu_time(start_time)

  call initialize(temperature_previous)

  do while ( worst_dt > temp_tolerance )

    do j=1,width
      do i=1,height
        temperature(i,j) = 0.25* (temperature_previous(i+1,j)&
                          + temperature_previous(i-1,j)&
                          + temperature_previous(i,j+1)&
                          + temperature_previous(i,j-1))
      enddo
    enddo

    worst_dt=0.0

    do j=1,width
      do i=1,height
        worst_dt = max( abs(temperature(i,j) - &
                        temperature_previous(i,j)),&
                    worst_dt )
        temperature_previous(i,j) = temperature(i,j)
      enddo
    enddo

    if( mod(iteration,100).eq.0 ) then
      call track_progress(temperature, iteration)
    endif

    iteration = iteration+1

  enddo

  call cpu_time(stop_time)

  print*, 'Max error at iteration ', iteration-1, ' was ', &
          worst_dt
  print*, 'Total time was ',stop_time-start_time, ' seconds.'
end program serial
```

```fortran
subroutine initialize( temperature_previous )
  implicit none
  integer, parameter              :: width=1000
  integer, parameter              :: height=1000
  integer                         :: i,j
  double precision, dimension(0:height+1,0:width+1) :: &
                    temperature_previous

  temperature_previous = 0.0

  do i=0,height+1
    temperature_previous(i,0) = 0.0
    temperature_previous(i,width+1) = (100.0/height) * i
  enddo

  do j=0,width+1
    temperature_previous(0,j) = 0.0
    temperature_previous(height+1,j) = ((100.0)/width) * j
  enddo
end subroutine initialize

subroutine track_progress(temperature, iteration)
  implicit none
  integer, parameter              :: width=1000
  integer, parameter              :: height=1000
  integer                         :: i,iteration

  double precision, dimension(0:height+1,0:width+1) :: &
        temperature

  print *, '------- Iteration number: ', iteration, ' ------'
  do i=5,0,-1
    write (*,'("("i4,",",i4,"):",f6.2,"   ")',advance='no') &
           height-i,width-i,temperature(height-i,width-i)
  enddo
  print *
end subroutine track_progress
```

4.1.2 COMPILING THE CODE

Take a few minutes to make sure you understand the code fully. In addition to the main loop, you have a small bit of initialization, a timer to aid in optimizing, and a basic output routine. This code compiles as simply as

```
pgcc laplace.c
```

Here it is for the PGI compiler:

```
pgcc laplace.f90
```

We use PGI for performance consistency in this chapter. Any other standard compiler would work the same. If you run the resulting executable, you will see something like this:

```
. . .
. . .
---------- Iteration number: 3200 ------------
. . . [998,998]: 99.18  [999,999]: 99.56  [1000,1000]: 99.86
---------- Iteration number: 3300 ------------
. . . [998,998]: 99.19  [999,999]: 99.56  [1000,1000]: 99.87

Max error at iteration 3372 was 0.009995
Total time was 21.344162 seconds.
```

The output shows that the simulation looped 3,372 times before all the elements stabilized (to within our 0.01 degree tolerance). If you examine the full output, you can see the elements converge from their zero-degree starting point.

The times for both the C and the Fortran version will be very close here and as you progress throughout optimization. Of course, the time will vary depending on the CPU you are using. In this case, we are using an Intel Broadwell running at 3.0 GHz. At the time of this writing, it is a very good processor, so our eventual speedups won't be compared against a poor serial baseline.

This is the last time you will look at any code outside the main loop. You will henceforth exploit the wonderful ability of OpenACC to allow you to focus on a small portion of your code—be it a single routine, or even a single loop—and ignore the rest. You will return to this point when you are finished.

4.2 Creating a Naive Parallel Version

In many other types of parallel programming, you would be wise to stare at your code and plot various approaches and alternative algorithms before you even consider starting to type. With OpenACC, the low effort and quick feedback allow you to dive right in and try some things without much risk of wasted effort.

4.2.1 FIND THE HOT SPOT

Almost always the first thing to do is find the **hot spot**: the point of highest numerical intensity in your code. A profiler like those you've read about will quickly locate and rank these spots. Often, as is the case here, it is obvious where to start. A large loop is a big flag, and you have two of them within the main loop. This is where we focus.

4.2.2 IS IT SAFE TO USE KERNELS?

The biggest hammer in your toolbox is the `kernels` directive. Refer to Chapter 1 for full details on `kernels`. Don't resist the urge to put it in front of some large, nested loop. One nice feature about this directive is that it is safe out of the box; until you start to override its default behavior with additional directives, the compiler will be able to see whether there are any code-breaking dependencies, and it will make sure that the device has access to all the required data.

4.2.3 OPENACC IMPLEMENTATIONS

Let's charge ahead and put `kernels` directives in front of the two big loops. The C and Fortran codes become the code shown in Listings 4.5 and 4.6.

Listing 4.5 C Laplace code main loop with kernels directives

```
while ( worst_dt > TEMP_TOLERANCE ) {

   #pragma acc kernels
   for(i = 1; i <= HEIGHT; i++) {
      for(j = 1; j <= WIDTH; j++) {
         Temperature[i][j] = 0.25 * (Temperature_previous[i+1][j]
                           + Temperature_previous[i-1][j]
                           + Temperature_previous[i][j+1]
                           + Temperature_previous[i][j-1]);
      }
   }

   worst_dt = 0.0;

   #pragma acc kernels
   for(i = 1; i <= HEIGHT; i++){
      for(j = 1; j <= WIDTH; j++){
         worst_dt = fmax( fabs(Temperature[i][j]-
                           Temperature_previous[i][j]),
                     worst_dt);
         Temperature_previous[i][j] = Temperature[i][j];
      }
   }

   if((iteration % 100) == 0) {
      track_progress(iteration);
   }

   iteration++;
}
```

Listing 4.6 Fortran Laplace code main loop with kernels directives

```fortran
do while ( worst_dt > temp_tolerance )

    !$acc kernels
    do j=1,width
        do i=1,height
            temperature(i,j) =0.25*(temperature_previous(i+1,j)&
                            + temperature_previous(i-1,j)&
                            + temperature_previous(i,j+1)&
                            + temperature_previous(i,j-1))
        enddo
    enddo
    !$acc end kernels

    worst_dt=0.0

    !$acc kernels
    do j=1,width
        do i=1,height
            worst_dt = max( abs(temperature(i,j) - &
                            temperature_previous(i,j)),&
                        worst_dt )
            temperature_previous(i,j) = temperature(i,j)
        enddo
    enddo
    !$acc end kernels

    if( mod(iteration,100).eq.0 ) then
        call track_progress(temperature, iteration)
    endif

    iteration = iteration+1

enddo
```

The compilation is also straightforward. All you do is activate the directives using, for example, the PGI compiler, for the C version:

```
pgcc -acc laplace.c
```

Or for the Fortran version:

```
pgf90 -acc laplace.f90
```

If you do this, the executable pops right out and you can be on your way. However, you probably want to verify that your directives actually did something. OpenACC's defense against compiling a loop with dependencies or other issues is to simply ignore the directives and deliver a "correct," if unaccelerated, executable. With the PGI compiler, you can request feedback on the C OpenACC compilation by using this:

```
pgcc -acc -Minfo=acc laplace.c
```

Here it is for Fortran:

```
pgf90 -acc -Minfo=acc laplace.f90
```

Similar options are available for other compilers. Among the informative output, you see the "Accelerator kernel generated" message for both of your kernels-enabled loops. You may also notice that a reduction was automatically generated for `worst_dt`. It was nice of the compiler to catch that and generate the reduction automatically. So far so good.

If you run this executable, you will get something like this:

```
. . .
. . .
---------- Iteration number: 3200 ------------
. . .[998,998]: 99.18  [999,999]: 99.56  [1000,1000]: 99.86
---------- Iteration number: 3300 ------------
. . .[998,998]: 99.19  [999,999]: 99.56  [1000,1000]: 99.87

Max error at iteration 3372 was 0.009995
Total time was 35.258830 seconds.
```

This was executed on an NVIDIA K80, the fastest GPU available at the time of this writing. For our efforts thus far, we have managed to slow down the code by about 70 percent, which is not impressive at all.

4.3 Performance of OpenACC Programs

Why did the code slow down? The first suspect that comes to mind for any experienced GPU programmer is data movement. The device-to-host memory bottleneck is usually the culprit for such a disastrous performance as this. That indeed turns out to be the case.

You could choose to use a sophisticated performance analysis tool, but in this case, the problem is so egregious you can probably find enlightenment with something as simple as the PGI environment profiling option:

```
export PGI_ACC_TIME=1
```

If you run the executable again with this option enabled, you will get additional output, including this:

```
Accelerator Kernel Timing data
 main  NVIDIA  devicenum=0
  time(us): 11,460,015
```

```
 31: compute region reached 3372 times
  33: kernel launched 3372 times
   grid: [32x250]  block: [32x4]
     device time(us): total=127,433 max=54 min=37 avg=37
     elapsed time(us): total=243,025 max=2,856 min=60 avg=72
 31: data region reached 6744 times
  31: data copyin transfers: 3372
     device time(us): total=2,375,875 max=919 min=694 avg=704
  39: data copyout transfers: 3372
     device time(us): total=2,093,889 max=889 min=616 avg=620
 41: compute region reached 3372 times
  41: data copyin transfers: 3372
     device time(us): total=37,899 max=2,233 min=6 avg=11
  43: kernel launched 3372 times
   grid: [32x250]  block: [32x4]
     device time(us): total=178,137 max=66 min=52 avg=52
     elapsed time(us): total=297,958 max=2,276 min=74 avg=88
  43: reduction kernel launched 3372 times
   grid: [1]  block: [256]
     device time(us): total=47,492 max=25 min=13 avg=14
     elapsed time(us): total=136,116 max=1,011 min=32 avg=40
  43: data copyout transfers: 3372
     device time(us): total=60,892 max=518 min=13 avg=18
 41: data region reached 6744 times
  41: data copyin transfers: 6744
     device time(us): total=4,445,950 max=872 min=651 avg=659
  49: data copyout transfers: 3372
     device time(us): total=2,092,448 max=1,935 min=616 avg=620
```

The problem is not subtle. The line numbers 31 and 41 correspond to your two kernels directives. Each resulted in a lot of data transfers, which ended up using most of the time. Of the total sampled time of 11.4 seconds (everything is in microseconds here), well over 10s was spent in the data transfers, and very little time in the compute region. That is no surprise given that we can see multiple data transfers for every time a kernels construct was actually launched. How did this happen?

Recall that the kernels directive does the safe thing: When in doubt, copy any data used within the kernel to the device at the beginning of the kernels region, and off at the end. This paranoid approach guarantees correct results, but it can be expensive. Let's see how that worked in Figure 4.2.

What OpenACC has done is to make sure that each time you call a device kernels, any involved data is copied to the device, and at the end of the kernels region, it is all copied back. This is safe but results in two large arrays getting copied back and forth twice for each iteration of the main loop. These are two 1,000 × 1,000 double-precision arrays, so this is (2 arrays) × (1,000 × 1,000 grid points/array) × (8 bytes/grid point) = 16MB of memory copies every iteration.

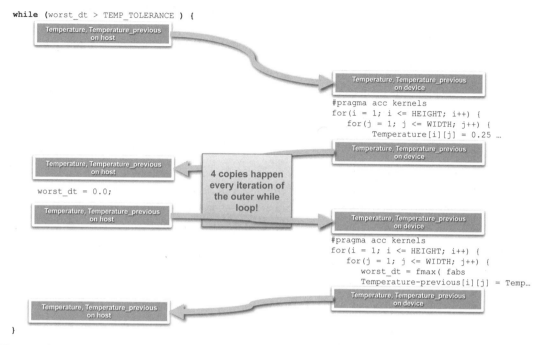

Figure 4.2 Multiple data copies per iteration

Note that we ignore `worst_dt`. In general, the cost of copying an 8-byte scalar (non-array) variable is negligible.

4.4 An Optimized Parallel Version

So far we have marked the parallel regions for acceleration. Now it is time to introduce data regions to optimize data transfers.

4.4.1 REDUCING DATA MOVEMENT

Now that you have identified the problem, you know you must apply some `data` directives. OpenACC lets you completely control the residency of the data. It has routines to set up data during program initialization, to automatically migrate data going into or out of any region or block of code, and to update at any given point in the code. So don't worry about what OpenACC *can* do. Worry about what you *want* to do.

Pause here and see whether you can come up with a strategy to minimize data movement. What directives does that strategy translate to? Feel free to experiment with the code on your own before reading the answer, which is provided later.

In general, we want the entire simulation to be executed on the device. That is certainly the ideal case and eliminates all the data transfer costs. But most of the time you can't achieve that objective; the entire problem may not fit in device memory, there may be portions of the code that must execute on the host, or IO may be required at some point.

But let's start with that objective in mind. If you load your data onto the device at the beginning of the main loop, when do you next need it on the host? Think the first iteration through as a start: there is no reason for the two big arrays to return to the host between the two kernels. They can stay on the device.

What about `worst_dt`? It is insignificant in size, so you don't care what it does as long as it is available when needed, as per the default `kernels` behavior. Once you start to use data regions, you uncouple the execution from the data regions and could prevent unnecessary data movement. Because there is no real performance gain, you won't override the default by including it in any `data` directives. It will continue to be set to 0 on the host, get to a maximum in the second nested loop (actually a reduction from all of the "local maximums" found by each processing element (PE) on the device), and get copied back to the host so that it can be checked as the condition to continue the `while` loop every iteration. Again, this is all default `kernels` behavior, so we don't worry about the details.

After that, you run into the output routine. It isn't an issue for the first 100 iterations, so let's ignore it for a moment and continue around the loop for the second iteration. At the start of the second iteration, you would like both big arrays to be on the device. That is just where you left them! So it looks as if you can just keep the data on the device between iterations of the `while` loop. The obvious `data` directives would be `data copy` clauses applied to the `while` loop.

```c
// C
#pragma acc data copy(Temperature_previous, Temperature)
while ( worst_dt > TEMP_TOLERANCE ) {
. . .
```

```fortran
! Fortran
!$acc data copy(temperature_previous, temperature)
do while ( worst_dt > temp_tolerance )
. . .
```

This is indeed the key. It will significantly speed up the code, and you will get the right answer at the end.

However, you do need to address that `track_progess()` output routine that gets invoked every 100 iterations. You need for the temperature to be back on the host at that point. Otherwise, the host copy of `temperature` will remain at the initial condition of all zeros until the data copy happens at the termination of the `while` loop, which is the end of the data region. Many programmers encounter this oversight when they apply the `data` directives, run the code to a quick completion in the expected 3,372 iterations, and assume victory, only to notice that all of their printed output has been zeros. Make sure you understand exactly how this happens, because it is a good example of what can occur when we decouple the data and execution regions using `data` directives.

The fix is easy. You just need an `update` at that point.

```
// C
. . .
if((iteration % 100) == 0) {
    #pragma acc update host(Temperature)
    track_progress(iteration);
}
. . .


! Fortran
. . .
if( mod(iteration,100).eq.0 ) then
    !$acc update host(temperature)
    call track_progress(temperature, iteration)
endif
. . .
```

It is important to realize that all the tools for convenient data management are already in OpenACC. Once you decide how you want to manage the data conceptually, some combination of `data copy`, `declare`, `enter/exit`, and `update` clauses should allow you to accomplish that as you wish. If you find yourself fighting the scope or blocking of your code to make the directives match your wishes, take a breath and ask yourself whether the other clauses will allow you to accomplish this more naturally.

4.4.2 EXTRA CLEVER TWEAKS

There is one more tweak you can apply to the code before you declare victory. If you look a little more carefully at the code, you might notice that you don't actually need to copy both big arrays into the `while` loop. It happens that `temperature_previous` is the array that is initialized in the initialization routine, and `temperature` uses these values to set itself in the first iteration. So you don't need to copy it in.

Continuing with that line of thought, you don't need for both arrays to exit the while loop with the final data; one will suffice. Once again, temperature_previous has the correct values so that you can abandon temperature on the device. This means that temperature is really just a temporary array used on the device, and there is no need to copy it in or out. That is exactly what the data create clause is for.

Note that this last optimization is really not very important. The big win was recognizing that you were copying the large arrays needlessly every iteration. You were copying two large arrays into and out of each of the two kernels each loop:

(2 arrays) × (in and out) × (2 pairs of loops) × (3,372 iterations) = 26,976 copies

Getting rid of all those transfers with a data copy was the big win. Using data create instead of copy for the Temperature array saved one copy in at the beginning of the entire run, and one copy out at the end. It wasn't significant. So don't feel bad if you didn't spot that opportunity.

Likewise, using an update for the track progress routine caused 33 transfers over the course of the run. It was a quick fix for the problem. In comparison to the original 26,876 copies, having 33 remaining is nothing. However now that you are down to one copy in and one copy out for the whole run, it does have an impact on the order of 5 percent of the new and significantly reduced total run time. Given the huge performance improvement you have achieved, you may not care, but for those of you seeking perfection, see Exercise 1 at the end of the chapter.

4.4.3 FINAL RESULT

Listing 4.7 shows the final C version of the OpenACC enabled routine, and Listing 4.8 shows the Fortran version.

Listing 4.7 Final C OpenACC Laplace code main loop

```
#pragma acc data copy(Temperature_previous), create(Temperature)
while ( worst_dt > TEMP_TOLERANCE ) {

    #pragma acc kernels
    for(i = 1; i <= HEIGHT; i++) {
        for(j = 1; j <= WIDTH; j++) {
            Temperature[i][j] = 0.25 * (Temperature_previous[i+1][j]
                                + Temperature_previous[i-1][j]
                                + Temperature_previous[i][j+1]
                                + Temperature_previous[i][j-1]);
        }
    }

    worst_dt = 0.0;
```

```
#pragma acc kernels
for(i = 1; i <= HEIGHT; i++){
    for(j = 1; j <= WIDTH; j++){
        worst_dt = fmax( fabs(Temperature[i][j]-
                               Temperature_previous[i][j]),
                         worst_dt);
        Temperature_previous[i][j] = Temperature[i][j];
    }
}

if((iteration % 100) == 0) {
#pragma acc update host(Temperature)
    track_progress(iteration);
}

iteration++;
}
```

Listing 4.8 Final Fortran OpenACC Laplace code main loop

```
!$acc data copy(temperature_previous), create(temperature)
do while ( worst_dt > temp_tolerance )

    !$acc kernels
    do j=1,width
        do i=1,height
            temperature(i,j) =0.25*(temperature_previous(i+1,j)&
                             + temperature_previous(i-1,j)&
                             + temperature_previous(i,j+1)&
                             + temperature_previous(i,j-1))
        enddo
    enddo
    !$acc end kernels

    worst_dt=0.0

    !$acc kernels
    do j=1,width
        do i=1,height
            worst_dt = max( abs(temperature(i,j) - &
                                temperature_previous(i,j)),&
                            worst_dt )
            temperature_previous(i,j) = temperature(i,j)
        enddo
    enddo
    !$acc end kernels

    if( mod(iteration,100).eq.0 ) then
        !$acc update host(temperature)
        call track_progress(temperature, iteration)
    endif

    iteration = iteration+1

enddo
!$acc end data
```

You compile exactly as before. If you again use the compiler verbose information option (-Minfo=acc for PGI), you see that the generated copies are now outside the while loop, as intended. Here is the result.

```
 .  .  .
 .  .  .
---------- Iteration number: 3200 ------------
 . . .[998,998]: 99.18   [999,999]: 99.56  [1000,1000]: 99.86
---------- Iteration number: 3300 ------------
 . . .[998,998]: 99.19   [999,999]: 99.56  [1000,1000]: 99.87

Max error at iteration 3372 was 0.009995
Total time was 1.054768 seconds.
```

This is much better. Table 4.1 sums it up. With only a handful of directives, you have managed to speed up the serial code more than 20 times. But you had to think about your data migration in order to get there. This is typical of accelerator development.

Table 4.1 Laplace code performance

OPTIMIZATION	TIME (SECONDS)	SPEEDUP
Serial	21.3	
kernels directive	35.2	0.60
data directives	1.05	20.3

To review, you looked for the large loops and placed kernels directives there. Then (prompted by terrible performance) you thought about how the data should really flow between the host and the device. Then you used the appropriate data directives to make that happen. Further performance improvements are possible (see the exercises), but you have achieved the lion's share of what can be done.

4.5 Summary

Here are all the OpenACC advantages you have used in this chapter.

- **Incremental optimization.** You focused on only the loop of interest here. You have not had to deal with whatever is going on in track_progress() or any other section of the code. We have not misled you with this approach. It will usually remain true for an 80,000-lines of code program with 1,200 subroutines. You may be able to focus on a single computationally intense section of the code to great effect. That might be 120 lines of code instead of our 20, but it sure beats the need to understand the dusty corners of large chunks of legacy code.

- **Single source.** This code is still entirely valid serial code. If your colleagues down the hall are oblivious to OpenACC, they can still understand the program results by simply ignoring the funny-looking comments (your OpenACC directives)—as can an OpenACC-ignorant compiler. Or a compute platform without accelerators. This isn't guaranteed to be true; you can utilize the OpenACC API instead of directives, or rearrange your code to make better use of parallel regions; and these types of changes will likely break the pure serial version. But it can be true for many nontrivial cases.

- **High level.** We have managed to avoid any discussion of the hardware specifics of our accelerator. Beyond the acknowledgment that the host-device connection is much slower than the local memory connection on either device, we have not concerned ourselves with the fascinating topic of GPU architecture at all.

- **Efficient.** Without an uber-optimized low-level implementation of this problem using CUDA or OpenCL, you have to take our word on this, but you could not do much better even with those much more tedious approaches. You can exploit the few remaining optimizations using some advanced OpenACC statements. In any event, the gains will be small compared with what you have already achieved.

- **Portable.** This code should run efficiently on any accelerated device. You haven't had to embed any platform-specific information. This won't always be true for all algorithms, and you will read more about this later in Chapter 7, "OpenACC and Performance Portability."

With these advantages in mind, we hope your enthusiasm for OpenACC is growing. At least you can see how easy it is to take a stab at accelerating a code. The low risk should encourage you to attempt this with your applications.

4.6 Exercises

1. We noted that the `track_progress` routine introduces a penalty for the periodic array copies that it initiates. However, the output itself is only a small portion of the full array. Can you utilize the `data` directive's array-shaping options to minimize this superfluous copy (see Section 1.3.4)?

2. The sample problem is small by most measures. But it lends itself easily to scaling. How large a square plate problem can you run on your accelerator? Do so, and compare the speedup relative to the serial code for that case.

3. This code can also be scaled into a 3D version. What is the largest 3D cubic case you can accommodate on your accelerator?

4. We have focused only on the main loop. Could you also use OpenACC directives on the initialize and output routines? What kinds of gains would you expect?

5. If you know OpenMP, you may see an opportunity here to speed up the host (CPU) version of the code and improve the serial performance. Do so, and compare to the speedup achieved with OpenACC.

Chapter 5

Compiling OpenACC

Randy Allen, Mentor Graphics

Getting eight independent oxen to work in unison is not simple. However, it is child's play compared with coordinating a thousand chickens. In either case, the problem is to harness independently operating beasts so that their efforts are coordinated toward achieving a single goal.

Exploiting parallelism—whether for pulling wagons or for speeding up computation—is challenging. At one level, it requires abstract thinking. Understanding the portions of an algorithm that can exploit parallelism—and, for that matter, creating an algorithm that can exploit parallelism—requires that you deal with problems at an abstract level. Gaining abstract understanding and designing algorithms are tasks best performed by humans.

At a different level, scheduling a thousand processors to coordinate effectively and arranging for data to be at the right place at the right time is complex. Complex, but only in its detail, not in its intellectual content. The human ability to manage detail of this complexity is at best spotty, but computers excel at exactly this.

Computers manage detail. Humans understand abstraction. Both are required for successful parallel execution. As with the gatekeeper and keymaster in *Ghostbusters*, it seems natural to get these two together. OpenACC does exactly that.

This chapter overviews the challenges that you must solve to effectively utilize massive parallelism and presents the theoretical foundations underlying solutions to those challenges. Then it closes with details of how compilers combine that theory with OpenACC directives to effect your requests and get effective speedup on parallel architectures.

5.1 The Challenges of Parallelism

Exploiting parallelism requires solving two challenges. First is figuring out the parts of the program that can be executed in parallel. Second is scheduling the parallel parts on the available hardware and getting needed data to the right place at the right time. A prerequisite for both is understanding the parallelism available in hardware.

The following section overviews that topic. Subsequent sections detail the process by which compilers map programs to parallelism, highlighting the type of information that they need to successfully effect a mapping. The following sections detail how OpenACC directives provide that information and how compilers use it to generate parallel code. OpenACC is not free, and the concluding sections detail the challenges introduced by OpenACC directives.

5.1.1 PARALLEL HARDWARE

At its most fundamental level, parallelism is achieved by replicating something. For computer hardware, that something is usually functional units. A **functional unit** may be an entire processor (including a program counter and branching logic), or a simple arithmetic unit (only arithmetic operations). The more replication you implement, the more operations that can be performed. However, just as chickens and oxen require coordination in the form of a harness and a driver, functional units need to be coordinated. Software can serve the role of the driver, but the harness, particularly for thousands of processors in GPUs, requires hardware support.

The simplest way of coordinating functional units is to link their execution so that all the units are executing the same instruction at the same time. This method is more or less required with arithmetic units, because arithmetic units rarely contain program counters. For processors, this method of coordination is often effected by having the processors share a single program counter. Sharing a single program counter is the approach taken in NVIDIA GPUs. Obviously, having processors redundantly execute the same instruction is productive only if each operates on different data. Following this approach, each chicken is essentially marching in lockstep.

An alternative is to have completely independent processors. Under that model, functional units are free to execute any instruction at any time on any data. No clock, program counter, or other tie constrains the functional units. At any given time, the processors may be executing different instructions on different data. In the pioneer analogy, each ox or chicken would be proceeding forward at its own pace, oblivious to the progress of the other animals.

Examples of functional units that concurrently execute the same instruction are vector units and lockstep processors. Generally, these are classified as single-instruction multiple-data (SIMD)[1] or single-instruction multiple-thread (SIMT).[2] The defining point semantically is simultaneous execution.

Examples of functional units that execute independently abound, and they are illustrated by virtually any processors connected by either an internal bus or an external network. The processors may share memory; memory may be distributed among them; or memory may be split between those two options. In any case, because the functional units are loosely connected, the relative order in which operations execute on two processors is indeterminate. This execution is multiple-instruction multiple-data (MIMD).[3]

GPUs contain both types of parallelism in their streaming multiprocessors (SMs) and warps. With an understanding of basic hardware parallelism, next we turn to understanding the mapping from programming languages to hardware.

5.1.2 MAPPING LOOPS

To productively utilize hundreds or thousands of processors, an application must be doing much computation. Scheduling that many processors requires regularity. Without regularity, many processors can be programmed to do only one task. Without regularity, processors are figuratively executing like chickens flying in random directions. For programming languages, "regularity" and "repetition" implies loops. And, unless an application is boringly repeating the same calculation, regularity also means arrays. Pragmatically speaking, effectively utilizing parallelism is a matter of mapping loops onto parallel hardware. Also pragmatically speaking, this mapping is performed by having processors execute loop iterations. In other words, the unit of regularity is the loop body, and the loop iterations are partitioned among the processors.

Loops in standard programming languages are, by definition, sequential (meaning that the iterations of the loop are executed in consecutive order). The semantics of

1. J. L. Hennessy and D. A. Patterson, *Computer Architecture: A Quantitative Approach*, second edition (San Francisco: Morgan Kaufmann, 1996).
2. M. McCool, J. Reinders, and A. Robison, *Structured Parallel Programming: Patterns for Efficient Computation* (San Francisco: Elsevier, 2013).
3. Hennessy and Patterson, *Computer Architecture*.

parallel hardware, by the adjective *parallel,* are not. Given that, it is not immediately obvious that loops can be directly mapped to parallel hardware. In fact, not all loops can be.[4]

Functional units that execute a single instruction implement simultaneous semantics. In terms of array accesses in loops, **simultaneous semantics** means that the behavior of the statement is defined by the final result obtained if all iterations of the loop are executed together. Consider the following C fragment:

```
for(i=0; i<n; i++) {
    a[i] = a[i] + 1;
}
```

Each element of a is incremented by 1. Because each element is accessed in only one loop iteration, the order in which the iterations occur is irrelevant. The loop may be iterated forward as written, backward, simultaneously (as with a vector processor or lockstep processor), or randomly (as with independent processors). The result will be the same.

This is not true of all loops. Here we change the fragment slightly:

```
for(i=1; i<n; i++) {
    a[i] = a[i-1] + 1;
}
```

This fragment sets each element of a to the value of its ordinal position (assuming elements are initially 0). Executed sequentially, a loop iteration picks up the value of a stored by the preceding iteration, increments it, and stores the result for the next iteration. Simultaneous execution changes the result. Executed simultaneously, all the initial values of a are fetched, then incremented, and finally stored. No updated values are used. Stated differently, every element of a is set to 1.

The reason this loop produces different results when executed simultaneously is that the loop body depends on values produced by previous iterations. When the loop executes simultaneously, the newly computed values are not available until the computation is complete. That is too late for the dependent iteration to use.

Because MIMD processors may execute loop iterations in any order, and because simultaneous execution is one possible order, not all sequential loops can be executed correctly on MIMD hardware. Sequential loops in which no statement depends on itself, directly or indirectly, may be executed simultaneously. The condition that determines whether sequential loops will execute correctly with

---

4. J. R. Allen and K. Kennedy, *Optimizing Compilers for Modern Architectures* (San Francisco: Morgan Kaufmann, 2001).

indeterminate execution order is more restrictive. A loop can be executed in MIMD fashion if and only if no memory location is written/read, read/written, or written/written on two different loop iterations. To illustrate the difference, the following can be executed correctly simultaneously but not indeterminately.

```
for(i=1; i<n; i++) {
    a[i] = b[i] + c[i];
    d[i] = a[i-1] + 1;
}
```

Executed simultaneously, all executions of the first statement complete before any of the second statement begin. The second statement correctly gets updated values. Executed indeterminately, loop iteration 2 (for instance) may execute before loop iteration 1 starts. If that happens, loop iteration 2 will incorrectly fetch old values of a.

5.1.3 MEMORY HIERARCHY

So far, parallelism has been discussed from a passive viewpoint. That is, you have seen methods that passively examine loops to uncover their semantics: A loop either is or is not acceptable for parallel execution. A more aggressive approach, undertaken by compilers, is to actively transform a nonparallel loop so that it can be correctly executed on parallel hardware.[5]

Consider the ideal parallel loop presented earlier, slightly modified:

```
for(i=0; i<n; i++) {
    t = a[i] + 1;
    a[i] = t;
}
```

Rather than use the result directly, the expression value is first stored into a **temporary**. Using temporaries in this fashion is a common coding style for users wary of compiler optimization. Excluding this temporary, the semantics of the loop are identical to those of the original.

Although the semantics are identical, the loop iterations as written cannot be correctly executed either simultaneously or indeterminately. The reason is the scalar temporary t. On a nonparallel machine, the temporary provides a location to hold the computation to avoid recomputing it. Executing the iterations in either simultaneous or indeterminate order, it is possible (and indeed probable) that multiple

5. Allen and Kennedy, *Optimizing Compilers for Modern Architectures*.

loop iterations will be stored into the temporary at roughly the same time. If so, the value fetched on an iteration may not be the proper one.

In the specific example, the obvious solution is to propagate the scalar forward. More generally, however, there may be many uses of t in the loop, in which case saving the results of the computation may be the most efficient approach. The more general solution is to expand the scalar to create a location for each loop iteration.

```
for(i=0; i<n; i++) {
    t[i] = a[i] + 1;
    a[i] = t[i];
}
```

A literal expansion illustrates the basic concept, but there are more efficient ways to achieve the end result.[6] The requirement is that each loop iteration (or thread) have a dedicated location for the value. On simultaneous architectures, the scalar is usually expanded into a vector register or equivalent in a transformation known as **scalar expansion**.[7] MIMD architectures usually provide individual processors with dedicated memory—memory *private* to that processor. Allocating the scalar to this storage (a transformation known as **privatization**) removes the bottleneck.[8]

5.1.4 REDUCTIONS

Simultaneous and indeterminate execution cover common forms of fully parallel loops. However, there are computations that are only partially parallel but that are important enough to merit special hardware attention. The most prevalent of these are reductions. **Reductions** are operations that reduce a vector or an array to a scalar. **Dot product** (a special version of a more general sum reduction) is one example:

```
t = 0;
for(i=0; i<n; i++) {
    t = t + a[i] * b[i];
}
```

Because of the update of t, these loop iterations obviously cannot be executed simultaneously or indeterminately. Locking access to the temporary before the fetch and releasing it after the update will eliminate the problem, but it effectively serializes the execution.

---

6. Allen and Kennedy, *Optimizing Compilers for Modern Architectures*.
7. M. J. Wolfe, *Optimizing Supercompilers for Supercomputers* (Cambridge, MA: MIT Press, 1989).
8. Allen and Kennedy, *Optimizing Compilers for Modern Architectures*.

Locking is necessary when results are accumulated in a globally accessible variable. Following the lead of the preceding section, if the accumulations are instead made to a private variable, no locking is necessary. The final accumulation into the global location, which does require locking, can then be performed outside the loop. Assuming tp is a private variable and that the outer brackets indicate the start of parallel execution, the following illustrates the transformation.

```
t = 0;
{
    tp = 0;
    for(i=0; i<n; i++) {
        tp = tp + a[i] * b[i];
    }
    lock(); t = t + tp; unlock();
}
```

This code may accumulate the sums in a different order from the original, because each individual private variable accumulates part of the overall sum. Although mathematical addition is associative, computer floating-point addition is not. This means that accumulating the sum in a different order may cause the results to vary slightly from the sequential result, and from run to run. Despite the possible variances, reductions consume enough computation in enough applications to justify this partial parallelism.

5.1.5 OPENACC FOR PARALLELISM

Given that the semantics of sequential loops differ from those of parallel hardware, it is not hard to see the role of OpenACC directives in exploiting parallelism in sequential programs. Programmers armed with OpenACC directives can use them to indicate parallel loops to the compiler, which can then take care of scheduling them.

The OpenACC gang and worker loop directives state that a loop will execute correctly regardless of the order in which the iterations are executed. Accordingly, such loops can be correctly executed on MIMD hardware. In fact, given that any iteration order is valid, gang and worker loops can also be executed simultaneously. This precipitates one of the decisions faced by a compiler (discussed later): Does it execute loops exactly as prescribed by directives (i.e., as gang and worker), or does it use the information to schedule loops as it sees fit (i.e., schedule a gang loop as gang, worker, and vector)? From a loop semantics viewpoint, gang and worker both imply indeterminate semantics. The difference between the two is that gang implies that there is more beneficial parallelism underneath.

The OpenACC vector `loop` directive states that a loop will execute correctly if the iterations are executed simultaneously. Accordingly, the loop can be executed on vector hardware or on the vector lanes of a GPU.

In OpenACC, a programmer can specify that a scalar variable be made `private` to a loop, directing the compiler to allocate a copy of the variable to local storage. By directing that the variable be made private, you are guaranteeing that this particular variable will not block parallelism, and that the move to `private` will preserve the semantics of the loop. For this to be true, the scalar must be used in one of only two ways: (a) The scalar must be defined on each loop iteration prior to any use, or (b) the scalar must not be assigned within the loop. You distinguish these two cases by indicating `firstprivate` for the latter, indicating that the private variable needs to be initialized with the value of the global location.

Reductions are indicated on a parallel loop by using a keyword (i.e., `sum`) indicating the kind of the reduction and the scalar that is the result of the reduction. With this information, the compiler knows to create a private copy of the reduction variable inside the parallel loop, initialize it according to the reduction kind, and create appropriate locking and updating of the associated global variable.

5.2 Restructuring Compilers

Previous sections present challenges that you must solve to effectively utilize parallelism: recognizing loops that can be executed as gang, worker, and vector loops; recognizing reductions; and placing variables appropriately in the memory hierarchy. These challenges are not new; parallel architectures have existed for decades, and every parallel architecture faces the challenges presented here. Compiler writers tend to be smart. Compiler research over those decades has resulted in a theoretical foundation to meet many of those challenges. To best apply OpenACC directives, you need to know where compilers can best be helped.

5.2.1 WHAT COMPILERS CAN DO

Fundamentally, executing a sequential loop simultaneously or indeterminately is reordering the execution of the loop. Compilers approach this reordering by creating a relation representing all the execution orderings in the sequential program that must be preserved for the computation results to be preserved. This relation is called **dependency.**[9] Here is an example of an ordering that must be preserved (i.e., a dependency):

```
t[i] = a[i] + 1;
a[i] = t[i];
```

The first statement computes a value of t[i] that is used by the second. As a result, their relative execution order must be preserved or else the second statement will use an incorrect value of t[i]. (Similarly, changing the relative execution order will also cause a[i] in the first statement to receive an incorrect value.) With dependency defined in this way, a compiler is free to reorder a program at will, as long as it does not violate any dependencies, and the results that are computed will remain unchanged. Dependency theory also includes the ability to attribute dependencies to specific loops, enabling more precise reordering.

Loop-based dependency enables an exact definition of sequential loops that can be correctly executed using simultaneous or indeterminate semantics. As a result, given an exact dependency graph, restructuring compilers can do a good job of determining loops that can be correctly executed as gang, worker, or vector loops. The problem is building an exact dependency graph for loops based on array references. In general, this problem is undecidable. Pragmatically, dependency theory has the mathematical foundations to deal with array subscripts that are linear functions of the loop induction variables, and that covers most loops encountered in practice. Based on this, dependency-based compilers can do a good, but not perfect, job on most programs.

Dependency is based on memory access. Two statements can be dependent only if they access a common memory location. Although the presence of a dependency limits the reordering that can be effected, it also implies that a memory location is reused between two statements. Compilers are able to utilize that reuse to find the best locations for variables in the memory hierarchy.

The scalar precursor of dependency is data-flow analysis, which summarizes the relationships between definitions and uses of scalar variables.[10] Data-flow analysis reveals whether a scalar is always defined before use in a loop (meaning it can be made private) or whether it needs initializing. Recognizing reductions is straightforward for humans, but the process is more abstract than it is mechanical, and

---

9. Allen and Kennedy, *Optimizing Compilers for Modern Architectures.*
10. S. S. Muchnick, *Advanced Compiler Design and Implementation* (San Francisco: Morgan Kaufmann, 1997).

general recognition is not simple for computers. Although it is not perfect, data-flow analysis does provide information necessary for recognizing most reductions.

With dependency and data-flow analysis, compilers can do a reasonable job exploiting parallel hardware. But they can't do everything.

5.2.2 WHAT COMPILERS CAN'T DO

With an exact dependency graph, compilers are perfect at uncovering potential parallelism from a semantic point of view. However, as noted earlier, creating an exact dependency graph is in general undecidable. In addition to the limitation mentioned earlier (array subscripts must be linear functions of the loop induction variables),[11] two programming constructs provide the biggest challenges for compilers: symbolic subscript expressions and aliasing.

Symbolic subscript expressions, wherein a loop variable's coefficient or other factor is unknowable at compile time, defy a compiler's best efforts. Such expressions arise more commonly than one might think, primarily because of multidimensional array references. In many cases, the symbolic expression involves physical quantities (e.g., mass or distance) that a user can reason about.

Aliasing, which occurs when the same memory location may have two or more references to it, is more subtle.[12] The following fragment illustrates aliasing and associated problems.

```
void copy(double a[], double b[], int n) {
    int i;
    for(i=0; i<n; i++)
        a[i] = b[i];
}
. . .
double x[100];
copy(&x[1], &x[0], 10);
```

Looking at the procedure `copy` in isolation, the loop appears parallelizable. But in fact, it's not. The reason is the way in which `copy` is called. The fact that a and b are different names for the same memory means that the statement depends on itself. Resolving aliases in a program is an NP-complete problem, where NP stands for nondeterministic polynomial time. Compilers must adopt a conservative approach (that is, compilers assume that the worst possible case is happening

---

11. Wolfe, *Optimizing Supercompilers for Supercomputers*.
12. K. D. Cooper and L. Torczon, *Engineering a Compiler* (San Francisco: Elsevier, 2004).

unless it can prove otherwise), and this means that, in most cases of possible aliasing, compilers must assume that a dependency exists.

Another symbolic area that creates problems for compilers is **symbolic loop bounds and steps.** Doing the best job of allocating loops to parallel hardware requires knowing roughly how many times the loops iterate. For instance, there is little point in scheduling a loop with only three iterations as a vector loop; the overhead of scheduling the loop will overwhelm the benefit. Given two potential candidates for vector execution, one that iterates 3 times and the other that iterates 128 times, the larger iteration loop is absolutely the better choice. However, the compiler can't make that choice without knowledge of the loop sizes, and if those sizes are symbolic, the compiler can only guess.

Compilers must work with the semantics of a computation as written and, in particular, with the semantics as expressed in a sequential language for OpenACC. Those semantics sometimes distort the mathematics underlying the physical phenomenon. Consider the following fragment:

```
for(i=1; i<m-1; i++) {
    for(j=1; i<n-1; j++) {
        a[i][j] = (a[i+1][j] + a[i-1][j] + a[i][j+1]
                + a[i][j-1]) / 4.0;
    }
}
```

This fragment is typical code used to solve differential equations, which have the property that at steady state, the value at a point is equal to the average value across a surrounding sphere. A compiler examining the fragment would correctly conclude that the statement depends upon itself in every loop and that it cannot be executed simultaneously or indeterminately. In fact, however, it can. The reason is that the fragment is converging toward a fixed point: when the values no longer change between iterations, a holds the solution. As a result, any errors that are encountered along the way by parallel execution are insignificant to the final solution. A human can readily recognize this; a compiler cannot.

The items in this section—symbolic expressions, aliasing, hidden semantics—are linked by a common theme: information. Compilers are not omniscient, and they must be conservative in their approach, so it's not surprising that information is a primary need. OpenACC is designed as a means for transferring this information from the programmer to the compiler.

5.3 Compiling OpenACC

OpenACC directives obviously simplify parts of the compilation process for GPU programs. Gang, worker, and vector directives tell the compiler whether a loop executes correctly in an indeterminate order, thereby eliminating the need for sophisticated dependency analysis and detailed loop analysis. Moreover, `private` clauses dictate precisely where variables need to be located in the memory hierarchy. Reduction recognition is tricky and detailed; the `reduction` clause eliminates the need for lots of checks normally employed by compilers to ensure correctness. Explicit directive control of memory transfers between host and device relieves the compiler of having to do detailed interprocedural analysis when it tries to optimize memory transfers.

Although it's easy to think that directives solve all the compiler's problems, that is not the case, and, in some cases, they complicate the compiler's work. The phrase *effective parallelism* has two parts: *parallelism*, which means getting an application to run in parallel, and *effective*, which means getting the application to run faster. Experienced programmers are aware that the two are not always the same. The ease of applying directives raises user expectations, making the compiler's job harder.

Some of the expected simplifications aren't necessarily simplifications. For instance, there are reasons to build a dependency graph beyond uncovering parallel loops. Users make mistakes in applying directives—mistakes that can be hard to debug by running the application. The compiler can help detect these at compile time only if it performs the analysis it would need to actually restructure the program.

Key challenges faced by an OpenACC-enhanced compiler are detailed next.

5.3.1 CODE PREPARATION

A compiler that uncovers parallel loops is almost certainly guaranteed to build a dependency graph. Although it is not necessarily wise to do so, the addition of OpenACC directives allow the compiler to bypass building the graph. However, less well known is the fact that such compilers also must implement a number of auxiliary transformations in order to support building the graph. These cannot be bypassed.

One example is auxiliary induction variable substitution. It is not uncommon for programmers who don't trust compiler optimization to perform optimizations by hand on their source code. Strength reduction is one example:

```
ix = 0;
iy = 0;
for(int i=0; i<n; i++) {
    y[iy] = y[iy] + alpha * x[ix];
    ix = ix + incx;
    iy = iy + incy;
}
```

What the user really intends is this:

```
for(int i=0; i<n; i++) {
    y[incy * i] = y[incy * i] + alpha * x[incx * i];
}
```

The programmer wrote the first form for efficiency. Additions are much cheaper than multiplications, so in terms of the integer support arithmetic, the first is faster (although a reasonable compiler will eventually generate that form regardless of what is written). The transformation that reduces the second form to the first form is known as **strength reduction** (replacing an operator with a cheaper operation). For vector or parallel execution, however, the second form is necessary, both to uncover the memory access strides through the vectors and to eliminate the scalar dependencies. This is true whether the parallelism is implicitly detected or explicitly stated by a directive. This transformation (known as **auxiliary induction variable substitution**)[13] as well as other preliminary transformations must be performed, either by the compiler or by the user.

5.3.2 SCHEDULING

Scheduling parallel and vector code involves balancing two conflicting forces. In one direction, parallelism is effective only when all processors are being productive. The best chance of keeping all processors busy is to make each instruction packet to be executed in parallel as small as possible, so that there are as many packets as possible. This approach means that as much code as possible will be ready to execute at any time. However, parallel execution does not come free; there is always some overhead involved in executing an instruction packet in parallel. Maximizing the number of packets maximizes the overhead. Effective scheduling therefore requires that you keep instruction packets small enough to balance the load across the processors, but large enough to minimize the overhead.

---

13. Wolfe, *Optimizing Supercompilers for Supercomputers.*

Most effective scheduling techniques are **dynamic:** they schedule work while the application is running. The alternative is **static** scheduling, wherein the compiler fixes the schedule for the application during the compilation process. Static scheduling introduces less overhead, because the compiler schedules the code directly with no overhead, whereas dynamic scheduling generally achieves better load balance, because it can adjust for execution changes based on input data.

OpenACC gangs require static scheduling on GPUs; workers can be dynamically scheduled. The result strikes an efficient point between overhead and load balance.

5.3.3 SERIAL CODE

GPUs start up in fully parallel mode, with all processors—blocks, warps, and vectors—executing the kernel. Its "natural" state is to be executing in parallel, and there is no one instruction that says, "Go serial." As a result, it is relatively simple to execute parallel code; accordingly, the more difficult task is to execute serial code. Assuming that workers are dynamically scheduled using a **bakery counter** (all loop iterations to be performed are placed in a queue; as a worker becomes free, the queue gives the worker an iteration to perform), serial code at the worker level is not difficult. When workers are working on a serial section, all processors except one (a **chief** processor) are held in a **pen**. When the chief processor encounters a worker loop, it adds the iterations to the queue and opens up the pen.

Serializing the vector lanes down to a single execution is more challenging. Making only one lane of a warp execute (making it effectively the "chief" lane) requires neutering the remaining lanes so that they do not execute. The pragmatic way of effecting this is to place a jump around the serial section of code, predicated on the `thread id`. For the zeroth thread (the chief lane), the jump is not taken; for all others it is. The result is similar to this:

```
if (thread_id == 0) {
    /* serial code */
}
/* back to full vector code */
```

The transformation is simple when performed on a single basic block (i.e., a group of instructions without control flow change; each instruction in the block is executed if and only if another instruction in the block is executed). But the process for handling multiple basic blocks with control flow change is more difficult.

An alternative implementation for GPUs with fully predicated instructions is to use a process known as **if conversion**.[14] If-conversion removes all branches in a section of code, replacing them with predicated instructions where the predicates exactly mimic the effects of the control flow. In optimizing compilers, if-conversion converts all control dependencies into data dependencies, thereby simplifying the construction of a dependency graph and allowing masked vector execution. It can produce the minimally necessary controlling condition for every statement, something that is not necessarily true for inserting jumps around serial blocks.

5.3.4 USER ERRORS

When optimizing a program, compilers analyze the program to uncover all the information they need to create more efficient forms of code. Compilers must be conservative; they do not effect an optimization unless they can absolutely prove that the change is safe. One would think that directives, including those in OpenACC, would save compilers the bother of implementing the analysis, given that the directives are providing the needed information. That approach works if the information provided by the user is correct. Unfortunately, users are not always perfect, and the coordination between OpenACC and user is not always perfect. Two critical areas compilers need to check are control flow and efficiency.

Control flow checks are useful because of the way in which GPUs implement control flow for simultaneous operations. When control flow splits (i.e., a conditional branch is encountered) the GPU continues; vector lanes that do not take the branch are enabled, and vector lanes that do take the branch are disabled. Eventually, the different paths should converge so that all vector lanes are again enabled. If that convergence does not occur, it prompts a condition known as **divergence**, and most likely it means that a valid program will hang at execution. Divergence normally does not happen with optimizing compilers under independent control, because compilers tackle only structured control flow, and divergence does not happen with structured programs. Users, however, are not limited to using structure programming or to placing directives around structured loops. Branches that terminate loops prematurely, particularly by branching prior to the loop, convolute convergence conditions.

---

14. Allen and Kennedy, *Optimizing Compilers for Modern Architectures.*

Efficiency is a second consideration, one that exposes a weakness in the directive strategy. At a coarse level, parallel performance[15] on virtually any parallel architecture is governed by a few simple principles.[16]

1. The outermost parallel loop should be the gang loop.

2. The next outermost parallel loop should be the worker loop.

3. If there is no other parallel loop, the outer loop should be both the gang and the worker loop.

4. Vector loops are most efficient when all the vectors access contiguous memory. In C, this means when the vector loop runs down the row with unit stride. In Fortran, this means when the vector loop runs down the column with unit stride.

5. Gang, worker, and vector loops all have a minimal size at which they become more efficient than scalar execution. Contrary to common conceptions, this size is usually more in the range of 5 to 10 than it is 2.

Note that compilers are proactive in trying to achieve these conditions. They will interchange loops to get a more profitable parallel loop to the outermost position or to get a better vector loop to an innermost position.

Although these principles are guiding, they are not absolute on every architecture. Directives in a program are usually immutable; as a result, they are not guaranteed to be optimally placed for every architecture. Compilers do have accurate models of architectures, so where they have full knowledge (e.g., loop lengths), they are better at loop selection than users.

One of the questions faced by compilers, given this, is whether the compiler should view OpenACC directives as prescriptive or descriptive. **Prescriptive** says that the user has prescribed exactly the desired mapping to hardware, and the compiler should follow it whether or not it is the most efficient. **Descriptive** says that the user has provided information to the compiler, describing the desired loop behavior, but the compiler should make the final decision. There are compilers supporting either strategy.

Whether it takes a prescriptive or a descriptive approach, a compiler should make the minimum check that the computation will speed up enough to justify the

---

15. We ignore, for the moment, memory concerns, something that definitely cannot be ignored in practice.
16. Allen and Kennedy, *Optimizing Compilers for Modern Architectures*.

download time to the device. If not, it makes more sense to execute the code on the host processor.

5.4 Summary

Exploiting parallelism with any number of processors is challenging, but it is particularly so when you are trying to effectively use hundreds or thousands of processors. The theme of this chapter is that effectively exploiting parallelism—particularly massive parallelism—is a job that requires cooperation of both the programmer and the compiler, and that OpenACC directives provide a firm basis for that cooperation. In doing so, you will be able to not only succeed in shepherding your one thousand chickens, but also see performance gains for your eight oxen.

The key challenges include recognizing loops (which observe simultaneous and indeterminate semantics, allocating variables to the proper level in the memory hierarchy) and recognizing and scheduling reductions. OpenACC directives help meet these challenges and allow programmers to help overcome the compiler's biggest weaknesses: aliasing, symbolic expressions, and hidden semantics. Although the use of OpenACC directives combined with a compiler is not a perfect solution, it greatly simplifies parallel programming and enables faster exploration of algorithms and loop parallelism to get the best possible performance.

5.5 Exercises

1. The OpenACC standard says that a `vector` loop cannot contain a `gang` or `worker` loop. Why?

2. Dr. Grignard, a longtime professor of parallel programming, has said, "If you can run a loop backwards (i.e., negating the step, starting with the upper bound, and ending at the lower) and you get the same result, you can run it correctly in vector." Is he right?

3. Dr. Grignard has also said that a loop that passes the test of running backward can also be run correctly as a gang loop. Is that correct?

4. The following procedure is one encoding of `daxpy`, a procedure for multiplying a scalar times a vector and adding the result to another vector (Alpha × X + Y).

```
void daxpy(int n, double alpha, double x[], int incx,
        double y[], int incy)
{
    for(int i=0; i<n; i++) {
        y[incy * i] = y[incy * i] + alpha * x[incx * i];
    }
}
```

5. Given the definition of `daxpy` as a procedure that adds two vectors, it seems natural to assume that the loop can be run in vector and in parallel.

   a. Can a compiler vectorize this loop as is?

   b. What should a compiler do if a user places a `vector` directive on the loop?

6. The text states that if a statement in a loop does not depend upon itself, then it can be executed simultaneously. Consider the following loop:

```
for(i=1; i<n; i++) {
    d[i] = a[i-1] + 1;
    a[i] = b[i] + c[i];
}
```

   There is a dependency from the second statement to the first, but neither statement depends upon itself. Can the statements be executed simultaneously? What should a compiler do if the user places a `vector` directive around the loop?

7. The text states that if there is a dependency in a loop caused by the loop, then the loop cannot be executed in gang or worker mode. Consider again the following loop:

```
for(i=1; i<n; i++) {
    d[i] = a[i-1] + 1;
    a[i] = b[i] + c[i];
}
```

   This loop carries a dependency from the second statement to the first. Can it be executed in gang or worker mode? If not, can you think of ways of changing it so that it can?

8. Following is a fairly standard coding of matrix multiply:

```
for(j=0; j<n; j++) {
    for(i=0; i<m; i++) {
        c[i][j] = 0;
        for(k=0; k<p; k++) {
            c[i][j] += a[i][k] * b[k][j];
        }
    }
}
```

What OpenACC directives would you place, and where, to get the best execution speed? Are there other changes you would make to the loops? Suppose the loop were instead written this way:

```
for(j=0; j<n; j++) {
    for(i=0; i<m; i++) {
        t = 0;
        for(k=0; k<p; k++) {
            t += a[i][k] * b[k][j];
        }
        c[i][j] = t;
    }
}
```

What would you do differently? Which version would you expect to execute faster, and why?

Chapter 6

Best Programming Practices

David Gutzwiller, NUMECA

Previous chapters have shown the details of how OpenACC can be used to identify and express parallelism in an algorithm, allowing portable heterogeneous execution. However, most real-world programming problems are far more complex than the provided code snippets and examples. Accelerating an existing application is often a bewildering and complex tradeoff of application performance, maintainability, and portability. Furthermore, in a professional programming environment developer time is a finite resource that must be taken into consideration.

This chapter introduces a set of best programming practices OpenACC developers should follow to achieve the best possible performance without major sacrifices in the maintainability and portability of their code, and yielding results in a minimum of developer time. It is impossible to establish a hard set of rules that will apply for all situations, but certain guidelines can be viewed as nearly universal. At the end of this chapter, you will understand these best practices:

- The necessity of baseline profiling

- The strategy of incremental acceleration and verification

- Techniques to maximize on-device computation

- Techniques to minimize data transfer and improve data locality

The concepts are demonstrated with a representative example: the parallel acceleration of a thermodynamic property table lookup and interpolation class, common in computational fluid dynamics solvers.

6.1 General Guidelines

Throughout this chapter, we explore techniques that can help OpenACC programmers maximize the performance of their applications. However, before we delve into the details of these techniques it is worthwhile to present a few general guidelines for heterogeneous programming. It is important to note that these guidelines are not specific to OpenACC or even specific to directive-based programming; they apply to any form of heterogeneous parallel programming.

Before attempting to accelerate code, you must understand how an application is consuming resources, such as how much time is spent in each function or loop, how frequently each function or loop is called, and how memory is being consumed. Taken together, this information is often referred to as an application's **profile,** and the process used to gather this information is known as **profiling.** A full exploration of the available profiling tools and techniques is outside the scope of this chapter, but most major compilers come packaged with capable profilers. Refer to Chapter 3 for information on profiling tools.

Basic flat profiles and call graphs are extremely useful when you are preparing a heterogeneous acceleration strategy. A **basic flat profile** usually contains the amount of time spent in each routine, both exclusive to the routine and in child routines, and the total number of times a routine is called. A **call graph** contains additional information about where in the call tree a routine is called. From this limited information, we can already identify promising application hot spots that are potential good locations to introduce acceleration. You should look for routines that have these characteristics:

- Are responsible for a large percentage of the application's run time

- Contain parallelizable math with a limited amount of other operations such as IO or MPI communication

- Are called a limited number of times

- Are preferably near the end of the call tree

Very lucky programmers may find a single hot spot that is responsible for the majority of the run time, in which case the next step is clear: Focus efforts on exposing the maximum amount of parallelism in the single hot spot. However, with most large research or industrial code, it is far more likely that the work will be spread across multiple loops and routines. In this situation achieving meaningful acceleration will require careful strategy.

6.1.1 MAXIMIZING ON-DEVICE COMPUTATION

The first principle of heterogeneous parallel programming is to maximize on-device computation. Conceptually, this may be viewed as an extension of Amdahl's law, which defines an application's maximum theoretical parallel speedup. From Amdahl's law, we know that with increasing parallel resources, an application's speedup will be limited by the execution time of any code running in serial. In a heterogeneous, CPU-accelerator architecture, this means that the accelerator will yield an impressive speedup only if a large percentage of the application's run time is eligible for parallel execution.

As an example, imagine an application profile showing 30 percent of the run time in thread-safe parallel loops, and the remaining 70 percent in serial operations such as IO or other nonparallelizable loops. This application would be limited to a speedup of ~1.4× and probably lower in practice. In this situation, your time would be better spent removing serial bottlenecks in the code before attempting a heterogeneous acceleration.

If an application's profile shows many small hot spots that sum to nearly 100 percent of the application's run time, the implication is clear: To achieve the best possible performance in the minimum amount of time, you should follow an acceleration strategy that offloads as many hot spots as possible to the accelerator device, rather than fine-tune any individual hot spot.

6.1.2 OPTIMIZING DATA LOCALITY

The second principle of heterogeneous parallel programming is to optimize data locality. This principle is sometimes presented as two different rules: Minimize data transfer, and maximize data reuse. No matter how it is presented, this principle aims to avoid the high cost of moving data between the various levels of a heterogeneous node's memory hierarchy. This movement includes transfers within a device memory hierarchy as well as the extremely costly transfers between the main system memory and the device memory, usually over a PCIe bus.

Optimizing for a device memory hierarchy is a complicated process that is both hardware and algorithm dependent, requiring you to adapt your algorithm for maximum arithmetical intensity (ratio of compute to data access). This presents somewhat of a portability problem, because it can be difficult or impossible to tune an algorithm for ideal performance on massively parallel accelerators as well as traditional CPUs. Depending on the application, it may be best to rely on the compiler's ability to optimize for the range of available accelerators, rather than tune the implementation for a specific target accelerator.

Minimizing the transfers between the main system memory and the device memory will improve performance on most hardware. These transfers are something OpenACC programmers can directly control, and effectively managing both the number and the size of these transfers is critical for effective accelerator use.

The most natural strategy for accelerating a large application is one of incremental acceleration and verification. With this approach, application hot spots are targeted one by one, starting with the most time-consuming routines or loops, which offer the greatest potential for acceleration. Each hot spot is first targeted independently, with all necessary data transferred to and from the device at the start and end of the routine or loop. This approach results in poor data locality and less than ideal performance, but it lends itself to easy verification of the targeted accelerated routines and is a useful first step.

The importance of frequent verification of results can't be overstated. It is critical to carefully verify the results of each accelerated routine or even each accelerated loop, demonstrating that the original and accelerated code yield the expected, deterministic results. Although this advice is valid for all forms of programming, it is even more important with heterogeneous, massively threaded models, where bugs often lead to unpredictable behavior rather than obvious crashes.

As the incremental acceleration progresses, an increasing number of compute regions will be offloaded to the device, and opportunities for improving data locality will appear. Data shared between multiple hot spots may be left on the device for an extended lifetime, or in some cases permanently. In practice, the incremental acceleration strategy has been shown to yield impressive application performance without massive disruptions in a typical industrial development cycle.[1]

---

1. D. Gutzwiller, R. Srinivasan, and A. Demeulenaere, "Acceleration of the FINE/Turbo CFD solver in a heterogeneous environment with OpenACC directives," in *Proceedings of the Second Workshop on Accelerator Programming Using Directives* (WACCPD '15) (2015).

> **Tip**
>
> Many current generation GPU accelerators perform best with single-precision math. However, some algorithms are susceptible to round-off error when run in single precision, which may yield small differences in CPU and the hybrid CPU-accelerator results. When verifying the results of an accelerated routine, make sure to compile in full double-precision mode to minimize the impact of these errors.

6.2 Maximize On-Device Compute

As previously mentioned, an application must provide an accelerator with as much compute work as possible. This means exposing all available parallelism in targeted loops and moving as many application hot spots as possible to the device. This section explores a few useful OpenACC features and concepts that help you maximize on-device compute without large-scale refactoring of your code.

6.2.1 ATOMIC OPERATIONS

Obtaining deterministic, repeatable results is mandatory for most scientific applications. Thus, problems can arise when non-thread-safe algorithms are offloaded to a massively parallel accelerator. Leaving these algorithms to be sequentially handled on the main CPU is an option, but following Amdahl's law this will degrade the overall speedup. Refactoring the offending algorithm for thread-safe execution may be the only option in some cases, and many coloring algorithms have been designed specifically for this goal.[2]

Before you resort to a time-intensive refactoring job, it is recommended to explore the use of the `acc atomic` directive. This directive ensures that a memory address is accessed or updated by no more than one thread at a time. Many seemingly unsafe algorithms can be made thread safe with careful use of this directive, often with negligible performance impact.

An example use of the `acc atomic` directive is shown in Listing 6.1. This example shows a flux summation loop, commonly used in unstructured finite-volume methods. In this algorithm, flux contributions from a finite volume's faces are summed

---

2. G. Rokos, G. Gorman, and P. H. Kelly, "A Fast and Scalable Graph Coloring Algorithm for Multi-core and Many-core Architectures," Lecture Notes in Computer Science Euro-Par 2015, *Parallel Processing* (2015): 414–425.

and stored. The parallel loop is over all mesh faces, and incorrect results will occur if multiple threads attempt to update the same volume concurrently. This algorithm may be made thread safe by the simple addition of `#pragma acc atomic` directly before each offending summation statement.

Listing 6.1 Atomic flux summation

```
#pragma acc parallel loop present(upVolume,downVolume,flux,. . .)
for (int iFace=0; iFace<nbFace; iFace++)
{
  int iUpVolume   = upVolume[iFace];
  int iDownVolume = downVolume[iFace];
  . . .
  < compute flux contributions >
  . . .
  #pragma acc atomic
  flux[iUpVolume]   -= contribution;
  #pragma acc atomic
  flux[iDownVolume] += contribution;
}
```

6.2.2 KERNELS AND PARALLEL CONSTRUCTS

Large-scale applications are likely to have many small execution hot spots rather than only a handful. Extending this concept, it is possible that any one of these high-cost routines will actually be composed of multiple smaller loops rather than a single monolithic loop. In situations like these, you should be aware of the differences between the parallel and kernels constructs.

The `kernels` directive, which can be applied to large blocks of code, instructs the compiler to identify possible parallelism and automatically implement data transfer and loop parallelism. The major benefit of this approach is that it allows parallelization of the code with a single construct, making it a low-risk approach that requires very little programmer time. The compiler will attempt to parallelize only loops that it can determine to be thread safe, and if multiple loops are present within a single kernel the compiler may be able to improve data locality automatically. However, the compiler may not be able to fully parallelize the code because of overly conservative analysis. The automatically generated data transfers may also be less than optimal for the same reasons. In practice, the kernels construct can often be used for a first implementation, allowing you to quickly see which loops the compiler can safely parallelize and which loops may require additional treatment. This resolves the problems mentioned earlier but allows for unsafe execution and potentially incorrect results.

Which option fits best depends on the application profile, the programming model, and your intended development time. It can be expected that the parallel construct, paired with carefully managed data regions, will lead to nearly optimal performance, but it will require a much more extensive development effort. This assertion is most apparent with complicated object-oriented programming models or code that contains extensive pointer indirection, which make it difficult for the compiler to determine which loops are eligible for safe, parallel execution. Finally, it is worth noting that the kernels construct may be interpreted differently by different compilers, resulting in different optimization, such as more or less effective data reuse. Whether this level of uncertainty is acceptable depends on the target end users and deployment strategy for your application.

6.2.3 RUNTIME TUNING AND THE IF CLAUSE

Following the incremental acceleration strategy, you will inevitably encounter code regions that offer only marginal potential for acceleration. There are many hardware and algorithmic factors that determine whether a particular loop or kernel will benefit from acceleration:

- The number of parallel loop iterations, depending on the size of the dataset

- The mathematical intensity of each loop iteration

- The number and size of necessary data transfers

- The speed and latency of the transfer bus (PCIe2, PCIe3, NVLink)

- The CPU model and performance

- The accelerator model and performance

- The number of processes concurrently offloading work to the accelerator

With so many competing factors, it becomes probable that some loops that benefit from accelerator execution with some datasets or hardware may actually result in an application slowdown in other scenarios. Targeting only loops that are guaranteed to result in a large speedup will result in low on-device computation and less-than-ideal performance. On the other hand, blindly accelerating all thread-safe loops without considering performance could be disastrous.

A runtime testing and tuning approach is one work-around for this problem. Although the details of the implementation vary from application to application, the basic concept is the same: At run time or during a trial execution, each parallel region should be launched and timed on both the CPU and the accelerator, including all necessary data transfers. From this comparative information, each region can be assigned to the CPU or the device, and the related data regions can be configured accordingly.

OpenACC has a simple `if` clause in place, for both kernels and parallel constructs, that facilitates conditional execution. An example of this approach follows in Listing 6.2, with a placeholder `accTimer` class used to gather and store comparative CPU and device execution times.

Listing 6.2 Runtime tuning and conditional execution

```
int accFlag = accTimer->getExecutionFlag();
accTimer->timerStart(accFlag);
#pragma acc parallel loop if(accFlag) copy(data)
for (int i=0; i<nbData; i++)
{
    < thread safe parallel work >
}
accTimer->timerStop(accFlag);
```

A runtime tuning approach has long-term benefits that could "futureproof" an application. Marginal loops can be adapted for accelerator execution on current low-end hardware without the risk of application slowdown. As future hardware with reduced data transfer or kernel startup overhead becomes available, these marginal loops will be automatically offloaded to the accelerator, improving the overall application speedup. The end user will benefit from improved performance with no additional development efforts.

6.3 Optimize Data Locality

The following sections show OpenACC techniques that you can use to improve data locality, which is the second principle for effective heterogeneous parallel programming. This discussion focuses primarily on the highest level of data locality: managing the transfer and lifetime of data on a platform with separate system and device memory. This level of data locality is something every OpenACC programmer will encounter, and properly optimizing is often the difference between an impressive speedup and a failed implementation.

6.3.1 MINIMUM DATA TRANSFER

When you are optimizing data transfers, it is prudent to note that performance is limited by more than the total size of the transferred data; the number of transfers and the number of device allocations are often more important. One example that clearly shows this is the offloading of solution quantities stored in a dynamically allocated two-dimensional array or in a one-dimensional linearized array, as shown in Listing 6.3. In this example, nbVar solution quantities are stored at nbPoints locations, so the total size for either data structure is nbVar*nbPoints.

Listing 6.3 2D and linearized 1D data structures

```
Int nbVar    = 6;
int nbPoints = std::atoi(argv[1]);

float** dataArray2D = new float*[nbVar];
for (int i=0; i<nbVar; i++) dataArray2D[i] = new float[nbPoints];

float* dataArray1D = new float[nbVar*nbPoints];
```

The time required to create and update the 2D and 1D data structures has been measured with increasing dataset sizes. These tests were performed on a Linux workstation with a PCIe3 transfer bus between the main memory and the device. As shown in Figure 6.1, the device offload time for the smaller datasets is dominated by the overhead of each distinct transfer. The 1D variant is guaranteed to be stored in a single contiguous block of memory and may be offloaded to the device with a single transfer, whereas the 2D variant is guaranteed to be only nbVar contiguous blocks of memory and must be offloaded accordingly. The impact is significant, leading to more than a 2× difference in offload time. With larger datasets the transfer time becomes linearly dependent on the total transfer size, and the performance difference of the two methods is diminished. From these results we can establish a few general guidelines for minimizing data transfer time.

- Transfer only the minimum data needed for your algorithm.

- Consider executing marginal parallel regions between computation hot spots on the device to avoid data transfer overhead.

- Aggregate small, unrelated data structures in a single transfer.

- If possible, refactor 2D arrays into linearized 1D arrays.

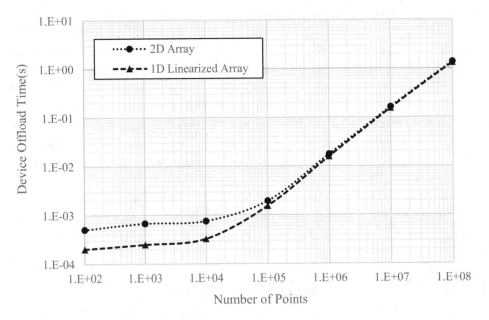

Figure 6.1 Solution array device offload demonstration

6.3.2 DATA REUSE AND THE PRESENT CLAUSE

Regardless of the application data structure, one of the best ways to minimize data transfer is to leave data on the device for as long as possible, allowing reuse by multiple compute regions. Many scientific applications utilize some data, such as mesh coordinates or topology data, which are unchanging over the life of a computation. In this situation, you need transfer the data only once. Most algorithms allow some level of data reuse, even if completely persistent device data is not possible because of a high memory footprint or mandatory host data updates.

The OpenACC `present` clause is used to indicate that data utilized in a parallelized loop already resides in device memory. This simple clause is often a positive indicator of well-optimized data locality. If the parallel regions in an application list most or all their associated data in a `present` clause, you can usually assume that data is being efficiently reused. The `present` clause works for many different data types, including arrays, structs, and even pointers to C++ objects.

Listing 6.4 demonstrates the use of the `present` clause for reuse of a data array in multiple parallel loops. In this example the unstructured `enter data` and `exit data` directives are used. Structured data regions can also be used to the same effect.

Listing 6.4 Data reuse and the present clause

```
#pragma acc enter data copyin(data[:nbData])
#pragma acc parallel loop present(data)
for (int i=0; i<nbData; i++)
{
    < thread-safe parallel work on data>
}
#pragma acc parallel loop present(data)
for (int i=0; i<nbData; i++)
{
    < more thread-safe parallel work on data>
}
#pragma acc exit data copyout(data[:nbData])
```

6.3.3 UNSTRUCTURED DATA LIFETIMES

OpenACC supports two types of data lifetimes: structured and unstructured. Structured data regions must begin and end within the same scope, effectively created and destroyed within the same routine. This is accomplished by using `enter data` and `exit data` as given earlier. This classic approach is well suited to procedural programming models with a clean call tree, allowing improved data locality through the use of nested structured data regions.

However, object-oriented programming models often have much more complicated call trees wherein dynamically allocated data is created and destroyed in different scopes. Nested, structured data regions are not applicable, resulting in many small structured data regions and poor data locality. Unstructured data regions solve this problem, allowing the creation, update, and deletion of device data at any point in the code. This is particularly useful when applied to C++ classes where data lifetimes are governed by the object's constructor and destructor. The C++ example at the end of this chapter makes extensive use of unstructured data regions.

6.3.4 ARRAY SHAPING

An application with well-optimized data locality likely has array data created on the device in one routine, and updated or otherwise managed in a different routine. In large C applications, it is common for array pointers to be passed through a call tree as arguments, and in C++ applications the same effect can be achieved by hosting a pointer as a class member. The pointer does not indicate the size of data, and with the pointer alone the compiler cannot interpret data management directives. The programmer needs to provide additional shape information to the `data` clause. The shape specification may describe the entire size of the array or a subarray, allowing you to efficiently update the minimum amount of data necessary. Array shaping also applies for multidimensional arrays, allowing you to selectively transfer or update portions of a large, multidimensional array.

Tip

A common pitfall comes from syntax differences between the Fortran and C/C++ array shape specification. Many legacy applications contain both Fortran and C modules with shared data structures, so to avoid data transfer bugs, you need to take extra care with array shaping. In Fortran the shape specification is `data(startIndex:endIndex)`, and in C/C++ the specification is `data[startIndex:count]`.

6.4 A Representative Example

Many of the concepts and techniques described in this chapter are applicable only to large, real-world code. Convincingly demonstrating the concepts with small code snippets is not always possible, and you need to imagine the following example within the scope of a much larger application. This example shows the heterogeneous CPU+GPU adaptation of a thermodynamic fluid property table, with lookup and interpolation via OpenACC directives. For this example we use the community edition of the PGI V16.10 compiler on a CentOS Linux system.[3] GNU gprof V2.23 is used for the baseline CPU profiling. All performance data come from a workstation pairing an Intel Xeon E5-2620 CPU with a NVIDIA Tesla K20 GPU. You are encouraged to compile and run the provided codes on your system.

6.4.1 BACKGROUND: THERMODYNAMIC TABLES

Increasingly, computational fluid dynamics (CFD) solvers are being used to analyze problems with complicated fluid properties such as fluids in phase change, supercritical fluids, and even combustion. Traditional methods for computing fluid state quantities (such as the ideal gas law) are inexpensive but not accurate enough for these problems. Advanced thermodynamic models exist, but they are not well suited for direct integration into a CFD solver iteration loop.[4,5]

---

3. https://www.pgroup.com/products/community.htm.
4. R. Pecnik, E. Rinaldi, and P. Colonna, "Computational Fluid Dynamics of a Radial Compressor Operating with Supercritical CO2," *Journal of Engineering for Gas Turbines and Power* 134(12) (2012): 122301-122301-8.
5. C. Lettieri, D. Yang, and Z. Spakovszky, "An Investigation of Condensation Effects in Supercritical Carbon Dioxide Compressors," *Journal of Engineering for Gas Turbines and Power* 137(8) (2015): 082602-082602-8.

A common technique in industrial CFD solvers is to provide a database of precomputed fluid state tables from which requested quantities may be interpolated. The tables are selectively refined to capture regions of rapid fluid property change, resulting in irregularly spaced axes. Over the life of a computation, the fluid state is updated thousands of times for potentially millions of mesh points, resulting in billions of table lookup and interpolation calls and perhaps resulting in a significant solver hot spot. This example covers the profiling, GPU acceleration, and optimization of a simple 2D fluid property interpolation table.

6.4.2 BASELINE CPU IMPLEMENTATION

For this example, we focus on a simplified 2D table lookup and interpolation in which the value of single unknown fluid property is retrieved from a table of two known quantities. The example program is broken into three main sections.

- Function `int main(int argc,char *argv[])`. This is the main function representing a simplified CFD solver. An iteration loop exists in which a single fluid state variable, density, is updated based on provided pressure and temperature values. In a real solver the iteration loop would contain many routines, some of them run on the CPU and others offloaded to the GPU. Thus, the host and device copies of the density, pressure, and temperature arrays must be updated every solver iteration.

- Class `LookupTable2D`. The `LookupTable2D` class houses the table data and contains methods to interpolate a value Z from provided X and Y values. For this example the `interpolate` method is simply a weighted average of nearby table points.

- Function `int bisection(float, float*, int)`. The stand-alone `bisection` function uses a bisection algorithm to find the subinterval of an unevenly spaced table axis containing the specified known quantity. A single table interpolation implies two calls to the `bisection` function: once to find the X axis subinterval, and once to find the Y axis subinterval.

6.4.3 PROFILING

Before attempting to accelerate the baseline CPU code, you must determine how the application is consuming resources, in particular the execution time. For the profiling run we use a dataset size that is representative of a small CFD simulation: $1e^5$ (105) points and $1e^3$ (103) iterations. The provided source file `ThermoTables_CPU.C` can be compiled and profiled with the following commands:

```
[user@hostname]$   pgc++ --c++11 -pg ThermoTables_CPU.C -o out_CPU
[user@hostname]$   ./out_CPU 100000 1000
[user@hostname]$   gprof out_CPU gmon.out > profile.txt
```

The first lines of the output `profile.txt` file shows a flat profile. The "percent time" and "self seconds" columns indicate that most of the program execution time comes from determining table subintervals in the `bisection` function and performing the weighted average in the `LookupTable2D::interpolate` method. At first glance this indicates that this program has multiple execution hot spots, but upon closer inspection we determine that the `bisection` method is called from within `interpolate`, and in fact this is a single hot spot. Careful reading of the call-graph output confirms this. The `interpolate` method is called millions of times, so finding parallelizable loops within the method is unlikely. However, the `main` function, which calls `interpolate`, may be a feasible point in the call tree to expose parallelism.

```
Flat profile:
  %   cumulative   self              self     total
 time   seconds   seconds    calls  ns/call  ns/call  name
52.33      8.32      8.32 100000000    83.20   156.70  interpolate(. . .)
46.23     15.67      7.35 200000000    36.75    36.75  bisection(. . .)
 0.82     15.80      0.13                               main
  . . .

  . . .
Call graph:
index % time    self  children    called     name
[1]     99.4    0.13    15.67                  main [1]
                8.32     7.35 100000000/100000000  interpolate(. . .) [2]
  . . .
-------------------------------------------------
                8.32     7.35 100000000/100000000  main [1]
[2]     98.6    8.32     7.35 100000000              interpolate(. . .) [2]
                7.35     0.00 200000000/200000000  bisection(. . .) [3]
```

6.4.4 ACCELERATION WITH OPENACC

Inside the main function you see a loop over the number of solver iterations. This is a time marching procedure wherein the flow quantities are updated based on previous values. It is fundamentally not a parallelizable loop. Nested within the iteration loop is a loop wherein `nbData` pressure values are retrieved from a temperature and density table. The update for any pressure value is independent of the other pressure values, so this loop can be parallelized.

It is obvious that the `temp`, `rho`, and `pres` arrays must be offloaded to the GPU. Less obviously, `presFromRhoTemp`, a pointer to a `LookupTable2D` object instantiated on the heap, must also be offloaded. To handle this you need to implement dedicated device data management methods in the `LookupTable2D` class. In these methods, shown in Listing 6.5, you create unstructured data regions that manage all the necessary class data and the `this` pointer, allowing member data access within class methods. Note the use of array shape specification for the 1D and 2D member data arrays.

Listing 6.5 LookupTable2D GPU data management methods

```
void createDevice()
{
    #pragma acc enter data copyin(this)
    #pragma acc enter data copyin(_zVals[0:_nbDataX][0:_nbDataY])
    #pragma acc enter data copyin(_xVals[0:_nbDataX])
    #pragma acc enter data copyin(_yVals[0:_nbDataY])
}
void deleteDevice()
{
    #pragma acc exit data delete(_zVals[0:_nbDataX][0:_nbDataY])
    #pragma acc exit data delete(_xVals[0:_nbDataX])
    #pragma acc exit data delete(_yVals[0:_nbDataY])
    #pragma acc exit data delete(this)
}
```

It is then necessary within the main function to call the `createDevice()` method before the parallel loop, and call `deleteDevice()` afterward. For the solution arrays you can append the `copy` clause to the loop, as shown in Listing 6.6.

Listing 6.6 Parallel loop

```
presFromRhoTemp->createDevice();
#pragma acc parallel loop \
    copy(pres[nbData],temp[nbData],rho[nbData]) \
    present(presFromRhoTemp)
for (int i=0; i<nbData; i++)
{
    pres[i] = presFromRhoTemp->interpolate(temp[i],rho[i]);
}
presFromRhoTemp->deleteDevice();
```

Before compiling with OpenACC you must tell the compiler how to handle method and function calls within the parallel region. The same directive can be used for both the class method `interpolate` and the stand-alone `bisection` function. Placing the `#pragma acc routine seq` directive on the line before each proto-type instructs the compiler that the routine will be launched on the device sequen-tially by each thread. Now you can compile and compare the CPU-only CPU+GPU performance.

```
[user@hostname]$  pgc++ --c++11 ThermoTables_OpenACC.C -o out_CPU
[user@hostname]$  pgc++ --c++11 -acc ThermoTables_OpenACC.C
                  -o out_GPU
[user@hostname]$  time ./out_CPU 100000 1000
real      0m13.858s
user      0m13.851s
sys       0m0.000s
[user@hostname]$  time ./out_GPU 100000 1000
real      0m2.378s
user      0m1.952s
sys       0m0.406s
```

At first glance, these results look great. The OpenACC implementation has resulted in an approximately 6× global speedup. However, this first test is run on a single CPU core, and the Xeon E5-2620 has six cores, making the comparison incomplete. You can use the OpenACC multicore target option to generate threaded code for the CPU, similar to widely used OpenMP parallelism.

```
[user@hostname]$  pgc++ --c++11 -acc -ta=multicore
                  ThermoTables_OpenACC.C-o out_CPU_Multicore
[user@hostname]$  time ./out_CPU_Multicore 100000 1000
real      0m2.376s
user      0m14.143s
sys       0m0.004s
```

From the multicore results, you see much less favorable results. The first OpenACC implementation with the table interpolation on the GPU yields performance much better than a single CPU core, but nearly identical to the six CPU cores. Additional optimizations are needed to obtain a worthwhile speedup.

6.4.5 OPTIMIZED DATA LOCALITY

Your first OpenACC implementation has poor data locality. All of the 2D table data and the flow quantity arrays are copied to and from the GPU every solver iteration. A few straightforward optimizations are possible, described here and shown in Listing 6.7.

- The table class is unchanged over the length of the computation and should be copied to the device before the main iteration loop and deleted afterward.

- Similarly, the three quantity arrays can be permanently created on the device outside the main iteration loop.

- Inside the iteration loop, the quantities can be selectively updated: density and temperature on the device, and the pressure on the host.

Listing 6.7 Parallel loop with improved data locality

```
presFromRhoTemp->createDevice();
#pragma acc enter data \
    create(pres[0:nbData],temp[0:nbData],rho[0:nbData])
for (int iter=0; iter<nbIter; iter++)
{
    #pragma acc update device(rho[0:nbData],temp[0:nbData])
    #pragma acc parallel loop present(presFromRhoTemp,pres,temp,rho)
    for (int i=0; i<nbData; i++)
    {
        pres[i] = presFromRhoTemp->interpolate(temp[i],rho[i]);
    }
    #pragma acc update host(pres[0:nbData])
}
#pragma acc exit data \
    delete(pres[0:nbData],temp[0:nbData],rho[0:nbData])
presFromRhoTemp->deleteDevice();
```

The results of the improved data locality are significant, reducing the execution time of this test from 2.38 seconds to 0.75 seconds. This represents a greater than 3× reduction in execution speed compared with the multithreaded six-core CPU results. In a full CFD solver many more hot spots would exist in the iteration loop, with some eligible for parallel execution and others not eligible. The same selective quantity update shown here could be extended to the additional routines, and, with a sufficient number of hot spots eligible for acceleration, it will be possible to skip certain updates, further improving data locality.

6.4.6 PERFORMANCE STUDY

The performance tests thus far have focused on a single dataset with 1e5 points. In a general-purpose CFD solver, the dataset size can vary significantly. This is true even within a single computation in which multiple refinement levels can be used to improve convergence, a system known as **multigrid.**

It is therefore worthwhile to investigate how the OpenACC implementation performs with varying dataset sizes. Figure 6.2 shows that datasets smaller than 1e3 points will experience a slowdown on the GPU compared with the six-core CPU, whereas datasets larger than 1e5 points will experience a roughly 3× speedup.

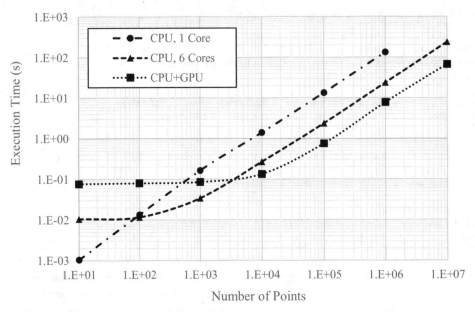

Figure 6.2 Table interpolation performance study

Tip

Depending on your hardware and operating system, there may be a significant over-head incurred when the accelerator is initialized. The PGI `pgcudainit` utility can be used to reduce this overhead and obtain more accurate results. Also, the command line `time` utility may not be able to obtain accurate timings with small datasets. The c++ 11 `std::chrono::high_resolution_clock` utility library can be used to obtain very high-resolution timing data for targeted regions.

6.5 Summary

Best programming practices for effective heterogeneous development with OpenACC are meant to yield meaningful performance improvements without major sacrifices to the maintainability and portability of the code, and with a minimum amount of programmer time. These practices provide a conceptual foundation that an OpenACC programmer can use to accelerate any large scientific application.

6.6 Exercises

1. In the table interpolation example, a random dataset of density and temperature values are generated. Using a small set of hard-coded input density and temperature values, verify that the CPU, multicore CPU, and CPU+GPU versions of the code yield identical output pressure values.

2. Offloading the table interpolation to the GPU has been shown to be inefficient with datasets smaller than 1e3 points. Use the `if` clause to conditionally skip data transfer and GPU execution for small datasets.

3. The dataset size cutoff for effective GPU acceleration varies, depending on your system hardware. Implement a runtime tuning class to conditionally skip GPU execution based on comparative CPU and GPU execution times gathered over a specified number of solver iterations.

4. The `#pragma acc routine seq` directive is applied to the `bisection` function to specify that the routine should be run in serial by each GPU thread. Is it possible to expose additional parallelism within the loop in this routine? Why or why not?

Chapter 7

OpenACC and Performance Portability

Graham Lopez and Oscar Hernandez, Oak Ridge National Laboratory

This chapter discusses the performance portability of directives provided by OpenACC to program various types of machine architectures. This includes nodes with attached accelerators: self-hosted multicores (e.g., multicore-only systems such as the Intel Xeon Phi) as well as GPUs. Our goal is to explain how to successfully use OpenACC for moving code between architectures, how much tuning might be required to do so, and what lessons we can learn from writing performance portable code. We use examples of algorithms with varying computational intensities for our evaluation, because both compute and data-access efficiency are important considerations for overall application performance. We explain how various factors affect performance portability, such as the use of tuning parameters, programming style, and the effectiveness of compilers' flags in optimizing and targeting multiple platforms.

7.1 Challenges

Performance portability has been identified by the high-performance computing (HPC) community as a high-priority design constraint for next-generation systems such as those currently being deployed in the Top500 (a list that ranks systems by using the Linpack benchmark)[1] as well as the exascale systems upcoming in the next decade. This prioritization has been emphasized because software development and maintenance costs are as large or larger than the cost of the system itself, and ensuring performance portability helps protect this investment—for example, by ensuring the application's usability if one architecture goes away or a new one becomes available.

Looking forward, we are seeing two main node-architecture types for HPC: one with heterogeneous accelerators (e.g., IBM Power-based systems with multiple NVIDIA Volta GPUs; Sunway accelerator architecture), and the other consisting of homogeneous architectures (e.g., third-generation Intel Xeon Phi-based nodes, Post-K ARM, etc.). At present it is a nontrivial task to write a performance portable application that targets these divergent hardware architectures and that makes efficient use of all the available computational resources (both at the node level and across nodes). It is clear that applications need to be written so that the parallelism can be easily decomposed and mapped with at least three levels of parallelism: across nodes, within the nodes (thread-level parallelism), and vector-level parallelism (fine-grained or SIMD-level parallelism).

The latest OpenACC 2.5 specification defines a directive-based programming API that can target the thread and vector levels, and it accommodates both traditional shared-memory systems and accelerator-based systems. However, we have also learned that performance portability depends on the quality of the implementation of the compilers and their ability to generate efficient code that can take advantage of the latest architectural features on different platforms. Shared-memory programming has been available in, and has been the main focus of, the industry-standard OpenMP specification for more than a decade, but the recent introduction of an offloading model in OpenMP poses the question, Is the accelerator model suitable to target both shared-memory and accelerator-based systems?

In this chapter, we show how OpenACC can be used as a single programming model to program host multicore, homogeneous, and heterogeneous accelerators, and we discuss the potential performance or productivity tradeoffs. We highlight how OpenACC can be used to program a micro-kernel called the Hardware Accelerated Cosmology Code (HACCmk), which is sensitive to vector-level parallelism (e.g., vectorization, warps, SMTs/SIMD, etc.).

We use the PGI and Cray compilers (see Section 7.3.4, "Data Layout for Performance Portability," later in this chapter for versions) to target OpenACC both on CPUs and on NVIDIA GPU hardware platforms. We compare the performance of

---

1. https://www.top500.org/project/.

the OpenACC versions versus baseline platform-optimized code written in multi-threaded OpenMP 3.1. Another approach to measure performance portability of the code is to compare the performance results to the machine theoretical peak floating-point operations per second (FLOPS) (for compute-bound kernels) or bandwidth (for memory-bound kernels) across the target architectures.

We summarize these experiences to reflect the current state of the art for achieving performance portability using OpenACC.

7.2 Target Architectures

To demonstrate performance portability using OpenACC, we use two target architectures: x86_64 with attached NVIDIA GPUs, and x86_64 only (multicore). The work can also be extended to target self-hosted Intel Xeon Phi KNL processors. At the time of this writing, support for Knights Landing (KNL) was not generally available with the PGI compilers.

7.2.1 COMPILING FOR SPECIFIC PLATFORMS

OpenACC is an open standard that is not tied to a specific architecture or software stack, but in this chapter we focus primarily on the PGI compiler, because it currently provides the most general performance portability. At this time, other available implementations, such as Cray, are more specialized in purpose, and upcoming implementations, such as that in the GNU compilers, are not yet as robust across multiple architectures.

7.2.2 X86_64 MULTICORE AND NVIDIA

In the PGI compiler, in addition to the `-acc` switch to enable general OpenACC support, there are flags that can further direct the generation of target code. Here we explain an example of how to use the PGI compiler to generate an executable that is suitable for various types of host CPU and NVIDIA accelerator platforms.

The default PGI behavior for the `-acc` flag is to create a unified "fat" binary that includes both host serial CPU and multiple targets of varying compute capabilities (cc20, cc35, cc50, etc.). This same behavior can be obtained by using, for instance, the flag `-ta=tesla,host`. At run time, the default OpenACC `device_type` will be NVIDIA unless no NVIDIA targets are available, in which case the `device_type` will be HOST.

Users can modify the default by either compiling to a specific target (such as
`-ta=tesla:cc60` for the Pascal architecture, or `-ta=multicore` for a parallel
CPU version); calling `acc_set_device_type()` in the program; or setting the `ACC_`
`DEVICE_TYPE` environment variable to have an effect on the default device type.

To take advantage of recent unified memory capabilities in the NVIDIA architecture,
you can add the flag `-ta=tesla:managed`.

In the near future, OpenACC parallelization for KNL will be supported by the PGI
compiler, furthering its capabilities toward performance portability.

7.3 OpenACC for Performance Portability

When targeting multiple architectures you must be aware of how the programming model maps to the target architecture. One important factor for high performance is efficient use of the memory systems. In this section, we examine how the
OpenACC memory model can be mapped to the various memory architectures.

7.3.1 THE OPENACC MEMORY MODEL

OpenACC uses a copy-in and copy-out data regions memory model to move data
to local (otherwise known as **affine**) memories of the accelerator. These data
regions can be thought of as user-managed caches. The interesting property of
this memory model is that it can be mapped efficiently to a variety of architectures.
For example, on shared memory, the data regions can be either ignored or used
as prefetching hints. On systems that have discrete memories, data regions can
be translated to data transfer APIs using a target runtime (e.g., CUDA, OpenCL,
etc.). On partially shared memory systems, the `data` directives can be either used
or ignored, depending on whether the thread that encounters the data region can
share data with the accelerator (e.g., unified memory, managed memory, etc.).

OpenACC data regions can be synchronized with the host memory. All data movement between host memory and device memory is performed by the host through
runtime library calls that explicitly move data between the memories (or ignored in
shared memory), typically by using direct memory access (DMA) transfers.

7.3.2 MEMORY ARCHITECTURES

Following is a list of various types of system memory.

- **Discrete memories.** These systems have completely separate host and device memory spaces that are connected via, for example, PCIe or NVLINK. This memory architecture maps well to the OpenACC data regions' copy-in and copy-out memory model.

- **Shared memory.** In these systems, all of the cores can access all of the memory available in the system. For example, traditional shared multicore systems (Intel KNL self-hosted, etc.) fit into this category. This model maps well to OpenACC, because the data region directives can be ignored or used as hints to the compiler to do prefetching.

- **Partially shared memories.** In this scenario, some of the system memory is shared between the host and the accelerator threads. Each device may have its own local memories but accesses a portion of memory that is shared. Future OpenACC specifications will support this by allowing data regions to be optionally ignored or used for prefetching if the thread of a host shares the same address space as the thread of the device. Currently, this is supported in the PGI compiler using the `-ta=tesla:managed` flag for dynamic allocated memory, and on systems where sharing is possible, as in the case of NVIDIA managed memory supported by software (e.g., CUDA Managed Memory over PCIe, or NVLINK).

7.3.3 CODE GENERATION

The best way to generate performance portable code is to use and tune the OpenACC `acc loop` directive, which can be used to distribute the loop iterations across gangs, workers, or vectors. The `acc loop` directive can also be used to distribute the work to gangs while the loop is still in worker-single and vector-single mode. For OpenACC, it is possible in some cases to apply `loop` directives such as `tile` to multiple nested loops to strip-mine the iteration space that is to be parallelized.

The OpenACC compilers also accept `gang`, `worker`, or `vector` clauses to pick the correct level of parallelism. If you specify only `acc loop`, the compiler decides how to map the iteration space to the target architecture based on its cost models and picks the right type of scheduling across gangs, workers, or vectors. This is an important feature of OpenACC, because it gives the compiler the freedom to pick how to map the loop iterations to different loop schedules, and that helps generate performance portable code while taking advantage of the target accelerator architecture.

However, in some cases the compiler cannot do the best job in generating the correct loop schedules. For these cases, you can improve the loop scheduling by adding clauses such as `gang`, `worker`, or `vector` to the OpenACC loops. In cases of perfectly nested parallel loops, OpenACC also supports the use of the `tile` clause to schedule nested loops to a given level of parallelism (e.g., gang or vector).

7.3.4 DATA LAYOUT FOR PERFORMANCE PORTABILITY

It's important to decide how the layout of data structures affects performance portability. Structures of arrays are in general more suitable for GPUs as long as the data access to the arrays is contiguous (memory coalescing). This is a good layout optimization for throughput-driven architectures. On the other hand, arrays of structures are also good for caching structure elements to cache lines, a layout that is important for latency-driven architectures common to host CPUs. Interestingly, we have noted that in some cases, improving data layouts on GPUs can also benefit the multicore case, but not as commonly the other way around.

We note that high-level frameworks for data abstractions (e.g. Kokkos,[2] SYCL,[3] etc.) can be useful to explore these types of issues related to data structure layouts, but they come at the cost of making the compilation process and compiler analysis more complex.

7.4 Code Refactoring for Performance Portability

To study the performance portability of accelerator directives provided by OpenACC, we use a kernel from the HACC HPC cosmology application. This kernel is part of the CORAL benchmarks suite.

---

2. http://www.sciencedirect.com/science/article/pii/S0743731514001257.
3. http://www.open-std.org/jtc1/sc22/wg21/docs/papers/2016/p0236r0.pdf.

7.4.1 HACCMK

HACC is a framework that uses N-body techniques to simulate fluids during the evolution of the early universe. The HACCmk[4] microkernel is derived from the HACC application and is part of the CORAL benchmark suite. It consists of a short-force evaluation routine which uses an $O(n^2)$ algorithm using mostly single-precision floating-point operations.

The HACCmk kernel as found in the CORAL benchmark suite has shared memory OpenMP 3.1 implemented for CPU multicore parallelization, but here we convert it to OpenACC 2.5. The kernel has one parallel loop over particles that contain a function call to the bulk of the computational kernel. This function contains another parallel loop over particles, resulting in two nested loops over the number of particles and the $O(n^2)$ algorithm, as described by the benchmark. A good optimizing compiler should be able to generate performance portable code by decomposing the parallelism of the two nested loops across threads and vector lanes (fine-grained parallelism). For vector (or SIMD-based) architectures, the compiler should aim at generating code that exploits vector instructions having long widths. For multithreaded or SMT architectures, it should exploit thread-level parallelism and smaller vector lanes.

As shown in Listing 7.1, the OpenACC version of the HACCmk microkernel, we parallelize the outer loop level using the `acc parallel loop` directive. The inner loop is marked by using an `acc loop` with `private` and `reduction` clauses. We intentionally do not specify any loop schedule in both `acc` loops to allow the compiler to pick the best schedule for the target architecture (in this case the GPU or multicore). We did this both to test the quality of the optimization of the OpenACC compiler and to measure how performance portable OpenACC is across architectures.

Listing 7.1 OpenACC version of the HACCmk microkernel

```
#pragma acc parallel private(dx1,dy1,dz1) \
                      copy(vx1,vy1,vz1) \
                      copyin(xx[0:n],yy[0:n],zz[0:n])
#pragma acc loop
  for ( i = 0; i < count; ++i) {
      const float ma0 = 0.269327, ma1 = -0.0750978,
      ma2 = 0.0114808, ma3 = -0.00109313,
      ma4 = 0.0000605491, ma5 = -0.00000147177;
      float dxc, dyc, dzc, m, r2, f, xi, yi, zi;
```

---

4. https://asc.llnl.gov/CORAL-benchmarks/Summaries/HACCmk_Summary_v1.0.pdf.

Listing 7.1 OpenACC version of the HACCmk microkernel (*continued*)

```
      int j;
      xi = 0.; yi = 0.; zi = 0.;
#pragma acc loop  private(dxc, dyc, dzc, r2, m, f) \
                  reduction(+:xi,yi,zi)
   for ( j = 0; j < n; j++ )      {
     dxc = xx[j] - xx[i];
     dyc = yy[j] - yy[i];
     dzc = zz[j] - zz[i];

     r2 = dxc * dxc + dyc * dyc + dzc * dzc;
     m = ( r2 < fsrrmax2 ) ? mass[j] : 0.0f;
     f =  powf( r2 + mp_rsm2, -1.5 )
          - ( ma0 + r2*(ma1 + r2*(ma2 + r2*(ma3
          + r2*(ma4+ r2*ma5)))));
     f = ( r2 > 0.0f ) ? m * f : 0.0f;
      xi = xi + f * dxc;
       yi = yi + f * dyc;
       zi = zi + f * dzc;
      }
     dx1 = xi;
     dy1 = yi;
     dz1 = zi;
   }
     vx1[i] = vx1[i] + dx1 * fcoeff;
     vy1[i] = vy1[i] + dy1 * fcoeff;
     vz1[i] = vz1[i] + dz1 * fcoeff;
}
```

HACCmk is an extremely interesting case study, because to work with performance portable codes, the compiler must successfully vectorize all the statements of the inner procedure (generate vector instructions) or generate efficient multithreaded or SMT code. For this code, performance portability depends on the quality of the compiler implementation and its ability to vectorize code or to generate multithreaded (SMT) code for GPUs. To get good performance on the CPU and Xeon Phi, we also need to make sure that there is a vector implementation of the `powf`, which belongs to the C math library `math.h`.

7.4.2 TARGETING MULTIPLE ARCHITECTURES

Achieving performance portability with OpenACC depends on how the compiler lowers (translates) and maps the parallelism specified by OpenACC to the target architecture. When we compile HACCmk with the PGI compiler and target a K20x NVIDIA GPU, we get the following output:

```
pgcc -acc -Minfo -O3 -c main.c -o main.o
main:
   203, Loop not vectorized: data dependency
```

```
        Loop unrolled 4 times
        FMA (fused multiply-add) instruction(s) generated
211, Generated an alternate version of the loop
        Generated vector simd code for the loop
222, Memory set idiom, loop replaced by call to __c_mset1
223, Memory copy idiom, loop replaced by call to __c_mcopy1
239, Generating implicit copyin(mass[:n])
        Generating copy(vx1[:],vy1[:],vz1[:])
        Generating copyin(xx[:n],zz[:n],yy[:n])
        Accelerator kernel generated
        Generating Tesla code
    242, #pragma acc loop gang /* blockIdx.x */
    257, #pragma acc loop vector(128) /* threadIdx.x */
        Generating reduction(+:xi,zi,yi)
```

When you compile HACCmk with the PGI compiler and target an AMD Bulldozer architecture, you get the following compiler output:

```
pgcc -acc -Minfo -O3 -ta=multicore -c main.c -o main.o
main:
    188, Loop not vectorized/parallelized:
        contains a parallel region
    203, Loop not vectorized: data dependency
        Loop unrolled 4 times
        FMA (fused multiply-add) instruction(s) generated
    211, Generated an alternate version of the loop
        Generated vector simd code for the loop
    222, Memory set idiom, loop replaced by call to __c_mset1
    223, Loop unrolled 8 times
    239, Generating Multicore code
        242, #pragma acc loop gang
    257, Loop is parallelizable
        Generated vector simd code for the loop containing
        reductions and conditionals
        Generated 4 prefetch instructions for the loop
        FMA (fused multiply-add) instruction(s) generated
    301, Generated vector simd code for the loop containing
        reductions
        Generated 3 prefetch instructions for the loop
        FMA (fused multiply-add) instruction(s) generated
```

Notice that for these two architectures, PGI translates the outer OpenACC loop to gang-level parallelism (loop 239) and translates the inner loop to vector-level parallelism (loop 257). However, one of the main differences is the vector_length used. For the GPU version, the vector length is 128, whereas the CPU version is based on the size of the vector register for AVX (256-bits). In this case the vector_length is 8 (for 8 floats vector instructions). Also notice that to efficiently vectorize the inner loop for multicores, generation of vector predicates and intrinsics is needed (e.g., powf()).

We specified different vector lengths using OpenACC, but for both cases (GPU and multicore) the PGI compiler always picked 128 (for the GPU) and 4 (for the multi-core) architecture. The compiler's internal cost models picked the right length for the different architectures and optionally decided to ignore the clauses provided by the user, as reported in the output from −Minfo shown earlier.

To control the number of threads spawned on the multicore platforms, you use the ACC_MULTICORE environment variable. However, this variable is a PGI extension and not part of the OpenACC standard. You should use this flag if you want to control the number of threads to be used on the CPU. If the flag is not specified, the CPU will use the maximum number of threads available on the target multicore architecture.

7.4.3 OPENACC OVER NVIDIA K20X GPU

We ran HACCmk on the OLCF Titan Cray XK7 supercomputer, which consists of a cluster of AMD Interlagos host CPUs connected to NVIDIA K20x GPUs. For the Oak Ridge Leadership Computing Facility (OLCF) Titan system, a compute node consists of (a) an AMD Interlagos 16-core processor with a peak flop rate of 140.2 GF and a peak memory bandwidth of 51.2 GB/sec, and (b) an NVIDIA Kepler K20x GPU with a peak single- or double-precision flop rate of 3,935/1,311 GF and a peak memory bandwidth of 250 GB/sec. For this platform, Cray compilers were used, with versions 8.5.0, and PGI 16.5 / 17.1.

Figure 7.1 shows the HACCmk speedup of the OpenACC version when running on an NVIDIA K20x GPU, as compared with the OpenMP shared-memory version running on an AMD Bulldozer processor using 8 host CPU threads (because each floating-point unit is shared between 2 of the 16 physical cores). The OpenACC version always outperformed the shared-memory version running on the CPU. This is what we would expect given the K20x compute capabilities. When we compare the results using different compilers, we observed less OpenACC speedup when using the PGI 16.5 compiler. These results highlight the fact that performance portability of code also depends on the quality of the compiler optimizations, because more hints may be needed to generate performance portable code, depending on the compiler.

7.4.4 OPENACC OVER AMD BULLDOZER MULTICORE

Figure 7.2 shows the HACCmk speedup of OpenACC (multicore) over OpenMP 3.1 using 8 threads when running on a Bulldozer AMD using 8 cores using PGI 17.1. We used the OpenACC environment flag ACC_NUM_CORES=8 to specify 8 OpenACC

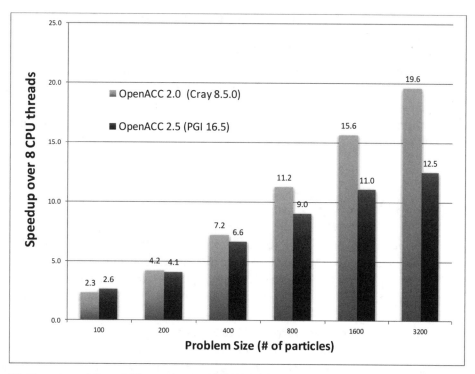

Figure 7.1 Speedup of OpenACC running on NVIDIA K20x GPUs when compared to OpenMP shared memory running on Bulldozer AMD CPU using 8 threads

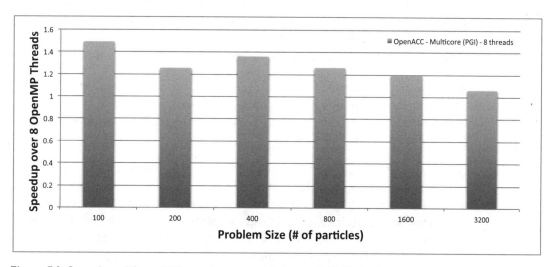

Figure 7.2 Speedup of OpenACC running on a Bulldozer AMD CPU when compared to OpenMP shared memory running on a Bulldozer AMD CPU using 8 threads

threads on the CPU. The OpenACC version outperformed the OpenMP 3.1 version. One of the reasons is that our OpenACC version inlines the inner loop (compared to the OpenMP 3.1 version) and provides more information to the vectorization phase of the compiler, including information about reductions. We also notice that when the problem size increases, the OpenACC improvement in terms of speedup becomes less profitable (from 1.49 to 1.06) as we saturate the memory bandwidth. The Cray 8.8.5 compiler did not support the mode of targeting OpenACC to multicore.

7.5 Summary

It is possible to achieve improved performance portability across architectures when you use OpenACC. Performance of OpenACC depends on the ability of the compiler to generate good code on the target platform. For example, we observed a significant performance variation when we compiled OpenACC with Cray 8.5.0 compared with the PGI 16.5. Further investigation showed a significant performance variation when we tried PGI 16.7. This tells us that compilers play a significant role in the level of performance portability of a programming model. To write performance portable code, it is important to specify where the parallelism in the code is (e.g., via `#pragma acc loop`) without specifying clauses that affect how the parallelism is mapped to the architecture. For example, specifying hints such as the OpenACC `vector_length` can help achieve good performance on an architecture, but, at the same time, it can possibly hinder performance on another one. However, sometimes these hints are necessary when the compiler cannot efficiently map the parallelism to the target platform.

When we compiled OpenACC to multicore, which in this case corresponded to the shared-memory host CPU, the PGI compiler ignored the data region directives. These included any `#pragma acc data` directives or clauses that move data to or from the accelerator.

Not only is the `#pragma acc loop` directive extremely useful for performance portability (to specify parallelism for offloading to accelerators), but also, depending on the implementation, it can be critical if you are to achieve good levels of multithreading and vectorization. It can help compilers identify the parallelism in the code when they cannot figure it out automatically, and this is important for optimizations such as automatic vectorization. Compilers cannot yet consistently identify these opportunities in all cases, so hints must be used to ensure that vectorization is used where appropriate. Although GPUs do not have vector units, the `#pragma` `acc loop` directive can be used to help identify parallelism that can be mapped to grids, thread blocks, and potential very fine-grained parallelism that can be executed by SMT threads (e.g., GPU warps).

We noticed better performance when using OpenACC (multicore) versus OpenMP 3.1 baseline when running in an AMD Bulldozer processor using 8 cores using PGI 17.1. One of the possible reasons for this behavior is that OpenACC provides more information to the vectorization phase of the compiler, including information about reductions. Being able to specify another level of parallelism in OpenACC that maps to vector instructions was an advantage. At the time of this writing, the Cray compiler didn't allow the ability to generate OpenACC code that targets multicore processors.

7.6 Exercises

1. How many levels of parallelism can be specified using OpenACC?

2. Which of the following directives is the most performance portable?

   a. `#pragma acc parallel loop`

   b. `#pragma acc parallel loop gang`

   c. `#pragma acc parallel loop vector`

   d. `#pragma acc parallel loop vector vector_length(N)`

3. Which of the following memory models does OpenACC support? Describe any limitations that apply to those models that are supported.

   a. Shared memory

   b. Discrete memory

   c. Partially Shared Memory

4. Which of the following clauses can be used to tune for a specific architecture?

   a. Specifying a `vector_length()`

   b. Specifying the number of gangs, workers, or vectors

   c. `acc copyin` and `copyout`

d. All of the above

e. None of the above

5. Is an OpenACC compiler allowed to

a. Ignore directives specified by the user

b. Change values in directives provided by the user

c. Both

d. Neither

Chapter 8

Additional Approaches to Parallel Programming

Christian Trott, Sandia National Laboratories[1]

In addition to OpenACC, several established and emerging parallel programming models are relevant for HPC. This chapter overviews the most important ones and discusses similarities and differences between them and OpenACC. In particular, this chapter highlights where the models differ only in syntax and where they diverge semantically. It also serves as a short translation guide, providing code examples for the most common parallel programming concepts.

8.1 Programming Models

This section offers a short description of each of the most relevant programming models. For this purpose, the models are also distinguished with respect to their implementation strategy (language features, directives, language extensions, or C++ abstraction), and their supported parallelization models (thread parallelism, task parallelism, and data parallelism).

1. Sandia National Laboratories is a multimission laboratory managed and operated by Sandia Corporation, a wholly owned subsidiary of Lockheed Martin Corporation, for the U.S. Department of Energy's National Nuclear Security Administration under contract DE-AC04-94AL85000.

In **thread parallelism** models, parallelism is introduced via concurrent execution of streams, which can coordinate via data exchange or explicit synchronization. Thread parallelism models are the most flexible way of expressing parallelism and can be used to implement both data parallelism and task parallelism execution schemes. However, these models are also the most cumbersome to use when you are implementing math or science algorithms.

Task parallelism–based systems are also flexible. They handle both functional and data parallelism. Furthermore, they can naturally expose parallelism in situations with complex data and synchronization dependencies.

Data parallelism is the most constrained model but is simpler to use than thread parallelism, and generally it has less runtime overhead than task parallelism–based systems. Data parallelism models describe work mainly via an index space, which can be iterated over in parallel. This does not necessarily mean that the iteration scheme is directly associated with a corresponding data structure. The data could be calculated during the execution of the program based on the iteration index.

Some programming models provide capabilities from all three areas. For example, OpenMP allows for thread parallelism and data parallelism as well as task parallelism.

As noted, all types of programming models can be implemented through various means.

Language features are the capabilities within the language itself that allow expressions of parallelism. Examples of those are the `DO CONCURRENT` concept in Fortran 2008, `std::thread` in C++11, and `for_each` in C++17. The advantage of using programming models that are implemented as language features is that they are part of the official programming language standard. Usually this means that they work well together with all other capabilities of a language. Additionally, they don't require any other third-party tools in addition to the compiler itself. However, native parallelism in language standards is usually many years behind programming models implemented through other means with respect to its scope.

OpenACC is one example of the directive-based approach. Directives have the benefit that they can be ignored if the code is compiled in an environment that does not require the parallelism, or where no compiler exists that understands the directives. Furthermore, it is usually possible to incrementally introduce directives into an application. In addition to OpenACC, the most widely used directive-based programming model is OpenMP.

Language extensions add capabilities to an existing programming language that are not part of the language standard. These require specialized compilers, which often are provided only by a single party. Examples are CUDA, OpenCL, and C++ AMP. Applications written in those models cannot be compiled by standard compilers, something that can lead to a vendor lock-in. Often these models have restrictions with respect to which language features can be utilized within parallel regions of the code.

The last set of programming models is implemented through **C++ abstractions.** With its **template** mechanism, C++ can be used to implement new concepts that have the look and feel of built-in language features from the perspective of an application developer. Although it is possible to achieve similar things via macros in pure C, the template mechanism is more flexible and less error prone. The C++ abstractions are usually layered over multiple other programming models and thus you can provide access to vendor-specific tool chains without locking the application itself into them.

For example, Kokkos, from the Sandia National Laboratories, provides back ends for CUDA, OpenMP, C++ threads, and serial execution, only one of which needs to be available on a given platform to compile and execute an application. The particular features of these back ends are abstracted, allowing the programmer to write code as if it were native C++. Other examples of this approach are RAJA and TBB.

Table 8.1 lists the various types of programming models, supported languages, and architectures these models can target.

Table 8.1 Programming models

MODEL	IMPLEMENTATION	SUPPORTED LANGUAGES	TARGET ARCHITECTURES
OpenACC	Directives	Fortran, C, C++	CPUs, GPUs, OpenPOWER
OpenMP	Directives	Fortran, C, C++	CPUs, Xeon Phi, GPUs
CUDA	Language extension	(Fortran), C, C++	GPUs (NVIDIA)
OpenCL	Language extension	C, (C++)	GPUs, (CPUs), FPGAs
C++ AMP	Language extension	C++	CPUs, GPUs
Kokkos	C++ abstraction	C++	CPUs, GPUs
RAJA	C++ abstraction	C++	CPUs, GPUs
TBB	C++ abstraction	C++	CPUs
C++17	Language feature	C++	CPUs
Fortran 2008	Language feature	Fortran	CPUs

8.1.1 OPENACC

Although OpenACC is extensively described in previous chapters, it is worthwhile to identify its properties relative to other programming models discussed in this chapter. OpenACC is a data parallel programming model designed to provide performance portability across various hardware architectures. As such it has provided data management directives from its inception. The semantics of OpenACC directives are generally less restrictive than OpenMP semantics, allowing for more flexible mapping of algorithmic parallelism to the available hardware execution resources. A large number of concepts (though not syntax) introduced by OpenACC are now part of OpenMP 4. More information about OpenACC can be found at http://www.openacc.org.

8.1.2 OPENMP

OpenMP is arguably the most mature of the shared-memory parallel programming models. As with OpenACC, it is a directive-based model that is available in Fortran, C, and C++. The OpenMP standard is defined by a consortium (OpenMP Architecture Review Board (ARB)) that has many members, including major hardware and software vendors such as Intel, IBM, AMD, NVIDIA, ARM, Oracle, and Fujitsu. As such, OpenMP is widely supported across the vast majority of all hardware platforms as well as on all major operating systems. All major compilers relevant for HPC support OpenMP directives, including GCC, Clang, Intel, IBM, Cray, and PGI.

In 1997, OpenMP was targeted for simple data parallel multiprocessing on CPUs, and thus its concepts and semantics are geared toward the existence of heavyweight threads. In fact, OpenMP has supported direct thread parallel algorithms from the start. In version 4.0, released in 2013, concepts were added to enable the support of heterogeneous architectures, including designs that contain accelerators. A significant number of new directives were introduced that support massively parallel algorithms on lightweight threads.

In its current iteration, version 4.5, OpenMP provides a rich set of parallel execution capabilities as well as data management capabilities for two-level memory systems. It also supports task parallelism in addition to data and thread parallel constructs.

Because OpenMP is one of the most mature shared-memory programming models, extensive documentation and training material is available, and many scientific libraries and applications are parallelized with OpenMP (www.openmp.org).

8.1.3 CUDA

CUDA is a language extension for C and C++ to enable support for using NVIDIA GPUs. It was initially released in 2007 to exploit the increased flexibility of NVIDIA GPUs, allowing them to be used for general-purpose programming instead of only graphic computations. CUDA is designed to exploit massive parallelism by using inherent hierarchies. It expresses parallelism through a grid of thread blocks, where only threads within the same block can synchronize with each other. Furthermore, threads within a block are organized in so-called warps, which execute instructions in lockstep.

Therefore, CUDA can be considered a hybrid data and thread parallel programming model at its core. **Interthread block** parallelism corresponds more closely to pure data parallelism: You specify how many blocks need to be executed (the index space), but CUDA does not promise anything with respect to the order of execution nor the number of concurrently executing thread blocks. **Intrathread block** parallelism, on the other hand, is thread parallelism: You specify how many threads are concurrently executing, and those threads can interact via memory as well as synchronization constructs.

You make data management explicit by using special allocators and deep copy function calls. There are no built-in data constructs (other than for special access operations such as noncoherent constant loads), so higher-level structures must be built from raw pointers.

The CUDA ecosystem provides a comprehensive set of scientific libraries that help with implementing complex applications. These include BLAS and solver libraries as well as comprehensive data analytics and artificial intelligence libraries.

Note that the CUDA programming model was also adopted to Fortran in the PGI compiler suite. More resources for CUDA are provided at http://www.nvidia.com/cuda.

8.1.4 OPENCL

With its introduction in 2008, OpenCL tried to fill the need for a programming model that allows applications to run across a wide range of hardware architectures. As an open standard released by the Khronos Group, it was soon supported by all major hardware companies, including Intel, NVIDIA, AMD, and IBM. Conceptually OpenCL has a lot of similarities to CUDA, a natural consequence of its desire to support GPU-type architectures. OpenCL provides a hybrid data/thread parallel model equivalent to CUDA. Work is scheduled in workgroups, with threads inside a workgroup providing a thread parallel programming environment, while interwork-group parallelism is data parallel.

Generally, OpenCL is more verbose than CUDA: Data management, execution resource management, and work dispatch are somewhat more complicated. Kernel code is generally compiled just in time. C++ inside the kernels is supported only as of the OpenCL 2.1 standard, which was released in November 2015. Data management revolves around `cl_mem` handles, which are used in lieu of raw pointers. Higher-level data structures must be built on top of those.

To address shortcomings of OpenCL in a C++ environment, a new standard called SYCL is being developed. SYCL provides a C++ abstraction on top of OpenCL.

Within the area of HPC, OpenCL is significantly less common than CUDA or OpenACC programs. Current trends indicate that the availability of OpenMP 4.5 will further reduce the relevance of OpenCL in HPC, because OpenMP 4.5 will be supported across all major hardware platforms. OpenCL's home page can be found at http://www.khronos.org/opencl.

8.1.5 C++ AMP

C++ AMP is a language extension to C++ introduced by Microsoft. Its goal is to make the compute capabilities of GPUs available inside C++ applications, but it can also be used to parallelize algorithms for the CPU. Its look and feel is very close to the C++ abstractions discussed next, but C++ AMP introduces a couple of keywords that make it a language extension. Consequently, applications that use C++ AMP can be compiled only with the Microsoft C++ compiler (disregarding some experimental compilers). To learn more about C++ AMP, visit https://msdn.microsoft.com/en-us/library/hh265136.aspx.

8.1.6 KOKKOS

Developed at Sandia National Laboratories, Kokkos is a programming model intended for writing performance portable HPC applications. It is implemented as a C++ abstraction layer and provides pure data parallel concepts, task parallelism, and hybrid data/thread parallel and task/thread parallel capabilities. One differentiator of Kokkos is its comprehensive data abstraction layer. The model can handle deep multilevel memory hierarchies as well as hybrid architectures having more than two types of execution resources.

The programming model Kokkos has been under development since 2011 and has been considered production ready since 2015. It is now the default model for Sandia's extensive application portfolio for implementing shared-memory parallelism.

Parallel work is dispatched via patterns such as `parallel_for`, `parallel_reduce`, and `task_spawn` in combination with execution policies, which specify the iteration scheme and where to execute work.

Data abstractions are handled mostly via the **view abstraction**, which is a multidimensional array abstraction with view semantics. A particular feature of **views** is their memory layout abstraction, which allows you to specify the index mapping to memory location. Views also implement the concepts of memory spaces as well as access traits such as atomic operations. Kokkos itself and libraries related to it (such as profiling tools and math libraries) are available at https://github.com/kokkos.

8.1.7 RAJA

Like Kokkos, RAJA is a programming model providing performance portability for applications through C++ abstractions. RAJA was developed at the Lawrence Livermore National Laboratory and is used to port HPC applications to run on new supercomputer designs. RAJA focuses on parallel execution and provides mechanisms to customize iteration schemes for specific applications. Although RAJA itself does not handle data management, libraries built on top of RAJA (such as CHAI) are being developed with more comprehensive data abstractions. RAJA is available at https://github.com/llnl/raja.

8.1.8 THREADING BUILDING BLOCKS

Threading Building Blocks (TBB) was developed by Intel to make threading more accessible in C++. It is also one of the first programming models implemented as a C++ abstraction layer. TBB provides support for a wide range of algorithmic concepts, including nested loops, reductions, and scans. In addition, TBB implements a set of higher-level data structures useful in threaded applications. This includes parallel hash maps, vectors, and queues. The basic execution mechanism is built on a task-scheduling mechanism that uses work stealing. The parallel patterns are utilized to submit tasks to a scheduler in bulk. The current implementation supports CPUs as well as manycore architectures and is available through multiple compilers, including the Intel compiler, GCC, and Microsoft Visual C++ (https://www.threadingbuildingblocks.org).

8.1.9 C++17

With the C++11 standard, the C++ standards committee has begun to address the need for shared-memory parallelism on modern computing systems by introducing `std::thread`. Although these capabilities allow for expressing thread parallelism similar to using POSIX threads, they do not allow for the use of hybrid compute architectures such as systems with CPUs and GPUs. This starts to change with C++17, which introduces fundamental data parallel constructs. Such constructs allow significantly more freedom to map parallel work onto various execution resources.

In C++17 only the very basics have been introduced. It provides a `for_each` function that takes an **execution policy** as the first argument. This execution policy states the allowable parallelization semantics for the provided index range. Technically these semantics allow for executing on a GPU, given a coherent memory subsystem, but at this point no compilers are available to exploit that possibility. The C++ committee is working on extending the scope of the available parallelization capabilities. The proposals are strongly influenced by programming models implemented as C++ abstraction layers. Indeed, many developers of those abstraction layers explicitly state that they consider their models as prototypes for a future C++ standard.

8.1.10 FORTRAN 2008

Fortran 2008 added a simple parallel loop concept called DO CONCURRENT. Although this is a necessary start, its applicability is limited because it does not provide reduction mechanisms or shared-memory atomics (although there are some limited atomic operation capabilities for Fortran coarrays). Therefore, this parallelism mechanism is rarely used. Fortran 2015 extends the existing coarray capabilities, thereby enabling parallelization across a whole machine. It is part of the class of partitioned global address space (PGAS) models and thus not very comparable to the node-level parallel models discussed in this chapter.

8.2 Programming Model Components

This section compares syntax and availability for some of the major concepts for programming models. In the syntax in Table 8.2, an X is shown only if it is a first-class feature of the programming model or if a straightforward mapping exists from a first-class feature of the model. For that reason, reductions are not given for many models. Although you can implement them through a combination of parallel loops, temporary data buffers, and serial loops, they are not an actual concept in many models and hence are shown as (X). For example, CUDA and OpenCL do not provide reductions. Also, most of the syntax examples are shown in C/C++ because only OpenMP, OpenACC, and Fortran 2008 have support for Fortran.

Table 8.2 Programming models: List of concept coverage

MODEL	PARALLEL LOOPS	PARALLEL REDUCTION	TIGHTLY NESTED LOOPS	NON-TIGHTLY NESTED LOOPS	TASK PARALLELISM	DATA ALLOCATIONS	DATA TRANSFERS
OpenACC	X	X	X	X	—	X	X
OpenMP	X	X	X	X	X	X	X
CUDA	(X)	—	(X)	(X)	—	X	X
OpenCL	(X)	—	(X)	(X)	—	X	X
C++ AMP	X	—	X	—	—	X	X
Kokkos	X	X	X	X	X	X	X
RAJA	X	X	X	—	—	—	—
TBB	X	X	X	X	X	X	—
C++17	X	—	—	—	(X)	X	(X)
Fortran 2008	X	—	—	—	—	X	(X)

8.2.1 PARALLEL LOOPS

Parallel loops are arguably one of the most useful and common parallel programming concepts in HPC applications. Consequently, parallel loops can be expressed in all of the parallel programming models cited here, albeit with different syntax. The purpose of a parallel loop is to map the execution of an index range to available execution resources.

In most models, parallel loops are a **first-class concept**, meaning that there is a specific syntax explicitly designed for parallelizing a loop over an index range. The exceptions are CUDA and OpenCL, which, as previously discussed, are hybrid data/thread parallel models. In both cases, part of the index to execution resources mapping must be carried out explicitly by the application.

Furthermore, there are differences in semantics with respect to the independence of iterations. Some models stipulate that iterations must be independent, whereas others allow for certain types of dependency. In this context, it is particularly important to know that the standard `parallel for` loop of OpenMP has semantics that allow for limited dependencies between loop iterations (as of OpenMP 4.5). Because of those semantics, it is not necessarily legal to map such a marked loop to vector units of a compute architecture or to threads of a GPU. OpenMP 4.0 introduced a syntax that allows such mapping.

A simple example of parallel loops is a vector addition, which as a plain C/C++ code can be written this way:

```
void axpby(int N, double * z, double alpha, double* x,
                               double beta, double* y) {
    for(int i = 0; i<N; i++)
        z[i] = alpha * x[i] + beta * y[i];
}
```

In this archetypal loop, every iteration is independent of every other (assuming z, x, and y do not alias each other). No matter the order in which loop iterations are executed, the output is bitwise the same. The conversion of this loop to all the discussed programming models is shown in Table 8.3.

Table 8.3 Mapping of a simple loop to the presented parallel programming models

MODEL	SYNTAX
OpenACC	```void launch (int N, [ARGS]) { #pragma acc parallel loop for(int i=0; i<N; i++) {/*. . .*/} }```
OpenMP (CPU only)	```void launch (int N, [ARGS]) { #pragma omp parallel for for(int i=0; i<N; i++) {/*. . .*/} }```
OpenMP	```void launch (int N, [ARGS]) { #pragma omp teams distribute parallel for for(int i = 0; i<N; i++) {/*. . .*/} }```
CUDA	```__global__ void foo(int N, [ARGS]) { int i = blockIdx.x * blockDim.x + threadIdx.x; if(i<N) {/*. . .*/} } void launch (int N, [ARGS]) { foo<<<(N+255)/256,256>>>(N, [ARS]); }```

| OpenCL | ```
__kernel void foo(T0 Arg0, T1 Arg1 [.ARGS] ) {
  int i = get_global_id(0); {/*. . .*/}
}

void launch (int N, T0 Arg0, T1 Arg1 [,ARGS]) {
    cl_kernel kernel = clCreateKernel(program, "foo", NULL);
    clSetKernelArg(kernel, 0, sizeof(T0), &Arg0);
    clSetKernelArg(kernel, 1, sizeof(T1), &Arg1);
    /*. . .*/
    clEnqueueNDRangeKernel(queue, kernel, 1, NULL,
                          &N, NULL, 0, NULL, NULL);

    clfork(stdgpu,0,krn,&ndr,CL_EVENT_NOWAIT);
}
``` |
|---|---|
| C++17 | ```
void launch (int N, [ARGS]) {
    for_each(par_unseq,begin(range),end(range),[&] (int i
        {/*. . .*/});
}
``` |
| Fortran | ```
DO CONCURRENT (i = 1:N)
    . . .
END DO
``` |
| C++ AMP | ```
void launch (int N, [ARGS]) {
    extent<1> range(N);
    parallel_for_each(range, [=] (index<1> idx) restrict(amp)
        { int i = idx[0]; {/*. . .*/} });
}
``` |
| Kokkos | ```
void launch (int N, [ARGS]) {
    parallel_for(N, KOKKOS_LAMBDA (int i) {/*. . .*/});
}
``` |
| RAJA | ```
void launch (int N, [ARGS]) {
    forall<cuda_exec<256>>(0, N, [=] RAJA_DEVICE (int i)
        {/*. . .*/});
}
``` |
| TBB | ```
void launch (int N, [ARGS]) {
    parallel_for(0, N, [=] (int i) {/*. . .*/});
}
``` |

8.2.2 PARALLEL REDUCTIONS

Parallel reductions combine a parallel loop with a reduction, such as computing a sum or finding the maximum value of a property computed in each loop iteration. Such reductions are commonplace occurrences in most scientific and engineering applications. A simple example is computing the dot product of two vectors.

```
double dot(int N, double* x, double* y) {
    double result = 0.0;
    for(int i=0; i<N; i++)
        result += x[i] * y[i];
    return result;
}
```
```

Simply parallelizing this loop would result in race conditions for the update of `result` and thus would produce the wrong answer.

Even though parallel reduction is commonplace, only about half of the programming models listed in this section provide a first-class concept of a reduction. In particular, CUDA and OpenCL, as well as C++17 and Fortran 2008, do not have native support for reductions. Implementing high-performing reductions in these models is a nontrivial endeavor. It requires a combination of multiple parallel loops, use of atomic operations, and thread parallel programming techniques such as tree reductions, which heavily utilize pairwise barriers between threads.

Another concern is which operations a model supports for reductions and on which data types these operations can work. Most models provide built-ins for numeric scalar types (such as integer or floating-point scalars) and a set of common operations (sum, max, min). Furthermore, some models such as OpenMP, Kokkos, and RAJA allow user-defined reduction operations and reduction types. Table 8.4, with syntax examples, demonstrates a max reduction.

Table 8.4 Syntax for max reduction using various programming models

MODEL	SYNTAX
| OpenACC | ```
double launch (int N, [ARGS]) {
    double result;
    #pragma acc parallel loop reduction(max: result)
    for(int i = 0; i<N; i++) {/*. . .*/}
}
``` |
| OpenMP | ```
double launch (int N, [ARGS]) {
    double result;
    #pragma omp teams distribute parallel for \
            reduction(max: result)  map(tofrom: result)
    for(int i = 0; i<N; i++) {/*. . .*/}
}
``` |
| Kokkos | ```
double launch (int N, [ARGS]) {
    double result; Max<double> max(result);
    parallel_reduce(N, KOKKOS_LAMBDA (int i, double& lmax)
        {/*. . .*/},
    max);
    return result;
}
``` |
| RAJA | ```
double launch (int N, [ARGS]) {
    ReduceMax<cuda_reduce<256>,double> max_val(0.0)
    forall<cuda_exec<256>>(0, N, [=] RAJA_DEVICE (int i) {
        /*. . .*/
        max_val(value_i);
    });
    return max_val.get();
}
``` |

TBB	`double launch (int N, [ARGS]) {`
	    `return tbb::parallel_reduce(tbb::blocked_range<int>(0,N), 0.0,`
	       `[&] (const tbb::blocked_range<int>& r, double lmax)->double`
	       `{`
	          `for(int i = r.begin(); i<r.end(); i++) {/*. . .*/}`
	          `return lmax;`
	       `}, std::max<double>());`
	`}`

8.2.3 TIGHTLY NESTED LOOPS

Another common algorithmic structure is tightly nested or multidimensional loops. These are constructs wherein multiple loops are nested without any intervening instructions. An example of this are structured grid-based applications, with the execution iterating over a 2D or 3D index space. Providing a first-class feature for this class of algorithms can help improve performance by exposing more parallelism as well as enabling loop tiling and similar compiler optimization techniques.

Many programming models support tightly nested loop constructs explicitly or allow for easy mapping. A simple example of tightly nested loops is a matrix addition, wherein each iteration is completely independent of every other one.

```
void matadd(int N0, int N1, double** C, double alpha,
            double** A, double beta, double** B) {
  for(int i0 = 0; i0 < N0; i0++)
    for(int i1 = 0; i1 < N1; i1++)
      C[i0][i1] = alpha * A[i0][i1] + beta * B[i0][i1];
}
```

As with simple loops, each iteration is completely independent and can be executed in any order. Programming models that support both reductions and tightly nested loops usually also support their combination. Table 8.5 shows the syntax for tightly nested loops using various programming models.

Table 8.5 Syntax for tightly nested loops using various programming models

MODEL	SYNTAX

OpenACC	`void launch (int N0, int N1, [ARGS]) {`
	    `#pragma acc parallel loop collapse(2)`
	    `for(int i0=0; i0<N0; i0++)`
	       `for(int i1=0; i1<N1; i1++) {/*. . .*/}`
	`}`

OpenMP	`void launch (int N0, int N1, [ARGS]) {`
	    `#pragma omp teams distribute parallel for collapse(2)`
	    `for(int i0=0; i0<N0; i0++)`
	       `for(int i1=0; i1<N1; i1++) {/*. . .*/}`
	`}`

Table 8.5 Syntax for tightly nested loops using various programming models (*continued*)

CUDA	```__global__ void foo(int N1, [ARGS]) {```
	``` int i0 = blockIdx.x;```
	``` for(int i1=threadIdx.x; i1<N1; i1+= blockDim.x) {/*. . .*/}```
	```}```
	
	```void launch(int N0, int N1,[ARGS]) { foo<<<N0, 256>>>(N1, [ARS]); }```

OpenCL	```__kernel void foo(T0 Arg0, T1 Arg1 [,ARGS]) {```
	``` int i0 = get_global_id(0);```
	``` int i1 = get_global_id(1);```
	``` {/*. . .*/}```
	```}```
	
	```void launch (int N0, int N1, T0 Arg0, T1 Arg1 [,ARGS]) {```
	``` cl_kernel kernel = clCreateKernel(program, "foo", NULL);```
	``` clSetKernelArg(kernel, 0, sizeof(T0), &Arg0);```
	``` clSetKernelArg(kernel, 1, sizeof(T1), &Arg1);```
	``` /*. . .*/```
	``` int DIM[2] = {N0,N1};```
	``` clEnqueueNDRangeKernel(queue, kernel, 2, NULL,```
	``` &DIM, NULL, 0, NULL, NULL);```
	```}```

C++ AMP	```void launch (int N0, int N1, [ARGS]) {```
	``` extent<2> range(N0,N1);```
	``` parallel_for_each(range, [=] (index<2> idx) restrict(amp) {```
	``` int i0 = idx[0]; int i1 = idx[1] {/*...*/}```
	``` });```
	```}```

Kokkos	```void launch (int N0, int N1, [ARGS]) {```
	``` parallel_for(MDRangePolicy<Rank<2>>(N0,N1),```
	``` KOKKOS_LAMBDA (int i0, int i1) {/*. . .*/});```
	```}```

RAJA	```void launch (int N0,int s0, int N1, int s1, [ARGS]) {```
	``` forallN<NestedPolicy<ExecList<cuda_threadblock_x_exec<16>,```
	``` cuda_threadblock_y_exec<16>>>> (```
	``` RangeStrideSegment(0, N0, s0),```
	``` RangeStrideSegment(0, N1, s1),```
	``` [=] RAJA_DEVICE (int i0, int i1) {/*. . .*/});```
	```}```

TBB	```void launch (int N0, int N1, [ARGS]) {```
	``` parallel_for(blocked_range2d<int>(0, N0, 0, N1)```
	``` [](const blocked_range2<int> &r) {```
	``` for(int i0=r.pages.begin(), i0 < r.pages.end(); i0++)```
	``` for(int i1=r.rows.begin(), i1 < r.rows.end(); i0++)```
	``` {/*. . .*/}```
	``` });```
	```}```

8.2.4 HIERARCHICAL PARALLELISM (NON-TIGHTLY NESTED LOOPS)

In cases where loops are not tightly nested but contain intervening code between loop levels, as well as in cases where the parallel patterns on each loop level are different, hierarchical parallelism is an appropriate concept. For example, in a matrix vector product (GEMV), the inner loop is a reduction whose result is written into another vector.

```
void gemv(int N0, int N1, double* y,
          double alpha, double** A, double* x) {
    for(int i0 = 0; i0 < N0; i0++) {
        double y_i0 = 0;
        for(int i1 = 0; i1 < N1; i1++)
            y_i0 += A[i0][i1] * x[i1];
        y[i0] = alpha * y_i0;
    }
}
```

You could express this as a tightly nested loop for serial execution by simply adding onto `y[i0]` in the inner loop, but this would assume that all elements of `y` are zero. For parallel execution this approach would result in write conflicts, because all the iterations of the inner loop would update the same value. Although true tightly nested loops allow for reductions, it would need to be a reduction over the entire index space. In the case of the matrix vector multiplication, you are confronted with a set of independent reductions, and hence it falls into the category of non-tightly nested loops.

One important distinction between programming models is the semantics of how hierarchical parallelism is provided. In OpenMP, nested levels of parallelism are forklike or joinlike constructs, which potentially spawn new threads. At a minimum, the state of the outer scope must be replicated on all threads for the inner scope.

In Kokkos, on the other hand, hierarchical parallelism is provided through the `team` interface. A work item is given to a team of threads, with all threads active for the lifetime of the work item. Nested parallel constructs thus are required only to compute their loop bounds and can go right on computing. In fact, a nested `parallel_for` can even be nonblocking. On the other hand, this makes it necessary to use execution restriction capabilities in the outer scope—for example, if a contribution to some global object should be made only once per work item. Table 8.6 shows the syntax for non-tightly nested loops using various programming models.

Table 8.6 Syntax for non-tightly nested loops using various programming models

MODEL	SYNTAX
OpenACC	```void launch (int N0, int N1, [ARGS]) {
#pragma acc parallel loop gang
for(int i0=0; i0<N0; i0++) {
/*. . .*/
#pragma acc loop vector reduction(+:y_i0)
for(int i1=0; i1<N1; i1++) {/*...*/}
/*. . .*/
}
}```
OpenMP	```void launch (int N0, int N1, [ARGS]) {
#pragma omp target teams distribute
for(int i0=0; i0<N0; i0++) {
/*. . .*/
#pragma omp parallel for
for(int i1=0; i1<N1; i1++) {/*...*/}
/*. . .*/
}
}```
CUDA	```__global__ void foo(int N1, [ARGS]) {
    int i0 = blockIdx.x;
    /*. . .*/
    for(int i1=threadIdx.x; i1<N1; i1+= blockDim.x) {/*. . .*/}
    /*. . .*/
}

void launch (int N0, int N1,[ARGS]) {foo<<<N0, 256>>>(N1, [ARS]); }``` |
| OpenCL | ```__kernel void foo(int N1, T0 Arg0, T1 Arg1 [,ARGS]) {
    int i0 = get_global_id(0);
    for(int i1 = get_local_id(1); i1<N1; i1+= get_local_size(1);
        {/*. . .*/}
}

void launch (int N0, int N1, T0 Arg0, T1 Arg1 [,ARGS]) {
    cl_kernel kernel = clCreateKernel(program, "foo", NULL);
    clSetKernelArg(kernel, 0, sizeof(int), &N1);
    clSetKernelArg(kernel, 1, sizeof(T0), &Arg0);
    clSetKernelArg(kernel, 2, sizeof(T1), &Arg1);
    /*. . .*/
    int DIM[2] = {N0,256};
    clEnqueueNDRangeKernel(queue, kernel, 2, NULL,
                        &DIM, NULL, 0, NULL, NULL);
}``` |

| Kokkos | ```
void launch (int N0, int N1, [ARGS]) {
    parallel_for(TeamPolicy< >(N0,AUTO),
        KOKKOS_LAMBDA (TeamPolicy<>::member_type& team) {
            int i0 = team.league_rank();
            /*. . .*/
            parallel_for(TeamThreadRange(team, N1), [&] (int i1) {
                /*. . .*/
            });
            /*. . .*/
        });
}
``` |
|---|---|
| TBB | ```
void launch (int N0, int N1, [ARGS]) {
    parallel_for( 0, N0, []( const int i0 ) {
        /*. . .*/
        parallel_for( 0, N1, []( const int i1 ) {/*. . .*/});
            /*. . .*/
    });
}
``` |

8.2.5 TASK PARALLELISM

The fundamental idea of task parallelism is that you do not prescribe parallelism to the runtime, but rather you describe units of work and their interdependency. Then a runtime can figure out how to map these units of work—or tasks—to execution resources.

There are several advantages to task-based parallelism. First, it allows for straightforward load balancing, similar to using a dynamic schedule for data parallelism. Second, task parallelism can affect implicit loop or kernel fusion. Consider a sequence of a vector addition and calculation of the norm of the resulting vector. If the vector length is split into chunks and if those chunks are dispatched as tasks, then a subtask of the norm calculation depends only on the subtask of the vector update with the same index range. Scheduling these two tasks one immediately after the other makes the norm calculation use values coming from the cache. If instead the entire index range first must go through the vector update, those values will have been evicted again. Whether the runtime can exploit these possibilities is less clear.

A third benefit of task parallelism is that it naturally allows for functional parallelism. This capability can help expose more parallelism and help with goals such as overlapping communication with computation.

Several programming models allow for variants of task parallelism, including OpenMP, Kokkos, TBB, and C++11. Only Kokkos provides task mechanisms that can run on CPU and GPU architectures.

The main mechanisms of task parallelism are spawning tasks, futures to wait on, dependencies, and potentially a mechanism to preempt an active task (i.e., pause its execution to wait for a child task). Arguably TBB tasking is the most comprehensive of the four models mentioned here, followed by Kokkos, which provides mechanisms to generate dynamic task-directed acyclic graphs (DAG). OpenMP tasking is significantly more limited in that it does not provide the future concept. The only kind of dependencies allowed are a parent task waiting on its children or a dependency on data regions. Furthermore, OpenMP tasks must be launched inside an OpenMP parallel region, and upon exiting the scope, a barrier ensures that all tasks are finished. That means that it is not possible to write unstructured code (as is often the case in C++) that can generate task trees. C++17 tasks do provide the future concept but are otherwise basic. For example, there is no mechanism to provide a future as a dependency to a new task for the purpose of scheduling order.

Because of the significant differences among the models, often it is not possible to express task-based code implemented by one model in another model.

8.2.6 DATA ALLOCATION

If a programming model supports heterogeneous architectures with multiple memory levels, it must provide ways to allocate data in these different levels. Such memory hierarchies exist in two of today's HPC architectures: systems with CPUs and GPUs, and Intel Xeon Phi systems, which come with high-bandwidth memory and capacity memory on the same socket. Different models handle this in different ways. You can use the pragma-based approaches in a way that data transfers are implicit; you do this by adding directives to parallel regions that state the read-write access. Using this capability eliminates the need for explicit allocations in the different memory spaces. In contrast to that are usage modes wherein data allocations are explicitly done for every memory level. Note that some of these architectures can be put into a mode wherein the faster level of the memory hierarchy simply acts as a cache. In those cases, no special treatment of data is necessary, usually at the cost of performance. Table 8.7 shows syntax for allocation of data using various programming models.

Table 8.7 Syntax for data allocation using various programming models

MODEL	SYNTAX
OpenACC	```void foo(..) {` ` double* device_data = (double*) acc_malloc(N*sizeof(double));` ` //. . .` ` acc_free(device_data);` `}```
OpenMP	```void foo(..) {` ` double* device_data = (double*) omp_target_alloc(` ` N*sizeof(double), omp_get_default_device());` ` //. . .` ` omp_target_free(device_data, omp_get_default_device());` `}```
CUDA	```void foo(..) {` ` double* a; cudaMalloc(&a, N*sizeof(double);` ` //. . .` ` cudaFree(a);` `}```
OpenCL	```void foo(..) {` ` cl_mem a = clCreateBuffer(context, CL_MEM_READ_WRITE,` ` N*sizeof(double), NULL, NULL);` ` //. . .` ` clReleaseMemObjecy(a);` `}```
C++ AMP	```void foo(..) {` ` array<double,1> a(N);` ` //Deallocates at end of scope` `}```
Kokkos	```void foo (..) {` ` View<double*, MemSpace> a("A",N);` ` View<double*, MemSpace>::HostMirror h_a =` ` create_mirror_view(a);` ` //Deallocates on its own after falling out of scope` `}```
TBB	```void foo(..) {` ` double* a =` ` (double*) scalable_aligned_malloc(N*sizeof(double),64);` ` //. . .` ` scalable_aligned_free(a);` `}```

8.2.7 DATA TRANSFERS

In addition to data allocations, a programming model that supports memory hierarchies needs to facilitate data transfers across memory spaces. Depending on the model, these transfers can be explicit or implicit. Furthermore, some models, such as OpenMP and OpenACC, provide multiple ways for achieving similar outcomes through both a function-based API and a directive-based interface. The directive-based interface in those cases is scope based. This means that copies to the device happen when execution enters the scope, and copies from the device occur upon exiting the scope. It also means that the device allocations are valid only for that scope. Table 8.8 shows the syntax for data transfer using various programming models.

Table 8.8 Syntax for data transfers using various programming models

MODEL	SYNTAX
OpenACC (directive structured)	```void foo(int N, double* a) { #pragma acc data copy(a[0:N]) { // . . . } }```
OpenACC (directive unstructured)	```void foo(int N, double* a) { #pragma acc enter data copyin(a[0:N]) // . . . #pragma acc update self(a[0:N]) // . . . #pragma acc exit data copyout(a) }```
OpenACC (API)	```void foo(int N, double* host_data, double* device_data) { acc_memcpy_to_device(device_data, host_data, N*sizeof(double)); // . . . acc_memcpy_from_device(host_data, device_data, N*sizeof(double)); }```
OpenMP (directive)	```void foo(int N, double* a) { #pragma omp target data map(tofrom: a[0:N]) { // . . . } }```
OpenMP (API)	```void foo(int N, double* host_data, double* device_data) { omp_target_memcpy(device_data, host_data, N*sizeof(double), 0, 0, omp_get_default_device(), omp_get_initial_device()); //... omp_target_memcpy(host_data, device_data, N*sizeof(double), 0, 0, omp_get_initial_device(), omp_get_default_device()); }```
CUDA	```void foo(int N, double* host_data, double* device_data) { cudaMemcpy(device_data, host_data, N*sizeof(double), cudaMemcpyDefault); // . . . cudaMemcpy(host_data, device_data, N*sizeof(double), cudaMemcpyDefault); }```

| OpenCL | ```
void foo(int N, double* host_data, cl_mem device_data) {
    clEnqueueWriteBuffer(queue, device_data, CL_TRUE, 0,
        sizeof(double) * N, host_data, 0, NULL, NULL);
    //. . .
    clEnqueueReadBuffer(queue, device_data, CL_TRUE, 0,
        sizeof(double) * N, host_data, 0, NULL, NULL);
}
``` |
|--------|----------|
| Kokkos | ```
void foo (HostViewT host_data, DeviceViewT device_data) {
    deep_copy(device_data, host_data);
    //. . .
    deep_copy(host_data, device_data);
}
``` |

8.3 A Case Study

This case study looks at the linear solver portion of MiniFE, from the Mantevo suite of miniapps. Mantevo provides proxy applications for several scientific programs implemented in various programming models. MiniFE is a proxy for finite element applications. It constructs a heat conduction system and then uses a simple conjugate gradient solver to compute the solution. A **conjugate gradient solver** (CG solve) consists of three fundamental mathematical operations: vector additions, dot product, and (sparse) matrix vector multiplications. These three operations make use of the most common programming model components: parallel loops, parallel reductions, and (non-tightly) nested loops. In addition, data allocation and data transfers are potentially necessary when execution enters into the solver.

For this case study, MiniFE was stripped of its MPI component, and the CG solve was modified to call functions that take simple pointers as input instead of the default vector and matrix classes otherwise used in MiniFE. Note that the solver has a certain amount of extra code for collecting timing information. But no allocated data are accessed outside the three math functions other than for data allocation and transfer. In the following, the implementations of the vector addition, the dot product, and the sparse matrix multiplication are given for several models. The vector addition is a simple elementwise operation, which can be expressed as a straightforward parallel loop. The dot product requires a reduction over the iteration space. The sparse matrix vector multiplication has non-tightly nested loops, with the inner loop being a reduction.

The code is available at the book's repository (see the Preface), and the file containing all the programming model-specific code is `src/cg_solve.h`. The rest of the application is largely unchanged from the original MiniFE version and is the same code for all variants.

8.3.1 SERIAL IMPLEMENTATION

The CG solve algorithm requires a few temporary vectors, which MiniFE allocates at its start. Furthermore, for the serial implementation we extract the raw pointers of the data arrays used for the algorithm from the vector and matrix classes of MiniFE. The matrix is stored in the so-called compressed sparse row (CSR) format. It consists of three arrays: an array with all the nonzero values of the matrix, wherein entries from the same row are consecutively stored; an array with the corresponding column indexes; and an array that contains the offsets into those arrays, where each row starts.

```
double* r = new double[nrows];
double* p = new double[ncols];
double* Ap = new double[nrows];

double* x = &x_in.coefs[0];
const double* b = &b_in.coefs[0];

const double* A_vals = &A.packed_coefs[0];
const int* A_cols = &A.packed_cols[0];
const int* A_rows = &A.row_offsets[0];
```

The vector addition (AXPBY) in serial is a simple loop. There are six input parameters: the length of the vectors, the output vector z, the input vectors x and y, and their prefactors alpha and beta. Both x and y are read only and thus come in as const data. The name AXPBY comes from the math operation performed: z = a*x + b*y.

```
void axpby(int n, double* z, double alpha, const double* x,
                             double beta,  const double* y) {
    for(int i=0; i<n; i++)
        z[i] = alpha*x[i] + beta*y[i];
}
```

The dot product has only three input parameters: the length of the vectors, and two const pointers for the vectors:

```
double dot(int n, const double* x, const double* y) {
    double sum = 0.0;
    for(int i=0; i<n; i++)
        sum += x[i]*y[i];
    return sum;
}
```

The sparse matrix vector multiplication (SPMV) function is slightly more complex, featuring a nested reduction. In addition to the aforementioned three arrays representing the matrix, the SPMV function also takes the number of rows, the output vector y, and the right-hand side vector x as input.

```
void SPMV(int nrows, const int* A_row_offsets, const int* A_cols,
          const double* A_vals, double* y, const double* x) {
  for(int row=0; row<nrows; ++row) {
    double sum = 0.0;
    int row_start=A_row_offsets[row];
    int row_end=A_row_offsets[row+1];
    for(int i=row_start; i<row_end; ++i) {
      sum += A_vals[i]*x[A_cols[i]];
    }
    y[row] = sum;
  }
}
```

8.3.2 THE OPENACC IMPLEMENTATION

For the code to run on GPUs, a data region must be entered. Other than the x vector, the data do not need to be copied back from the device, so the `copyin` clause can be used. For the x vector the `copy` clause is used to retrieve the result from the device.

```
#pragma acc data \
    copyin(r[0:nrows], p[0:nrows],Ap[0:nrows], b[0:nrows], \
          A_vals[0:nnz], A_cols[0:nnz], A_rows[0:nrows+1]) \
    copy(x[0:nrows])
```

For the vector addition, the simple parallel loop construct is employed. Because the data were already transferred, the `present` clause is used to declare the arrays available.

```
void axpby(int n, double* z, double alpha, const double* x, double beta,
           const double* y) {
  #pragma acc parallel loop  present(x[0:n],y[0:n])
  for(int i=0; i<n; i++)
    z[i] = alpha*x[i] + beta*y[i];
}
```

The dot product is similar to the AXPBY function, with the addition of a reduction parameter.

```
double dot(int n, const double* x, const double* y) {
  double sum = 0.0;
  #pragma acc parallel loop reduction(+: sum) \
    present(x[0:n],y[0:n])
  for(int i=0; i<n; i++)
    sum += x[i]*y[i];
  return sum;
}
```

For the SPMV operation, a hierarchical operation is implemented wherein the outer loop is parallelized with gangs and workers, and the inner loop is parallelized with vector parallelism. To get good performance on GPUs, the number of workers and the vector length on the parallel region are explicitly defined. The `vector_length` of 8 is chosen to optimize performance and is mainly dependent on the number of nonzeros of a typical row of the matrix. In MiniFE that number is 27.

```
void spmv(int nrows, int nnz, const int* A_row_offsets,
         const int* A_cols,const double* A_vals, double* y,
         const double* x) {
   #pragma acc parallel num_workers(64) vector_length(8) \
          present(y[0:nrows], x[0:nrows], A_row_offsets[0:nrows+1], \
                  A_cols[0:nnz], A_vals[0:nnz])
   {
       #pragma acc loop gang worker
       for(int row=0; row<nrows; ++row) {
           const int row_start=A_row_offsets[row];
           const int row_end=A_row_offsets[row+1];

           double sum = 0.0;
           #pragma acc loop vector reduction(+: sum)
           for(int i=row_start; i<row_end; ++i) {
               sum += A_vals[i]*x[A_cols[i]];
           }
           y[row] = sum;
       }
   }
}
```

8.3.3 THE OPENMP IMPLEMENTATION

The OpenMP implementation provided here uses OpenMP 4.5 directives to provide portability. Thus, data transfers are necessary. In this case, it is sufficient to simply open a data region for the whole CG solve. Only the x vector needs to be copied back from the device, and hence everything else uses the `map(to:` clause.

```
#pragma omp target data \
        map(to: r[0:nrows], p[0:nrows],Ap[0:nrows], b[0:nrows], \
                A_vals[0:nnz], A_cols[0:nnz], A_rows[0:nrows+1]) \
        map(tofrom: x[0:nrows])
{
. . .
```

The AXPBY function is a simple parallel for usage. Here, the `data` clauses are added again, because they appear inside a function. The runtime should make sure that the data are not copied if the AXPBY function is called within a target data scope where the data is already present on the device.

```
void axpby(int n, double* z, double alpha, const double* x, double beta,
        const double* y) {
   #pragma omp target teams distribute parallel for map(from: z[0:n]) \
           map(to: x[0:n], y[0:n])
   for(int i=0; i<n; i++)
       z[i] = alpha*x[i] + beta*y[i];
}
```

The dot product function using OpenMP 4.5 directives also requires an explicit `tofrom` mapping of the reduction variable `sum`:

```
double dot(int n, const double* x, const double* y) {
    double sum = 0.0;
    #pragma omp target teams distribute parallel for \
            reduction(+: sum) map(tofrom: sum) \
            map(to: x[0:n], y[0:n])
    for(int i=0; i<n; i++)
        sum += x[i]*y[i];
    return sum;
}
```

As in the OpenACC variant, vector parallelism is used for the inner reduction in the SPMV algorithm, whereas the loop over the number of rows is spread over threads. It is worthwhile, though, to observe that removing the vector `reduction` clause on the inner loop improves performance on KNL.

```
void SPMV(int nrows, int nnz, const int* A_row_offsets,
          const int* A_cols, const double* A_vals, double* y,
          const double* x) {
    #pragma omp target teams distribute parallel for \
            map(from: y[0:nrows]) \
            map(to: x[0:nrows], A_row_offsets[0:nrows+1], \
                    A_cols[0:nnz], A_vals[0:nnz])
    for(int row=0; row<nrows; ++row) {
        const int row_start=A_row_offsets[row];
        const int row_end=A_row_offsets[row+1];

        double sum = 0.0;
        #pragma omp simd reduction(+: sum)
        for(int i=row_start; i<row_end; ++i) {
            sum += A_vals[i]*x[A_cols[i]];
        }
        y[row] = sum;
    }
}
```

8.3.4 THE CUDA IMPLEMENTATION

For the CUDA variant of the CG solve, first all necessary arrays must be allocated in the GPU memory. Then the input data are copied to the GPU before the actual CG solve is executed.

```
// Get Pointers to input data
double* h_x = &x_in.coefs[0];
const double* h_b = &b_in.coefs[0];
double* h_A_vals = &A.packed_coefs[0];
int* h_A_cols = &A.packed_cols[0];
int* h_A_rows = &A.row_offsets[0];

// Allocate Device Data
```

```
double* r; cudaMalloc(&r,nrows*sizeof(double));
double* p; cudaMalloc(&p,nrows*sizeof(double));
double* Ap; cudaMalloc(&Ap,nrows*sizeof(double));
double* x; cudaMalloc(&x,nrows*sizeof(double));
double* b; cudaMalloc(&b,nrows*sizeof(double));
double* A_vals; cudaMalloc(&A_vals,A_size*sizeof(double));
int* A_cols; cudaMalloc(&A_cols,A_size*sizeof(int));
int* A_rows; cudaMalloc(&A_rows,(nrows+1)*sizeof(int));

// Copy to Device
cudaMemcpy(x,h_x,nrows*sizeof(double),cudaMemcpyDefault);
cudaMemcpy(b,h_b,nrows*sizeof(double),cudaMemcpyDefault);
cudaMemcpy(A_vals,h_A_vals,A_size*sizeof(double),cudaMemcpyDefault);
cudaMemcpy(A_cols,h_A_cols,A_size*sizeof(int),cudaMemcpyDefault);
cudaMemcpy(A_rows,h_A_rows,(nrows+1)*sizeof(int),cudaMemcpyDefault);
```

The AXPBY function is a straightforward application of the parallel loop concept. The function is split into the dispatch code and the device kernel. The typical choice of 256 threads per block is made, and the vector length n is split over the necessary number of blocks. Because the vector length might not be a multiple of 256, an if condition is used to make sure that only the desired range is executed. The synchronization call after the kernel execution serves only timing purposes. Without it the timer after the call would be triggered before the kernel finishes, because its dispatch is asynchronous.

```
void __global__ axpby_kernel(int n, double* z, double alpha,
                             const double* x, double beta,
                             const double* y) {
    int i = blockIdx.x * blockDim.x + threadIdx.x;
    if(i<n)
        z[i] = alpha*x[i] + beta*y[i];
}

void axpby(int n, double* z, double alpha, const double* x,
           double beta, const double* y) {
    axpby_kernel<<<(n+255)/256,256>>>(n,z,alpha,x,beta,y);
    cudaDeviceSynchronize();
}
```

The dot product is significantly more complex. Because CUDA does not provide a native reduction capability, a two-step algorithm is implemented. First, within each block so-called shared memory is used to implement a tree reduction. Shared memory is local scratch memory that is private to the block of threads. Each block then writes out a single value to a buffer. The buffer is allocated in memory that is accessible from both device and host. Although the access is relatively slow from the GPU, its sparse use does not constitute significant overhead. In this case the synchronization is necessary, to ensure that the kernel has written all its results back to the buffer. Then the final reduction is performed serially on the host.

Note that the reduction method used here is intentionally simplistic and may not perform well. More complex reduction schemes using three or even four levels are deployed in practice (such as in the Kokkos model). In those schemes a hierarchical reduction is used that is aware of the fact that blocks consist of subgroups called warps, and the final reduction is performed by the last block to write back its partial result. Another noteworthy particularity of this algorithm is the artificial limitation of the number of blocks to 4,096. This allows for a fixed-length buffer, as well as limits the amount of data that needs to be transferred back to the host. Its drawback is that it limits the flexibility of the GPU's hardware scheduler, because fewer independent blocks of work exist. This scheme is often referred to as **block recycling.**

```
void __global__ dot_kernel(int n, const double* x,
                           const double* y, double* buffer) {
    int i_start = blockIdx.x * blockDim.x + threadIdx.x;
    double sum = 0;
    for(int i=i_start; i<n; i+=gridDim.x*blockDim.x)
        sum += x[i]*y[i];

    // Do Per Block Reduction
    __shared__ double local_buffer[256];
    local_buffer[threadIdx.x] = sum;
    int delta = 1;
    while(delta<256) {
        __syncthreads();
        if(threadIdx.x%(delta*2)==0)
            local_buffer[threadIdx.x] +=
                local_buffer[threadIdx.x+delta];
        delta*=2;
    }
    if(threadIdx.x==0)
        buffer[blockIdx.x] = local_buffer[0];
}


double dot(int n, const double* x, const double* y) {
    static double * buffer = NULL;
    if(buffer == NULL) {
        cudaMallocHost(&buffer,4096*sizeof(double));
    }

    int nblocks = 4096 * 256 < n?4096:(n+255)/256;
    dot_kernel<<<nblocks,256>>> (n,x,y,buffer);
    cudaDeviceSynchronize();

    double sum = 0.0;
    for(int i=0; i<nblocks; i++)
        sum += buffer[i];

    return sum;
}
```

The SPMV function is comparably simpler than the dot product because no global reduction is necessary. As with the AXPBY function, the outer loop is split over both the number of blocks and the threads within the block. In this case the second dimension of the block is used as part of that index range. But in contrast to the AXPBY function, a second dimension of the block is used for parallelism in the inner loop. The reason to use the x dimension for the parallelism of the inner loop is that threads with consecutive x indexes are part of the same warp. This means that they are synchronized and act as vector lanes on CPUs, something that allows the use of shuffle operations to implement the nested reduction. These shuffle operations allow for direct register exchange between threads within the same warp. Therefore, the number of threads for that x dimension must be a power of 2 smaller, or equal to 32. In this case 8 is chosen because it is empirically shown to be the best value for this operation, given the matrix structure of MiniFE with its typical 27 entries per row.

```
__global__ void spmv_kernel(int nrows, const int* A_row_offsets,
                            const int* A_cols,
                            const double* A_vals,
                            double* y, const double* x) {
  int row = blockIdx.x * blockDim.y + threadIdx.y;
  if(row>=nrows) return;

  int row_start=A_row_offsets[row];
  int row_end=A_row_offsets[row+1];
  double sum = 0.0;
  for(int i=row_start + threadIdx.x; i<row_end; i+=blockDim.x)
    sum += A_vals[i]*x[A_cols[i]];
  // Reduce over blockDim.x
  int delta = 1;
  while(delta < blockDim.x) {
    sum += __shfl_down(sum,delta,blockDim.x);
    delta*=2;
  }
  if(threadIdx.x == 0)
    y[row] = sum;
}

void SPMV(int nrows, const int* A_row_offsets, const int* A_cols,
          const double* A_vals, double* y, const double* x) {
  dim3 blocks((nrows+63)/64,1,1);
  dim3 threads(8,64,1);
  spmv_kernel<<<blocks,threads>>>
      (nrows, A_row_offsets, A_cols, A_vals, y, x);
  cudaDeviceSynchronize();
}
```

8.3.5 THE KOKKOS IMPLEMENTATION

As with the CUDA implementation, Kokkos requires data to be in its own allocations for Kokkos to run on GPUs. For this example, the use of simple one-dimensional Kokkos Views is sufficient. The incoming data are first wrapped into unmanaged views on the host; new views for both the incoming data and the temporary vectors are allocated in the default memory space; and then the input data are deep copied. In addition, Kokkos is explicitly initialized. Although this initialization call should usually be done right after the launch of the process, for the sake of simplicity we handle both initialization and finalization directly in the CG solve call. Note that here in the book the preceding Kokkos namespace qualifier has been removed.

```
initialize();

View<double*> r("r",nrows);
View<double*> p("p",nrows);
View<double*> Ap("Ap",nrows);

View<double*,HostSpace, MemoryTraits<Unmanaged> >
    h_x(&x_in.coefs[0], nrows);
View<double*> x("x",nrows);

View<const double*,HostSpace, MemoryTraits<Unmanaged> >
    h_b(&b_in.coefs[0], nrows);
View<double*> b("b",nrows);

View<double*,HostSpace, MemoryTraits<Unmanaged> >
    h_A_vals(&A.packed_coefs[0], A.packed_coefs.size());
View<double*> A_vals("A_vals", A.packed_coefs.size());

View<int*,HostSpace, MemoryTraits<Unmanaged> >
    h_A_cols(&A.packed_cols[0], A.packed_cols.size());
View<int*> A_cols("A_cols", A.packed_cols.size());

View<int*,HostSpace, MemoryTraits<Unmanaged> >
    h_A_rows(&A.row_offsets[0], nrows+1);
View<int*> A_rows("A_rows", nrows+1);


deep_copy(x,h_x);
deep_copy(b,h_b);
deep_copy(A_vals,h_A_vals);
deep_copy(A_cols,h_A_cols);
deep_copy(A_rows,h_A_rows);
```

The vector addition is again a simple parallel loop. The KOKKOS_LAMBDA macro adds the necessary function qualifiers when you are compiling with back ends such as CUDA, something that requires you to mark functions that need to be compiled for the GPU. The string is an optional, not necessarily unique, identifier used in Kokkos-aware profiling and debugging tools. The `fence` is added for timing purposes, because the `parallel_for` call is potentially asynchronous.

```
void axpby(int n, View<double*> z, double alpha,
           View<const double*> x, double beta,
           View<const double*> y) {
   parallel_for("AXpBY", n, KOKKOS_LAMBDA ( const int& i) {
       z(i) = alpha*x(i) + beta*y(i);
   });
   fence();
}
```

Because Kokkos, like OpenACC and OpenMP, supports reductions as a first-class concept, the dot product is straightforward as well. Kokkos assumes by default that a reduction is a sum. Hence it is not necessary to specify the actual reduction operation for the dot product.

```
double dot(int n, View<const double*> x, View<const double*> y) {
   double x_dot_y = 0.0;
   parallel_reduce("Dot",n,
                   KOKKOS_LAMBDA (const int& i,double& sum) {
       sum += x[i]*y[i];
   }, x_dot_y);
   fence();
   return x_dot_y;
}
```

For the SPMV operation two implementations are provided. The first uses simple flat parallelism on the outer loop, a technique that represents a straightforward port from the serial implementation and is enough to get good performance on CPUs.

```
void SPMV(int nrows, View<const int*> A_row_offsets,
          View<const int*> A_cols, View<const double*> A_vals,
          View<double*> y,
          View<const double*, MemoryTraits< RandomAccess>> x) {

   parallel_for("SPMV:Flat",nrows,
                KOKKOS_LAMBDA (const int& row) {
       const int row_start=A_row_offsets[row];
       const int row_end=A_row_offsets[row+1];
       double y_row = 0.0;
       for(int i=row_start; i<row_end; i++)
           y_row += A_vals(i)*x(A_cols(i));
       y(row) = y_row;
   } );
   fence();
}
```

Although this implementation is OK for CPUs, it is not good for GPUs because (a) it doesn't expose all available parallelism, and (b) it has uncoalesced data access for most arrays. To remedy this, a more flexible kernel is provided using hierarchical parallelism. But that exposes another issue: The inner loop is too small for an actual team of threads. Hence the approach taken subdivides rows into row-blocks, with each team handling one row-block. Kokkos's third level of hierarchical parallelism is then used to perform the reduction for each row. By choosing appropriate row-block and team-size parameters, we now allow this kernel to perform well across all architectures.

```
void SPMV(int nrows, View<const int*> A_row_offsets,
          View<const int*> A_cols, View<const double*> A_vals,
          View<double*> y,
          View<const double*, MemoryTraits< RandomAccess>> x) {

#ifdef KOKKOS_ENABLE_CUDA
    int rows_per_team = 64;
    int team_size = 64;
#else
    int rows_per_team = 512;
    int team_size = 1;
#endif

    parallel_for("SPMV:Hierarchy",
       TeamPolicy< Schedule< Static > >
       ((nrows+rows_per_team-1)/rows_per_team,team_size,8),
       KOKKOS_LAMBDA (const TeamPolicy<>::member_type& team) {
       const int first_row = team.league_rank()*rows_per_team;
       const int last_row = first_row+rows_per_team<nrows?
                            first_row+rows_per_team:nrows;
       parallel_for(TeamThreadRange(team,first_row,last_row),
          [&] (const int row) {
          const int row_start=A_row_offsets[row];
          const int row_length=A_row_offsets[row+1]-row_start;

          double y_row;
          parallel_reduce(ThreadVectorRange(team,row_length),
             [=] (const int i,double& sum) {
             sum += A_vals(i+row_start)*
                    x(A_cols(i+row_start));
          } , y_row);
          y(row) = y_row;
       });
    });
    fence();
}
```

8.3.6 THE TBB IMPLEMENTATION

The AXPBY implementation in TBB is almost identical to the Kokkos one, considering that both models provide a similar interface for parallel loops.

```
void axpby(int n, double* z, double alpha, const double* x,
           double beta, const double* y) {
```

```
    tbb::parallel_for(0,n,[&] (const int& i) {
        z[i] = alpha*x[i] + beta*y[i];
    });
}
```

The dot product is somewhat more involved. TBB does not provide its simple range interface for `parallel_reduce`; instead, you use the `blocked_range` policy. Furthermore, when compared to Kokkos, TBB does not assume a sum reduction as the default, and thus the reduction operation must be provided explicitly.

```
double dot(int n, const double* x, const double* y) {
    return tbb::parallel_reduce(tbb::blocked_range<int>(0,n),
            0.0,[&] (const tbb::blocked_range<int>& r,
            double lsum)->double {
        for(int i = r.begin(); i<r.end(); i++)
            lsum += x[i]*y[i];
        return lsum;
    }, std::plus<double>()
    );
}
```

For the SPMV again, two implementations are provided. The flat parallelism one can use the simple `parallel_for` for the outer loop:

```
void SPMV(int nrows, const int* A_row_offsets, const int* A_cols,
            const double* A_vals, double* y, const double* x) {
    tbb::parallel_for(0,nrows,[&] (const int& row) {
        double sum = 0.0;

        int row_start=A_row_offsets[row];
        int row_end=A_row_offsets[row+1];
        for(int i=row_start; i<row_end; ++i) {
            sum += A_vals[i]*x[A_cols[i]];
        }
        y[row] = sum;
    });
}
```

The other implementation, using a nested `parallel_reduce`, is provided mainly to highlight the pitfalls when using programming models outside their intended scenarios. Although functional, this implementation results in dramatically reduced performance. In fact, this implementation is significantly slower than even serial execution. This is caused by the fundamental design of TBB, which splits index ranges into chunks and gives them out as tasks to threads. Doing so comes with overhead that dwarfs the work per iteration for the inner loop of the reduction.

```
void SPMV(int nrows, const int* A_row_offsets, const int* A_cols,
            const double* A_vals, double* y, const double* x) {
    tbb::parallel_for(0,nrows,[&] (const int& row) {
        int row_start=A_row_offsets[row];
        int row_end=A_row_offsets[row+1];
```

```
      y[row] =
          tbb::parallel_reduce(tbb::blocked_range<int>
                                (row_start,row_end), 0.0,
      [&] (const tbb::blocked_range<int>& r,
            double lsum)->double {
          for(int i = r.begin(); i<r.end(); i++)
            lsum += A_vals[i]*x[A_cols[i]];
          return lsum;
      }, std::plus<double>()
      );
  )});
}
```

8.3.7 SOME PERFORMANCE NUMBERS

To demonstrate the real-world impact of the example, the following plots provide performance comparisons. The data are shown for two system sizes: 100^3 and 200^3 (use the $-nx$ option). Keep in mind that the results reflect not only the different semantics of the models but also the maturity of compilers and particular parameter choices. The comparatively bad performance of OpenMP on the NVIDIA P100 GPU, for example, is caused by a mixture of programming model semantics—which are less optimal for GPUs compared with OpenACC semantics—and the immaturity of the compiler and runtime. In particular, the simd statements had to be removed, because they led to compile time or runtime failures. Consequently, the work assignment can't match the one used in the OpenACC, CUDA, and the Kokkos versions, where the inner reduction is parallelized as well.

For the Power8 benchmark, the test runs had to be limited to a single socket, because the OpenMP and OpenACC code does not take care of proper first touch of the data. For Kokkos that is not an issue, because all the data are explicitly copied into Kokkos Views, which are first-touch initialized in parallel at construction time. To provide a fairer comparison of the runs, however, all models were restricted to a single socket. The best performance was generally achieved with two or four hyperthreads per core. Note that all code variants were compiled with the PGI and GNU compilers, respectively, to provide a fairer programming model comparison. The IBM XL compiler was not able to generate working OpenMP 4.5 code for the Power8 architecture. For the Serial and the Kokkos versions, it did work, though, and provided significant performance improvements (not shown in the plots).

Two semantic issues of the programming model hamper TBB on Intel KNL. The first significant issue is that TBB by default does not provide any thread-binding mechanisms. On an architecture such as Intel's KNL chip, that leads to severe performance degradation. The other issue is that TBB's internal implementation is task based, with the corresponding overhead. That makes nested parallelism significantly more expensive than, for example, in the Kokkos model. Thus, it is not suited for something like the inner loop of the SPMV function, which has only a few operations per iteration. The data shown here come from runs in which threads were properly pinned using additional code provided in the online repository (see the Preface).

> ### Note
>
> For the KNL data, the OpenACC code was compiled with PGI 17.3, with Intel Haswell CPUs as the target architecture. At the time of this writing, the KNL architecture is not yet explicitly supported by PGI. As with the OpenMP back end on GPUs, performance is expected to improve with future compiler versions.
>
> As mentioned previously, the OpenMP SPMV operation could have been improved by removing the SIMD reduction on the inner loop. This was not done for this comparison.

The data shown in Figures 8.1, 8.2, and 8.3 were collected using Intel 17.1, PGI 17.3, IBM XL 13.1.5, GCC 6.3, and CUDA 8.0.44, respectively. For detailed run settings, consult the Results folder in the online code repository (see the Preface).

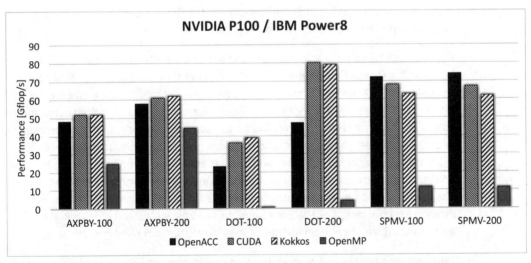

Figure 8.1 Performance comparison of different CG solve component implementations on an NVIDIA P100 GPU

Note: AXPBY is the vector addition, DOT the dot product, and SPMV the sparse matrix vector multiplication. Two different problem sizes are run: 100×100×100 cells and 200×200×200 cells.

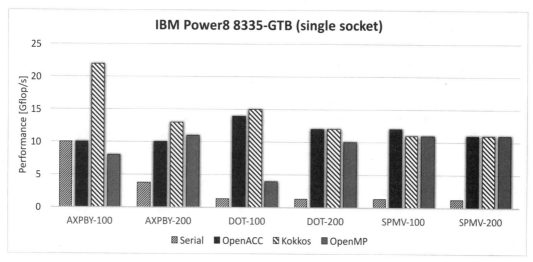

Figure 8.2 Performance comparison of different CG solve component implementations on an IBM Power8 CPU

Note: APBY is the vector addition, DOT the dot product, and SPMV the sparse matrix vector multiplication. Two different problem sizes are run: 100×100×100 cells and 200×200×200 cells. Except for the serial implementation, two or four threads were used on each of the eight cores.

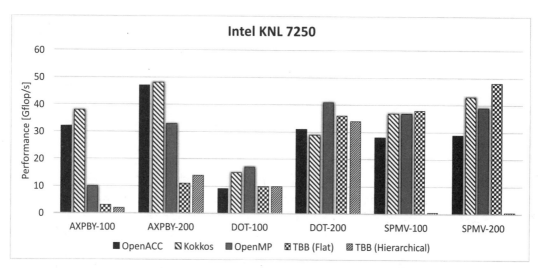

Figure 8.3 Performance comparison of different CG solve component implementations on an Intel Xeon Phi Knights Landing processor

Note: APBY is the vector addition, DOT the dot product, and SPMV the sparse matrix vector multiplication. Two different problem sizes are run: 100×100×100 cells and 200×200×200 cells.

8.4 Summary

Parallel programming concepts carry over to most programming models. Although syntax can be different, it should generally be recognizable to someone familiar with one or two of those models, and translating from one model to another should be straightforward. But as with many other things, the details matter. Design points for these models differ, and thus use cases might fit better or worse to any of these models. The main considerations for choosing a model are the maturity of the available software stack, the level of support by different vendors, and the likelihood of continued support in the future.

8.5 Exercises

1. Which of the following programming models do not support CPUs, manycore architectures, and GPUs?

    a. OpenACC

    b. OpenMP

    c. CUDA

    d. OpenCL

    e. Kokkos

    f. RAJA

    g. TBB

2. Which of these programming models provide task parallelism concepts?

    a. OpenACC

    b. OpenMP

    c. CUDA

    d. OpenCL

    e. Kokkos

    f. RAJA

    g. TBB

3. Which of these mathematical operations can be implemented with tightly nested loop constructs?

    a. Matrix-Vector multiplication

    b. Matrix-Matrix addition

    c. Matrix-Matrix multiplication

4. Which of the following operations involve a reduction?

    a. Computing the norm of a vector

    b. Finding the particle in a list close to a given set of coordinates

    c. Performing a matrix-matrix multiplication

    d. Computing the total kinetic energy of a set of particles

Chapter 9

OpenACC and Interoperability

Jiri Kraus, NVIDIA

One of the major strengths of OpenACC is that it is interoperable with native or low-level APIs to program the accelerator. This enables two important use cases:

- **Calling native device code from OpenACC.** This allows you to easily call into high-performance libraries, such as BLAS or FFT, or custom kernels using the native device API from an OpenACC program without introducing any unnecessary data staging.

- **Calling OpenACC code from native device code.** This also avoids unnecessary data staging.

This chapter explains how OpenACC interoperability works for both cases, covering the following:

- How OpenACC-managed accelerator memory can be used by kernels written in a native device API

- How OpenACC can work with memory managed by a native device API

- How native accelerator constructs, such as CUDA streams or device memory, can be mapped to the corresponding OpenACC constructs

This chapter primarily uses the NVIDIA CUDA platform targeting C in examples, but the presented concepts are easily transferable to other accelerator targets and languages supported by OpenACC.

9.1 Calling Native Device Code from OpenACC

This section explains by example how OpenACC interoperability works for calling native device code from OpenACC. The example targets NVIDIA GPUs using cuFFT, the NVIDIA CUDA Fast Fourier Transform (FFT) library. The methodology shown is transferable to other accelerator targets. The section explains the example application, then covers how OpenACC-managed accelerator memory can be used by kernels written in a native accelerator API, and closes with how CUDA streams can be mapped to OpenACC work queues, which is introduced in Chapter 10.

9.1.1 EXAMPLE: IMAGE FILTERING USING DFTS

The example application applies two filters to a gray scale image:

- A 5×5 Gaussian blur filter to remove image noise

- A 3×3 sharpening filter

The combination of these two filters is an edge detector. Example input and output images are shown in Figures 9.1 and 9.2.

A naive implementation could be to apply both filters in sequence, but a more computationally efficient method is to transfer both filters to the frequency domain by doing a **Discrete Fourier Transform** (DFT) using fast Fourier transforms (FFTs).[1] The advantage of this approach is that, under that form, both filters can be combined into a single pointwise complex multiplication in frequency space. Because the filters are independent of the input image, you can reuse them to apply them to multiple images, and thus you can amortize the preprocessing costs needed to prepare the filters if you are processing multiple images. Furthermore, you can process the image in chunks using the approach explained in Chapter 10, thus

---

1. C. V. Loan, *Computational Frameworks for the Fast Fourier Transform* (Philadelphia: Society for Industrial and Applied Mathematics, 1992).

Figure 9.1 Example input image
Image courtesy of NVIDIA.

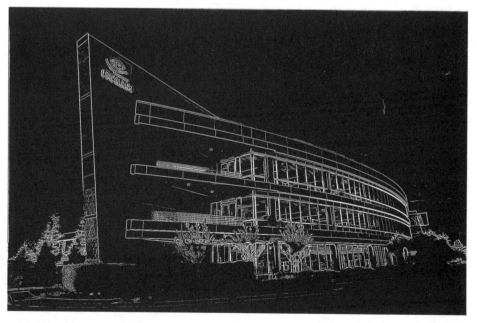

Figure 9.2 Example output image
Image courtesy of NVIDIA.

allowing you to reuse one filter for all image chunks. Working with small chunks also lowers the cost of preparing the filters in frequency space, because the filter size need only match the size of a single chunk and not of the whole image.

The processing flow of the example application is visualized in Figure 9.3. For the preprocessing, first the FFT plans for the real-to-complex (R2C) and complex-to-real (C2R) DFTs are created. These plans are used for transformations from real to frequency space and frequency space to real space, respectively. Independent of planning the DFTs, the filters need to be initialized in real space. After that, the filters are transformed and combined in frequency space with a pointwise complex multiplication.

You start processing the image by transforming the input image from real to frequency space using a DFT R2C transform. The combined filter is then applied to the image in frequency space by a pointwise complex multiplication. Then the filtered image is transformed back from frequency space to real space with a DFT C2R transform, and finally the output needs to be normalized. The normalization is necessary because cuFFT computes unnormalized DFTs.

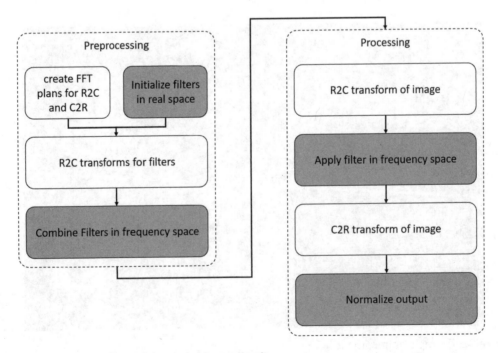

Figure 9.3 Processing flow of the example application

In Figure 9.3, the steps that are executed by a library are shown in white boxes, and the steps that are executed by kernels written in OpenACC are in shaded boxes. The data dependencies are depicted with arrows and highlight the fact that the input of each library call is produced by an OpenACC kernel and the output of each library call is consumed by an OpenACC kernel. Thus, for efficient execution the FFT library and OpenACC should share data. In the provided example code, data are managed by OpenACC and the called FFT library operates on the data. How that works is explained next.

9.1.2 THE HOST_DATA DIRECTIVE AND THE USE_DEVICE CLAUSE

In Section 2.6, *Data Environment of The OpenACC Application Programming Interface* (OpenACC-Standard.org, 2016), the following is specified.

> OpenACC supports systems with accelerators that have distinct memory from the host as well as systems with accelerators that share memory with the host. In the former case, called a non-shared memory device, the system has separate host memory and device memory. In the latter case, called a shared memory device as the accelerator shares memory with the host thread, the system has one shared memory.

The concept of separate accelerator and host memory is discussed earlier in this book. Because native or low-level accelerator models usually operate on accelerator memory, it is important to understand this concept and know how to obtain references to the different memories when you use nonshared memory devices.

OpenACC programs operate by default on the host version of all variables. Some directives are used to manage device instances of some host variables; other directives are also used to mark the code regions that will be executed on the device using the device instances of the host variables referenced in those code regions.

Listing 9.1 shows a simple example covering the different cases.

Listing 9.1 Simple data region example

```
1: int foo = 0;
2: #pragma acc data create( foo )
3: {
4:     foo = 1;
5:     #pragma acc parallel
6:     {
7:         foo = 2;
8:     }
9: }
```

The host variable `foo` is referenced three times in this example. Its initialization at line 1 is done outside all OpenACC context and so only concerns the host. The `data` directive in line 2 ensures that an instance of `foo` exists on the device for the duration of the block of code ranging from line 3 to line 9. However, the data directive is only about data management, and the associated code remains executed by the host; this means that `foo` in line 4 still refers to the host variable. Finally, the block of code from lines 6 to 8 is subject to the `parallel` directive in line 5, and this implies that this code is executed on the device. Consequently, line 7 refers to the device version of `foo`.

When you want to call into a library that is written using a low-level or native programming model and you expect references to accelerator memory, it is necessary to pass a reference to accelerator memory to the library instead of the reference to host memory. Using a parallel or kernels construct to perform the address translation is not possible, because the library call must be executed on the host. To solve that problem, OpenACC provides `host_data`, a construct whose body is executed on the host using the device addresses of all variables specified in its `use_device` clauses.

An example of this is given in Listing 9.2, where the pointers to device memory of `pic_real` and `pic_freq` are passed into the NVIDIA CUDA FFT Library cuFFT.

Listing 9.2 host_data use_device example

```
1: float * pic_real
2:    = (float*) malloc( r_size*sizeof(float) );
3: float complex * pic_freq
4:    = (float complex*) malloc( f_size*sizeof(float complex) );
5: #pragma acc data create( pic_real[0:r_size], \
6:                          pic_freq[0:f_size] )
7: {
8:     #pragma acc host_data use_device( pic_real, \
9:                                       pic_freq )
10:     {
11:         CUFFT_CALL( cufftExecR2C(r2c_plan,
12:                         pic_real,
13:                 (cufftComplex*) pic_freq) );
14:     }
15: }
```

The `host_data` construct with the `use_device` clause for `pic_real` and `pic_freq` in lines 8 and 9 tells the compiler to use pointers to the accelerator memory in the structured block, spawning lines 10–14. These pointers are then passed into the cuFFT call, spawning lines 11–13. On a shared-memory accelerator, the references within the `host_data` construct may be the same as outside the `host_data` construct, because the host and the device instances of a variable might be identical. However, there is no guarantee of that, because even on a shared-memory accelerator an OpenACC implementation might choose to create separate copies for performance reasons.

Alignment

The example program uses the C11 `float complex` type in OpenACC kernels to allow the use of the provided arithmetic operators for that type. In line 9 of Listing 9.2, it is therefore required to cast the pointer to `pic_freq` from C11 `float complex` to `cufftComplex`, both of which have the same size and data layout. In the scope of the shown code snippet this cast is safe, because sufficient alignment is provided by the OpenACC allocator for device memory. However, C11 `float complex` might *not* have the same alignment as `cufftComplex`. For example, with the PGI compiler on x86, the alignment requirement for `float complex` is 4 bytes, whereas the alignment requirement for `cufftComplex` is 8 bytes, because it is a `typedef` to the CUDA built-in type `float2`,[2] "B.3. Built-in Vector Types."

Low-level or native APIs typically allocate data with coarse alignment, meaning that such an alignment is typically not a problem. However, it can become an issue with a custom suballocator that does not guarantee sufficient alignment, or with user-defined types such as this:

```
struct foo {
    float weight;
    float complex data[512];
};
```

It is therefore recommended that you check for sufficient alignment to avoid this hard-to-debug issue:

```
#pragma acc host_data use_device( pic_real, pic_freq )
{
    assert( 0 == ((uintptr_t)pict_freq%alignof(cufftComplex)));
    CUFFT_CALL( cufftExecR2C(r2c_plan, pict_real,
                             (cufftComplex*) pic_freq) );
}
```

The OpenACC runtime library routine `acc_deviceptr` offers the same functionality as the `host_data` directive with the `use_device` clause. It returns the

---

2. *NVIDIA Documentation*, retrieved from Programming Guide :: CUDA Toolkit Documentation, http://docs.nvidia.com/cuda/cuda-c-programming-guide/index .html#built-in-vector-types.

device address for a given host address. Similarly, `acc_hostptr` returns the host address for a given device address.

9.1.3 API ROUTINES FOR TARGET PLATFORMS

Calls to the NVIDIA FFT library cuFFT are asynchronous with respect to the host—that is, they return immediately before the work has finished. To manage multiple independent streams of work, the CUDA platform offers the concept of **streams.** The `cufftSetStream` function provided by cuFFT needs to be called to control which CUDA stream will be used by the library. As explained in more detail in Chapter 10, OpenACC offers a similar concept with the `async` clause and work queues. In both concepts, work submitted to the same stream or work queue is guaranteed to be processed in order, and work submitted to different streams or work queues can be executed concurrently.

This arrangement poses a synchronization problem between OpenACC and asynchronous work submitted via native or low-level APIs such as CUDA, even if no streams or work queues are used explicitly in the program. The reason is that the code using the low-level API as well as OpenACC might internally use a work queue, a CUDA stream, or something similar, to use for work when nothing is specified. To the underlying platform, the work queue of OpenACC is independent of what a native library like cuFFT uses internally, so there is no synchronization between the two.

For the provided example code, this has the consequence that an OpenACC kernel launched after a DFT transform does not wait for that transform to finish and thus very likely operates on stale data.

To add the missing synchronization between the OpenACC runtime and libraries written in a native API, either you can map a native API stream or work queue to an OpenACC work queue identifier, or you can query the OpenACC runtime for the native API stream or work queue it uses internally for a given identifier.

In the case of the CUDA platform the OpenACC API calls are as follows.

- `acc_set_cuda_stream` tells the OpenACC runtime to use the given CUDA stream for the specified OpenACC work queue identifier.

- `acc_get_cuda_stream` queries the OpenACC runtime to identify the CUDA stream it uses for the given OpenACC work queue identifier.

As mentioned, even if no OpenACC work queue is explicitly used in the OpenACC part of the program, the OpenACC runtime implicitly uses a work queue. For compute constructs without any `async` clause, the internally used work queue can be accessed with the identifier `acc_async_sync`. In the case of CUDA, the call `acc_get_cuda_stream ( acc_async_sync )`, as shown in Listing 9.3, is used to access the CUDA stream that is used by OpenACC internally for compute constructs that do not use an `async` clause. By passing the return value of that call to `cufftSetStream`, the cuFFT work is submitted to the same work queue as the OpenACC compute constructs so that they don't start before the preceding work in cuFFT has finished.

Listing 9.3 acc_get_cuda_stream example

```
CUFFT_CALL( cufftSetStream(r2c_plan,
                    acc_get_cuda_stream ( acc_async_sync ) ) );
CUFFT_CALL( cufftSetStream(c2r_plan,
                    acc_get_cuda_stream ( acc_async_sync ) ) );
```

In addition to the API calls `acc_set_cuda_stream` and `acc_get_cuda_stream`, OpenACC offers `acc_get_current_cuda_device` (to get the CUDA device handle currently used) and `acc_get_current_cuda_context` (to access the CUDA context currently used).

There are similar API routines for other target platforms, such as OpenCL or Intel Coprocessor Offload Infrastructure.[3]

9.2 Calling OpenACC from Native Device Code

As with the possibility to call native accelerator kernels or libraries as described in the preceding section, it is also possible to use an OpenACC-generated kernel from an application written in a native or low-level accelerator API. This allows you to write libraries in OpenACC that are also usable from applications written with a native accelerator API, or to write a plugin in OpenACC for an application written with a native accelerator API. The principal issue is the same: For efficient execution, the code paths using the native accelerator API and OpenACC need to share data. Compared with the preceding section, the data are now managed by native

---

3. OpenACC-Standard.org, *The OpenACC Application Programming Interface Version 2.5,* June 2016, http://www.openacc.org/sites/default/files/OpenACC_2pt5.pdf, p. 112.

accelerator APIs and used by OpenACC. Similar to the `host_data` directive with the `use_device` clause, OpenACC has the `deviceptr` clause. An example of this is shown in Listing 9.4.

Listing 9.4 deviceptr clause example

```
double * x_d = (double*) acc_malloc( n*sizeof(double) );
double * y_d = (double*) acc_malloc( n*sizeof(double) );

#pragma acc kernels deviceptr(x_d,y_d)
for (int i = 0; i < n; i++)
{
    y_d[i] += x_d[i];
}
```

The `deviceptr` clause is allowed on structured data and compute constructs and `declare` directives. The `deviceptr` tells the compiler that no data management needs to be done for the pointers listed in the `deviceptr` clause—in other words, the listed pointers can be directly used in a kernel generated by the OpenACC compiler.

9.3 Advanced Interoperability Topics

This section covers two advanced OpenACC interoperability topics:

- How to use `acc_map_data` to make the OpenACC runtime aware of allocations managed by the application, a call that is useful for C++ classes and to make libraries OpenACC-aware

- How to call CUDA device routines from OpenACC kernels

9.3.1 ACC_MAP_DATA

In the preceding section, the `deviceptr` clause is introduced as a possibility to use data managed by native accelerator APIs in OpenACC. Using the OpenACC API calls `acc_map_data` and `acc_unmap_data`, you can achieve the same thing by making the OpenACC runtime aware of accelerator data that were allocated with the native accelerator API (or with `acc_malloc`) which is done by associating host and accelerator data allocations. This allows the following:

- Making the OpenACC runtime aware of device memory that is managed by an external library

- Implementing complex memory management techniques (such as double buffering) that cannot easily be done with OpenACC directives

- Ensuring that device memory is allocated with a specific alignment

Listing 9.5 shows an example of using `acc_map_data`.

Listing 9.5 acc_map_data clause example

```
1 : double * x = (double*) malloc(n*sizeof(double));
2 : double * y = (double*) malloc(n*sizeof(double));
3 :
4 : double * x_d = (double*) acc_malloc( n*sizeof(double) );
5 : double * y_d = (double*) acc_malloc( n*sizeof(double) );
6 :
7 : acc_map_data( x, x_d, n*sizeof(double) );
8 : acc_map_data( y, y_d, n*sizeof(double) );
9 :
10: #pragma acc kernels present(x[0:n],y[0:n])
11: for (int i = 0; i < n; i++)
12: {
13:     y[i] += x[i];
14: }
15:
16: acc_unmap_data( y );
17: acc_unmap_data( x );
18: acc_free( y_d );
19: acc_free( x_d );
```

In Listing 9.5, the application allocates host and accelerator data using `malloc` and `acc_malloc`, respectively, in lines 1–5. To use the host and accelerator data allocated that way in OpenACC directives, it is necessary to map the accelerator data (x_d and y_d) to the corresponding host data (x and y), something that is done with the calls to `acc_map_data` in lines 7 and 8. Listing 9.5 is equivalent to the code shown in Listing 9.6. This demonstrates that a call to `acc_map_data` is essentially equivalent to an `enter data` directive combined with the `create` clause, with the difference that no accelerator memory is allocated; instead, the pointer passed in as the second argument is used. So the calls `acc_map_data` to x and y can be used in OpenACC directives as if they are part of an enclosing data region. For example, in line 10 of Listing 9.5 the `present` clause can be used and the body of the loop spawning lines 11–14 operates on the memory allocated in lines 4 and 5.

Listing 9.6 acc_map_data clause example, equivalent code to Listing 9.5

```
1 : double * x = (double*) malloc(n*sizeof(double));
2 : double * y = (double*) malloc(n*sizeof(double));
3 :
```

Listing 9.6 acc_map_data clause example, equivalent code to Listing 9.5 *(continued)*

```
4 : #pragma acc enter data create(x[0:n],y[0:n])
5 :
6 : #pragma acc kernels present(x[0:n],y[0:n])
7 : for (int i = 0; i < n; i++)
8 : {
9 :     y[i] += x[i];
10: }
11:
12: #pragma acc exit data delete(x,y)
```

9.3.2 CALLING CUDA DEVICE ROUTINES FROM OPENACC KERNELS

In case you want to use an accelerator library that is callable from the accelerator or if a certain low-level accelerator feature is needed, you must call accelerator device routines from OpenACC kernels. This section describes how this can be done with the PGI OpenACC compiler and CUDA C/C++.

First, the CUDA C device function needs to be prepared. As shown in Listing 9.7, you need the extern "C" linkage specifier in order to avoid C++ name mangling and make the later mapping and linking steps work.

Listing 9.7 CUDA C device function with C linkage

```
extern "C"
__device__
float saxpy_dev(float a, float x, float y)
{
    return a * x + y;
}
```

The CUDA C device function needs to be compiled using the CUDA C/C++ compiler nvcc to an object using the -relocatable-device-code true command-line option. In this way, code is generated that later can be used by the device linker.

On the OpenACC side, it is necessary to put a routine directive in front of the function declaration as shown in Listing 9.8. The example tells the OpenACC compiler that at link time there will be a device-callable sequential routine with the name saxpy_dev. It is important that only the function declaration, and not the definition, appear in OpenACC code; otherwise there would be multiple definitions of the device function.

Listing 9.8 acc routine example

```
#pragma acc routine seq
extern "C" float saxpy_dev(float, float, float);
```

This routine can then be used in OpenACC compute constructs, as shown in Listing 9.9.

Listing 9.9 Using CUDA device functions in OpenACC compute constructs

```
#pragma acc parallel loop
for( i = 0; i < n; i++ )
{
    y[i] = saxpy_dev(2.0, x[i], y[i]);
}
```

The linking needs to be done with the PGI compiler using the `rdc` suboption to `-ta=tesla` and presenting the object file generated with `nvcc` containing the device code of `saxpy_dev` and the object file with the OpenACC code.

A fully working example of this is given in Chapter 10, and the example is available at https://github.com/jefflarkin/openacc-interoperability in `openacc_cuda_device.cpp`.

9.4 Summary

A powerful feature of OpenACC is its ability to be interoperable with native or low-level accelerator programming APIs. This capability is particularly important because it not only allows the use of highly tuned standard libraries (such as BLAS and FFT) from OpenACC code but also allows exploitation of libraries (such as MPI) that are aware of accelerators—for example, CUDA-aware MPI. In addition, interoperability with native accelerator programming APIs allows you to use OpenACC for productivity and performance portability without compromising performance. In cases where OpenACC cannot match the performance of native accelerator programming APIs, it is possible to use the native programming APIs.

OpenACC's ability to interoperate with native accelerator programming APIs increases productivity and improves performance.

9.5 Exercises

1. What happens if you remove the `acc host_data use_device` directives in the accompanying example code?

2. Change the code to call a host FFT library instead of cuFFT. What changes are necessary, and how do the runtime and the timeline tools (such as the NVIDIA Visual Profiler or `pgprof`) show the change?

3. What happens if you remove the calls to `CUFFT_CALL( cufftSetStream(r2c_plan, acc_get_cuda_stream ( acc_async_sync ) ) );` in the accompanying example code? Compare the timelines of both versions with the NVIDIA Visual Profiler or `pgprof`.

4. Is there a possible alternative to `CUFFT_CALL( cufftSetStream(r2c_plan, acc_get_cuda_stream ( acc_async_sync ) ) );`?

Chapter 10

Advanced OpenACC

Jeff Larkin, NVIDIA

With the basics of OpenACC programming well in hand, this chapter discusses two advanced OpenACC features for maximizing application performance. The first feature is asynchronous operations, which allow multiple things to happen at the same time to better utilize the available system resources, such as a GPU, a CPU, and the PCIe connection in between. The second feature is support for multiple accelerator devices. The chapter discusses two ways that an application can utilize two or more accelerator devices to increase performance: one using purely OpenACC, and the other combining OpenACC with the Message Passing Interface (MPI).

10.1 Asynchronous Operations

Programming is often taught by developing a series of steps that, when completed, achieve a specific result. If I add E = A + B and then F = C + D, then I can add G = E + F and get the sum of A, B, C, and D, as shown in Figure 10.1.

Our brains often like to think in an ordered list of steps, and that influences the way we write our programs, but in fact we're used to carrying out multiple tasks at the same time. Take, for instance, cooking a spaghetti dinner. It would be silly to cook the pasta, and then the sauce, and finally the loaf of bread. Instead, you will probably let the sauce simmer while you bake the bread and, when the bread is almost finished, boil the pasta so that all the parts of the meal will be ready when they are needed. By thinking about when you need each part of the meal and cooking the parts so that they all complete only when they are needed, you can cook the meal in less time than if you'd prepared each part in a separate complete step. You also

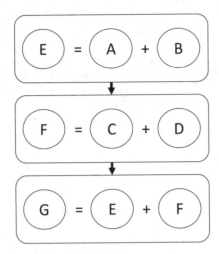

Figure 10.1 Summing four numbers step-by-step

would better utilize the kitchen by taking advantage of the fact that you can have two pots and the oven working simultaneously.

By thinking of your operations as a series of dependencies, rather than a series of steps, you open yourself to running the steps in potentially more efficient orders, possibly even in parallel. This is a different sort of parallelism than we have discussed so far in this book. The chapters before this one focus on **data parallelism,** or performing the same action on many different data locations in parallel. In the case of the spaghetti dinner analogy, we're discussing **task-based parallelism,** or exposing different tasks, each of which may or may not be data parallel, that can be executed concurrently.

Let us look at the spaghetti dinner example a little more closely. You can treat cooking the pasta, preparing the sauce, and baking the bread as three separate operations in cooking the dinner. Cooking the pasta takes roughly 30 minutes, because it involves bringing the water to a boil, actually cooking the pasta, and then draining it when it is done. Making the sauce takes quite a bit longer, roughly two hours from putting the sauce in a pot, adding seasoning, and then simmering so that the seasoning takes effect. Baking the bread is another 30-minute operation, involving heating the oven, baking the bread, and then allowing the bread to cool. Finally, when these operations are complete, you can plate and eat your dinner.

If I did each of these operations in order (in any order), then the entire process would take three hours, and at least some part of my meal would be cold. To understand the dependencies between the steps, let's look at the process in reverse.

1. To plate the meal, the pasta, sauce, and bread must all be complete.

2. For the pasta to be complete, it must have been drained, which requires that it has been cooked, which requires that the water has been brought to a boil.

3. For the sauce to be ready, it must have simmered, which requires that the seasoning has been added, and the sauce has been put into a pot.

4. For the bread to be done, it must have cooled, before which it must have been baked, which requires that the oven has been heated.

From this, you can see that the three parts of the meal do not need to be prepared in any particular order, but each has its own steps that do have a required order. To put it in parallel programming terms, each step within the larger tasks has a **dependency** on the preceding step, but the three major tasks are **independent** of each other. Figure 10.2 illustrates this point. The circles indicate the steps in cooking the dinner, and the rounded rectangles indicate the steps that have dependencies. Notice that when each task reaches the plating step, it becomes dependent on the completion of the other tasks. Therefore, where the rounded rectangles overlap is where the cook needs to **synchronize** the tasks, because the results of all three tasks are required before you can move on; but where the boxes do not cross, the tasks can operate **asynchronously** from each other.

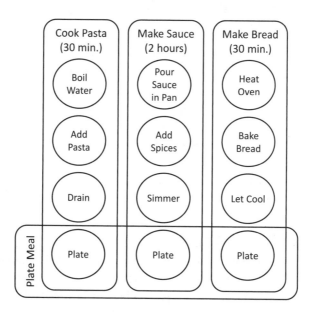

Figure 10.2 Dependency graph for spaghetti dinner example

Asynchronous programming is a practice of exposing the dependencies in the code to enable multiple independent operations to be run concurrently across the available system resources. Exposing dependencies does not guarantee that independent operations will be run concurrently, but it does enable this possibility. In the example, what if your stove has only one burner? Could you still overlap the cooking of the pasta with the simmering of the sauce? No, because both require the same resource: the burner. In this case, you will need to **serialize** those two tasks so that one uses the burner as soon as the other is complete, but the order in which those tasks complete is still irrelevant. Asynchronous programming is also the practice of removing synchronization between independent steps, and hence the term *asynchronous*. It takes great care to ensure that necessary synchronization is placed in the code to produce consistently correct results, but when done correctly this style of programming can better utilize available resources.

10.1.1 ASYNCHRONOUS OPENACC PROGRAMMING

By default, all OpenACC directives are synchronous with the host thread, meaning that after the host thread has sent the required data and instructions to the accelerator, the host thread will wait for the accelerator to complete its work before continuing execution. By remaining synchronous with the host thread OpenACC ensures that operations occur in the same order when run on the accelerator as when run in the original program, thereby ensuring that the program will run correctly with or without an accelerator.

This is rarely the most efficient way to run the code, however, because system resources go unused while the host is waiting for the accelerator to complete. For instance, on a system having one CPU and one GPU, which are connected via PCIe, then at any given time either the CPU is computing, the GPU is computing, or the PCIe bus is copying data, but no two of those resources are ever used concurrently. If we were to expose the dependencies in our code and then launch our operations asynchronously from the host thread, then the host thread would be free to send more data and instructions to the device or even participate in the calculation. OpenACC uses the `async` clause and `wait` directive to achieve exactly this.

Asynchronous Work Queues

OpenACC uses **asynchronous work queues** to expose dependencies between operations. Anything placed into the same work queue will be executed in the order it was enqueued. This is a typical first-in, first-out (FIFO) queue. Operations placed in different work queues can execute in any order, no matter which was enqueued first. When the results of a particular queue (or all queues) are needed, the programmer must *wait* (or synchronize) on the work queue (or queues). Referring to Figure 10.2, the rounded rectangles could each represent a separate work queue, and the steps should be put into that queue in the order in which they must be completed.

OpenACC identifies asynchronous queues with non-negative integer numbers, so all work enqueued to queue 1, for instance, will complete in order and operate independently of work enqueued in queue 2. The specification also defines several special work queues. If `acc_async_sync` is specified as the queue, then all directives placed into the queue will become synchronous with the host thread, something that is useful for debugging. If the queue `acc_async_noval` is used, then the operation will be placed into the default asynchronous queue.

The async Clause

Specific directives are placed into work queues by adding the `async` clause to the directive. This clause may be added to parallel and kernels regions and the `update` directive. This clause optionally accepts a non-negative integer value or one of the special values previously discussed. If no parameter is given to the `async` clause, then it will behave as if the `acc_async_noval` queue was specified, often referred to as the default queue. Listing 10.1 demonstrates the use of the `async` clause in C/C++, both with and without the optional parameter.

Listing 10.1 Example of async clause in C/C++

```
// The next directive updates the value of A on the device
// asynchronously of the host thread and in queue #1.
#pragma acc update device(A[:N]) async(1)
// The next directive updates the value of B on the device
// and may execute before the previous update has completed.
// This update has been placed in the default queue.
#pragma acc update device(B[:N]) async
// The host thread will continue execution, even before the
// above updates have.
```

The wait Directive

Once work has been made asynchronous, it's necessary to later synchronize when the results of that work are needed. Failure to synchronize will likely produce incorrect results. This can be achieved in OpenACC by using either the `wait` directive or the `wait` clause. The `wait` directive identifies a place in the code that the encountering thread cannot pass until all asynchronous work up to that point in the program has completed. The directive optionally accepts a work queue number so that the program waits only for the work in the specified work queue to complete, and not all asynchronous work. Listing 10.2 demonstrates the use of the `wait` directive in C/C++.

Listing 10.2 Example of wait directive in C/C++

```
// The next directive updates the value of A on the device
// asynchronously of the host thread and in queue #1.
#pragma acc update device(A[:N]) async(1)
// The host thread will continue execution, even before the
// above updates have completed.
// The next directive updates the value of B on the device
// and may execute before the previous update has completed.
// This update has been placed in queue #2.
#pragma acc update device(B[:N]) async(2)
// The next directive updates the value of C on the device
// and may execute before the previous update has completed.
// This update has been placed in the default queue.
#pragma acc update device(C[:N]) async
// When the program encounters the following directive, it will
// block further execution until the data transfer in queue #1
// has completed.
#pragma acc wait(1)
// When the program encounters the following directive, it will
// wait for all remaining asynchronous work from this thread to
// complete before continuing.
#pragma acc wait
```

Perhaps rather than insert a whole new directive into the code to force this syn-chronization, you would rather force an already existing directive to wait on a particular queue. This can be achieved with the `wait` clause, which is available on many directives. Listing 10.3 demonstrates this in both C and C++.

Listing 10.3 Example of wait directive in C/C++

```
// The next directive updates the value of A on the device
// asynchronously of the host thread and in queue #1.
#pragma acc update device(A(:N)) async(1)
// The next directive updates the value of B on the device
// and may execute before the previous update has completed.
// This update has been placed in queue #2.
#pragma acc update device(B[:N]) async(2)
// The host thread will continue execution, even before the
// above updates have completed.
// The next directive creates a parallel loop region, which it
// enqueues in work queue #1, but waits on queue #2. Queue 1
// will wait here until all prior work in queue #2 has completed
// and then continue executing.
#pragma acc parallel loop async(1) wait(2)
for (int i=0 ; i < N; i++) {
  C[i] = A[i] + B[i]
}
// When the program encounters the following directive, it will
// wait for all remaining asynchronous work from this thread
// into any queue to complete before continuing.
#pragma acc wait
```

Joining Work Queues

When placing work into multiple work queues, eventually you need to wait for work to complete in both queues before execution moves forward. The most obvious way to handle such a situation is to insert a `wait` directive for each queue and then move forward with the calculation. Although this technique works for ensuring correctness, it results in the host CPU blocking execution until both queues have completed and could create bubbles in one or both queues while no work is available to execute, particularly if one queue requires more time to execute than the other. Instead of using the host CPU to synchronize the queues, it's possible to join the queues together at the point where they need to synchronize by using an asynchronous `wait` directive. The idea of asynchronously waiting may seem counterintuitive, so consider Listing 10.4.

The code performs a simple vector summation but has separate loops for initializing the A array, initializing the B array, and finally summing them both into the C array. Note that this is a highly inefficient way to perform a vector sum, but it is written only to demonstrate the concept discussed in this section. The OpenACC directives place the work of initializing A and B into queues 1 and 2, respectively. The summation loop should not be run until both queues 1 and 2 have completed, so an asynchronous `wait` directive is used to force queue 1 to wait until the work in queue 2 has completed before moving forward.

On first reading, the asynchronous `wait` directive may feel backward, so let's break down what it is saying. First, the directive says to wait on queue 2, but then it also says to place this directive asynchronously into work queue 1 so that the host CPU is free to move on to enqueue the summation loop into queue 1 and then wait for it to complete. Effectively, queues 1 and 2 are joined together at the asynchronous `wait` directive and then queue 1 continues with the summation loop. By writing the code in this way you enable the OpenACC runtime to resolve the dependency between queues 1 and 2 on the device, for devices that support this, rather than block the host CPU. This results in better utilization of system resources, because the host CPU no longer must idly wait for both queues to complete.

Listing 10.4 Example of asynchronous wait directive in C/C++

```
#pragma acc data create(A[:N],B[:N],C[:N])
  {
#pragma acc parallel loop async(1)
  for(int i=0; i<N; i++)
  {
    A[i] = 1.f;
  }
#pragma acc parallel loop async(2)
  for(int i=0; i<N; i++)
  {
```

Listing 10.4 Example of asynchronous wait directive in C/C++ (*continued*)

```
    B[i] = 2.f;
  }
#pragma acc wait(2) async(1)
#pragma acc parallel loop async(1)
  for(int i=0; i<N; i++)
  {
    C[i] = A[i] + B[i];
  }
#pragma acc update self(C[0:N]) async(1)
  // Host CPU free to do other, unrelated work
#pragma acc wait(1)
  }
```

Interoperating with CUDA Streams

When developing for an NVIDIA GPU, you may need to mix OpenACC's asynchronous work queues with CUDA streams to ensure that any dependencies between OpenACC and CUDA kernels or accelerated libraries are properly exposed. Chapter 9 demonstrates that it is possible to use the `acc_get_cuda_stream` function to obtain the CUDA stream associated with an OpenACC work queue. For instance, in Listing 10.5, you see that `acc_get_cuda_stream` is used to obtain a CUDA stream, which is then used by the NVIDIA cuBLAS library to allow the arrays populated in queue 1 in OpenACC to then safely be passed between the asynchronous loop in line 6, the asynchronous library call in line 15, and the `update` directive in line 16. By getting the CUDA stream associated with queue 1 in this way, you can still operate asynchronously from the host thread while ensuring that the dependency between the OpenACC directives and the `cublas` function is met. This feature is useful when you are adding asynchronous CUDA or library calls to a primarily OpenACC application.

Listing 10.5 Example of acc_get_cuda_stream function

```
1    cudaStream_t stream = (cudaStream_t)acc_get_cuda_stream(1);
2    status = cublasSetStream(handle,stream);
3
4  #pragma acc data create(a[:N],b[:N])
5    {
6  #pragma acc parallel loop async(1)
7      for(int i=0;i<N;i++)
8      {
9        a[i] = 1.f;
10       b[i] = 0.f;
11     }
12
13 #pragma acc host_data use_device(a,b)
14     {
15       status = cublasSaxpy(handle, N, &alpha, a, 1, b, 1);
16 #pragma acc update self(b[:N]) async (1)
17 #pragma acc wait(1)
18   }
```

It is also possible to work in reverse, associating a CUDA stream used in an application with a particular OpenACC work queue. You achieve this by calling the `acc_set_cuda_stream` function with the CUDA stream you wish to use and the queue number with which it should be associated. In Listing 10.6, you see that I have reversed my function calls so that I first query which stream the `cublas` library will use and then associate that stream with OpenACC's work queue 1. Such an approach may be useful when you are adding OpenACC to a code that already has extensive use of CUDA or accelerated libraries, because you can reuse existing CUDA streams.

Listing 10.6 Example of acc_set_cuda_stream function

```
1   status = cublasSetStream(handle,stream);
2   acc_set_cuda_stream(1, (void*)stream);
3
4  #pragma acc data create(a[:N],b[:N])
5   {
6  #pragma acc parallel loop async(1)
7     for(int i=0;i<N;i++)
8     {
9        a[i] = 1.f;
10       b[i] = 0.f;
11    }
12
13 #pragma acc host_data use_device(a,b)
14    {
15       status = cublasSaxpy(handle, N, &alpha, a, 1, b, 1);
16    }
17 #pragma acc update self(b[:N]) async (1)
18 #pragma acc wait(1)
19   }
```

These examples strictly work on NVIDIA GPUs with CUDA, but OpenACC compilers using OpenCL have a similar API for interoperating with OpenCL work queues.

10.1.2 SOFTWARE PIPELINING

This section demonstrates one technique that is enabled by asynchronous programming: **software pipelining**. Pipelining is not the only way to take advantage of asynchronous work queues, but it does demonstrate how work queues can allow better utilization of system resources by ensuring that multiple operations can happen at the same time. For this example, we will use a simple image-filtering program that reads an image, performs some manipulations on the pixels, and then writes the results back out. Listing 10.7 shows the main filter routine, which has already been accelerated with OpenACC directives.

Listing 10.7 Baseline OpenACC image-filtering code

```
const int filtersize = 5;
const double filter[5][5] =
{
    0,   0,   1,   0,   0,
    0,   2,   2,   2,   0,
    1,   2,   3,   2,   1,
    0,   2,   2,   2,   0,
    0,   0,   1,   0,   0
};
// The denominator for scale should be the sum
// of non-zero elements in the filter.
const float scale = 1.0 / 23.0;

void blur5(unsigned restrict char *imgData,
 unsigned restrict char *out, long w, long h, long ch, long step)
{
  long x, y;

#pragma acc parallel loop collapse(2) gang vector \
            copyin(imgData[0:w * h * ch]) \
            copyout(out[0:w * h * ch])
  for ( y = 0; y < h; y++ )
  {
    for ( x = 0; x < w; x++ )
    {
      float blue = 0.0, green = 0.0, red = 0.0;
      for ( int fy = 0; fy < filtersize; fy++ )
      {
        long iy = y - (filtersize/2) + fy;
        for ( int fx = 0; fx < filtersize; fx++ )
        {
          long ix = x - (filtersize/2) + fx;
          if ( (iy<0)   || (ix<0) ||
               (iy>=h)  || (ix>=w) ) continue;
          blue   += filter[fy][fx] *
                    (float)imgData[iy * step + ix * ch];
          green += filter[fy][fx] *
                    (float)imgData[iy * step + ix * ch + 1];
          red    += filter[fy][fx] *
                    (float)imgData[iy * step + ix * ch + 2];
        }
      }
      out[y * step + x * ch]      = 255 - (scale * blue);
      out[y * step + x * ch + 1 ] = 255 - (scale * green);
      out[y * step + x * ch + 2 ] = 255 - (scale * red);
    }
  }
}
```

We start by analyzing the current application performance using the PGI compiler, an NVIDIA GPU, and the PGProf profiling tool. Figure 10.3 shows a screen shot of PGProf, which shows the GPU timeline for the filter application. For reference, the data presented is for a Tesla P100 accelerator and an 8,000×4,051 pixel image. Notice that copying the image data to and from the device takes nearly as much time as actually performing the filtering of the image. The program requires 8.8ms to copy the image to the device, 8.2ms copying the data from the device, and 20.5ms performing the filtering operation.

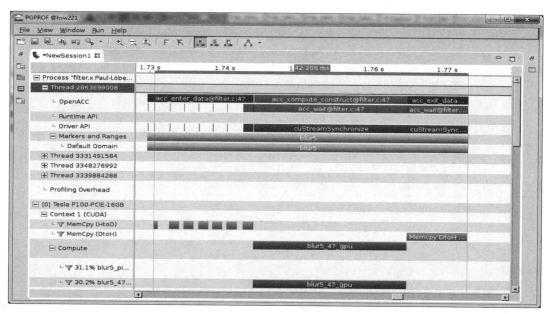

Figure 10.3 PGProf timeline for baseline image filter

The most significant performance limiter in this application is the time spent copying data between the CPU and the GPU over PCIe. Unfortunately, you cannot remove that time, because you do need to perform those copies for the program to work, so you need to look for ways to overlap the data copies with the GPU work. If you could completely overlap both directions of data transfers with the filtering kernel, then the total run time would drop to only 20.5ms, which is a speedup of 1.8×, so this is the maximum speedup you can obtain by optimizing to hide the data movement.

How can you overlap the data transfers, though, if you need to get the data to the device before you start and cannot remove it until you have computed the results? The trick is to recognize that you do not need *all* of the data on the device to proceed; you need only enough to kick things off. If you could break the work into discrete parts, just as you did with cooking dinner earlier, then you can operate on each smaller part independently and potentially overlap steps that do not require the same system resource at the same time. Image manipulation is a perfect case study for this sort of optimization, because each pixel of an image is independent of all the others, so the image itself can be broken into smaller parts that can be independently filtered.

Blocking the Computation

Before we can pipeline the operations, we need to refactor the code to operate on chunks, commonly referred to as blocks, of independent work. The code, as it is written, essentially has one block. By adding a loop around this operation and adjusting the bounds of the existing loops to avoid redundant work, you can make the code do exactly the same thing it does currently, but in two or more blocks. You write the code to break the operation only along rows, because this means that each block is contiguous in memory, something that will be important in later steps. It should also be written to allow for any number of blocks from one up to the height of the image, giving you maximum flexibility later to find just the right number of blocks. Listing 10.8 shows the new code with the addition of the blocking loop.

Listing 10.8 Blocked OpenACC image-filtering code

```
 1 void blur5_blocked(unsigned restrict char *imgData,
 2                    unsigned restrict char *out,
 3                    long w, long h, long ch, long step)
 4 {
 5   long x, y;
 6   const int nblocks = 8;
 7
 8   long blocksize = h/ nblocks;
 9 #pragma acc data copyin(imgData[:w*h*ch],filter) \
10                    copyout(out[:w*h*ch])
11   for ( long blocky = 0; blocky < nblocks; blocky++)
12   {
13     // For data copies we include the ghost zones for filter
14     long starty = blocky * blocksize;
15     long endy   = starty + blocksize;
16 #pragma acc parallel loop collapse(2) gang vector
17     for ( y = starty; y < endy; y++ )
18     {
19       for ( x = 0; x < w; x++ )
20       {
21         float blue = 0.0, green = 0.0, red = 0.0;
22         for ( int fy = 0; fy < filtersize; fy++ )
23         {
24           long iy = y - (filtersize/2) + fy;
25           for ( int fx = 0; fx < filtersize; fx++ )
26           {
27             long ix = x - (filtersize/2) + fx;
28             if ( (iy<0)  || (ix<0) ||
29                  (iy>=h) || (ix>=w) ) continue;
30             blue  += filter[fy][fx] *
31                      (float)imgData[iy * step + ix * ch];
32             green += filter[fy][fx] * (float)imgData[iy * step + ix *
```

```
33                         ch + 1];
34            red    += filter[fy][fx] * (float)imgData[iy * step + ix *
35                         ch + 2];
36            }
37          }
38          out[y * step + x * ch]       = 255 - (scale * blue);
39          out[y * step + x * ch + 1 ] = 255 - (scale * green);
40          out[y * step + x * ch + 2 ] = 255 - (scale * red);
41        }
42      }
43    }
44 }
```

There are a few important things to note from this code example. First, we have
blocked only the computation, and not the data transfers. This is because we want
to ensure that we obtain correct results by making only small changes to the code
with each step. Second, notice that within each block we calculate the starting and
ending rows of the block and adjust the y loop accordingly (lines 11–13). Failing to
make this adjustment would produce correct results but would increase the run
time proportionally to the number of blocks. With this change in place, you will see
later in Figure 10.4 that the performance is slightly worse than the original. This
is because we have introduced a little more overhead to the operation to manage
the multiple blocks of work. However, this additional overhead will be more than
compensated for in the final code.

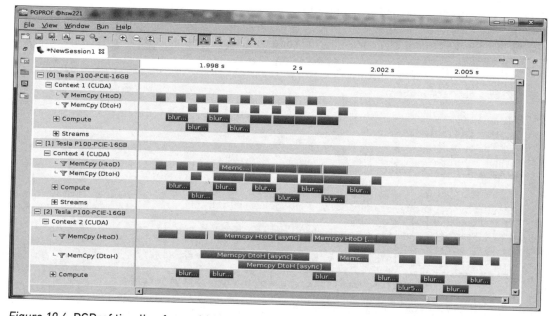

Figure 10.4 PGProf timeline for multidevice, software pipelined image filter

Blocking the Data Movement

Now that the computation has been blocked and is producing correct results, it's time to break up the data movement between the host and the accelerator to place it within blocks as well. To do this, you first need to change the data clauses for the imgData and out arrays to remove the data copies around the blocking loop (see Listing 10.9, line 9). This can be done by changing both arrays to use the create data clause. Next, you add two acc update directives: one at the beginning of the block's execution (line 17) to copy the input data from imgData before the computation, and another after the computation to copy the results back into the out array (line 48).

Our image filter has one subtlety that needs to be addressed during this step. The filter operation for element [i][j] of the image requires the values from several surrounding pixels, particularly two to left and right, and two up and down. This means that for the filter to produce the same results, when you copy a block's portion of imgData to the accelerator you also need to copy the two rows before that block and the two after, if they exist. These additional rows are frequently referred to as a **halo** or **ghost zone**, because they surround the core part of the data. In Listing 10.9, notice that, to accommodate the surrounding rows, the starting and ending rows for the update directive are slightly different from the starting and ending rows of the compute loops. Not all computations require this overlapping, but because of the nature of the image filter, this application does. The full code for this step is found in Listing 10.9.

Listing 10.9 Blocked OpenACC image-filtering code with separate update directives

```
1 void blur5_update(unsigned restrict char *imgData,
2     unsigned restrict char *out, long w, long h,
3     long ch, long step)
4 {
5   long x, y;
6   const int nblocks = 8;
7
8   long blocksize = h/ nblocks;
9 #pragma acc data create(imgData[w*h*ch],out[w*h*ch]) \
10                     copyin(filter)
11   {
12   for ( long blocky = 0; blocky < nblocks; blocky++)
13   {
14     // For data copies we include ghost zones for the filter
15     long starty = MAX(0,blocky * blocksize - filtersize/2);
16     long endy   = MIN(h,starty + blocksize + filtersize/2);
17 #pragma acc update \
18             device(imgData[starty*step:(endy-starty)*step])
19     starty = blocky * blocksize;
20     endy = starty + blocksize;
21 #pragma acc parallel loop collapse(2) gang vector
```

```
22      for ( y = starty; y < endy; y++ )
23      {
24        for ( x = 0; x < w; x++ )
25        {
26          float blue = 0.0, green = 0.0, red = 0.0;
27          for ( int fy = 0; fy < filtersize; fy++ )
28          {
29            long iy = y - (filtersize/2) + fy;
30            for ( int fx = 0; fx < filtersize; fx++ )
31            {
32              long ix = x - (filtersize/2) + fx;
33              if ( (iy<0)  || (ix<0) ||
34                   (iy>=h) || (ix>=w) ) continue;
35              blue  += filter[fy][fx] *
36                       (float)imgData[iy * step + ix * ch];
37              green += filter[fy][fx] *
38                       (float)imgData[iy * step + ix * ch + 1];
39              red   += filter[fy][fx] *
40                       (float)imgData[iy * step + ix * ch + 2];
41            }
42          }
43          out[y * step + x * ch]     = 255 - (scale * blue);
44          out[y * step + x * ch + 1 ] = 255 - (scale * green);
45          out[y * step + x * ch + 2 ] = 255 - (scale * red);
46        }
47      }
48 #pragma acc update self(out[starty*step:blocksize*step])
49    }
50    }
51 }
```

Again, you need to run the code and check the results before moving to the next step. You see in Figure 10.4 that the code is again slightly slower than the previous version because of increased overhead, but that will soon go away.

Making It Asynchronous

The last step in implementing software pipelining using OpenACC is to make the whole operation asynchronous. Again, the key requirement for making an operation work effectively asynchronously is to expose the dependencies or data flow in the code so that independent operations can be run concurrently with sufficient resources. You will use OpenACC's work queues to expose the flow of data through each block of the image. For each block, the code must update the device, apply the filter, and then update the host, and it must be done in that order. This means that for each block these three operations should be put in the same work queue. These operations for different blocks may be placed in different queues, so the block number is a convenient way to refer to the work queues. There is overhead involved in creating new work queues, so it is frequently a best practice to reuse some smaller number of queues throughout the computation.

Because we know that we are hoping to overlap a host-to-device copy, accelerator computation, and a device-to-host copy, it seems as if three work queues should be enough. For each block of the operation you use the block number, modulo 3 to signify which queue to use for a given block's work. As a personal preference, I generally choose to reserve queue 0 for special situations, so for this example we will always add 1 to the queue number to avoid using queue 0.

Listing 10.10 shows the code from this step, which adds the `async` clause to both `update` directives and the `parallel loop`, using the formula just discussed to determine the work queue number. However, one critical and easy-to-miss step remains before we can run the code: adding synchronization to the end of the computation. If we did not synchronize before writing the image to a file, we'd almost certainly produce an image that's only partially filtered. The `wait` directive in line 52 of Listing 10.10 prevents the host thread from moving forward until after all asynchronous work on the accelerator has completed. The final code for this step appears in Listing 10.10.

Listing 10.10 Final, pipelined OpenACC filtering code with asynchronous directives

```
 1 void blur5_pipelined(unsigned restrict char *imgData,
 2    unsigned restrict char *out, long w, long h,
 3    long ch, long step)
 4 {
 5   long x, y;
 6   const int nblocks = 8;
 7
 8   long blocksize = h/ nblocks;
 9 #pragma acc data create(imgData[w*h*ch],out[w*h*ch])
10   {
11   for ( long blocky = 0; blocky < nblocks; blocky++)
12   {
13     // For data copies we include ghost zones for the filter
14     long starty = MAX(0,blocky * blocksize - filtersize/2);
15     long endy   = MIN(h,starty + blocksize + filtersize/2);
16 #pragma acc update \
17             device(imgData[starty*step:(endy-starty)*step]) \
18             async(blocky%3+1)
19     starty = blocky * blocksize;
20     endy = starty + blocksize;
21 #pragma acc parallel loop collapse(2) gang vector \
22                       async(blocky%3+1)
23     for ( y = starty; y < endy; y++ )
24       {
```

```
25        for ( x = 0; x < w; x++ )
26        {
27          float blue = 0.0, green = 0.0, red = 0.0;
28          for ( int fy = 0; fy < filtersize; fy++ )
29          {
30            long iy = y - (filtersize/2) + fy;
31            for ( int fx = 0; fx < filtersize; fx++ )
32            {
33              long ix = x - (filtersize/2) + fx;
34              if ( (iy<0)  || (ix<0) ||
35                   (iy>=h) || (ix>=w) ) continue;
36              blue  += filter[fy][fx] *
37                      (float)imgData[iy * step + ix * ch];
38              green += filter[fy][fx] *
39                      (float)imgData[iy * step + ix * ch + 1];
40              red   += filter[fy][fx] *
41                      (float)imgData[iy * step + ix * ch + 2];
42            }
43          }
44          out[y * step + x * ch]     = 255 - (scale * blue);
45          out[y * step + x * ch + 1 ] = 255 - (scale * green);
46          out[y * step + x * ch + 2 ] = 255 - (scale * red);
47        }
48      }
49  #pragma acc update self(out[starty*step:blocksize*step]) \
50                  async(blocky%3+1)
51    }
52  #pragma acc wait
53    }
54 }
```

What is the net result of these changes? First, notice in Table 10.1 that the run time of the whole operation has now improved by quite a bit. Compared with the original version, you see an improvement of 1.8×, which is roughly what we predicted earlier for fully overlapped code. Figure 10.5 is another timeline from the PGProf, which shows that we have achieved exactly what we set out to do. Notice that nearly all of the data movement is overlapped with computation on the GPU, making it essentially free. The little bit of data transfer at the beginning and end of the computation is offset by a small amount of overlap between subsequent filter kernels as each kernel begins to run out of work and the next one begins to run. You can experiment with the number of blocks and find the optimal value, which may vary depending on the machine on which you are running. In Figure 10.5, we are obviously operating on eight blocks.

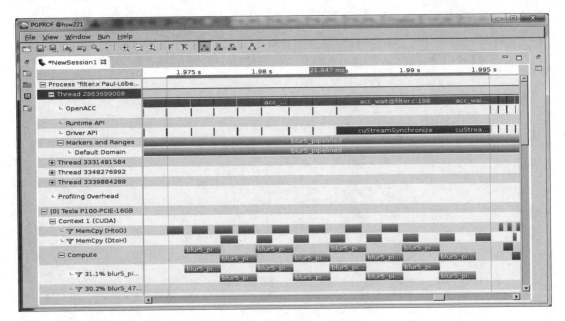

Figure 10.5 PGProf timeline for software pipelined image filter

Table 10.1 PGProf timeline for baseline image filter

OPTIMIZATION STEP	TIME (MS)	SPEEDUP
Baseline	43.102	1.00×
Blocked	45.217	0.95×
Blocked with update	52.161	0.83×
Asynchronous	23.602	1.83×

10.2 Multidevice Programming

Many systems are now built with not only one, but several accelerator devices. This section discusses ways to extend existing code to divide work across multiple devices.

10.2.1 MULTIDEVICE PIPELINE

In the preceding section, you modified an image-filtering program to operate over blocks of the image so that you could overlap the cost of transferring the requisite data to and from the device with computation on the device. Here is something to consider about that example: If each block is fully independent of the other blocks and manages its data correctly, do those blocks need to be run on the same device? The answer, of course, is no, but how do you send blocks to different devices using OpenACC?

To do that, OpenACC provides the `acc_set_device_num` function. This function accepts two arguments: a device type and a device number. With those two pieces of information, you should be able to choose any device in your machine and direct your work to that device. Once you have called `acc_set_device_num`, all OpenACC directives encountered by the host thread up until the next call to `acc_set_device_num` will be handled by the specified device. Each device will have its own copies of the data (if your program is running on a device that has a distinct memory) and its own work queues. Also, each host thread can set its own device number, something you'll take advantage of in this section.

The OpenACC runtime library provides routines for querying and setting both the device type (e.g., NVIDIA GPU, AMD GPU, Intel Xeon Phi, etc.) and the device number. With these API routines you can direct both your data and compute kernels to different devices as needed. Let us first look at the routines for querying and setting the device type.

Listing 10.11 demonstrates the usage of `acc_get_device_type` and `acc_set_device_type` to query and set the type of accelerator to use by default. Setting only the type means that the OpenACC runtime will still choose the specific device within that type to use. You can take even more control and specify the exact device number within a device type to use.

Listing 10.11 Example usage of setting and getting OpenACC device type

```
1 #include <stdio.h>
2 #include <openacc.h>
3 int main()
4 {
5   int error = 0;
6   acc_device_t myDev = -1;
7
8   acc_set_device_type(acc_device_nvidia);
9   myDev = acc_get_device_type();
10  if ( myDev != acc_device_nvidia )
11  {
12    fprintf(stderr, "Wrong device type returned! %d != %d\n",
13            (int)myDev, (int)acc_device_nvidia);
14    error = -1;
15  }
16  return error;
17 }
```

Listing 10.12 demonstrates the `acc_set_device_num` and `acc_get_device_num` routines. These listings also demonstrate the `acc_get_num_devices` routine, which is used to learn how many devices of a particular type are available. This information can be useful in ensuring that the application is portable to any machine, no matter how many accelerators are installed.

Listing 10.12 Example usage of getting the number of devices, setting the current device, and getting the current device number

```c
1 #include <stdio.h>
2 #include <openacc.h>
3 int main()
4 {
5   int numDevices = -1, myNum = -1;
6   numDevices = acc_get_num_devices(acc_device_nvidia);
7   acc_set_device_num(acc_device_nvidia,0);
8   myNum = acc_get_device_num(acc_device_nvidia);
9
10  printf("Using device %d of %d.\n", myNum, numDevices);
11
12  return 0;
13 }
```

Let's extend the pipelined example from the preceding section to send the chunks of work to all available devices. Although I am running on an NVIDIA Tesla P100, I don't want to assume that other users will have a machine that matches my own, so I will specify `acc_device_default` as my device type. This is a special device type value that tells the compiler that I don't care what specific device type it chooses. On my testing machine, I could also have used `acc_device_nvidia`, because that best describes the accelerators in my machine. I have chosen to use OpenMP to assign a CPU thread to each of my accelerator devices. This is not strictly necessary—a single thread could send work to all devices—but in my opinion this simplifies the code because I can call `acc_set_device` once in each thread and not worry about it again.

Listing 10.13 Multidevice image-filtering code using OpenACC and OpenMP

```c
1 #include <openacc.h>
2 #include <omp.h>
3 void blur5_pipelined_multi(unsigned restrict char *imgData,
4                            unsigned restrict char *out,
5                            long w, long h, long ch, long step)
6 {
7   int nblocks = 32;
8
9   long blocksize = h/ nblocks;
10 #pragma omp parallel \
11           num_threads(acc_get_num_devices(acc_device_default))
```

```
12   {
13     int myid = omp_get_thread_num();
14     acc_set_device_num(myid,acc_device_default);
15     int queue = 1;
16 #pragma acc data create(imgData[w*h*ch],out[w*h*ch])
17   {
18 #pragma omp for schedule(static)
19   for ( long blocky = 0; blocky < nblocks; blocky++)
20   {
21     // For data copies we include ghost zones for the filter
22     long starty = MAX(0,blocky * blocksize - filtersize/2);
23     long endy   = MIN(h,starty + blocksize + filtersize/2);
24 #pragma acc update device \
25                    (imgData[starty*step:(endy-starty)*step]) \
26                    async(queue)
27     starty = blocky * blocksize;
28     endy = starty + blocksize;
29 #pragma acc parallel loop collapse(2) gang vector async(queue)
30     for ( long y = starty; y < endy; y++ )
31     {
32       for ( long x = 0; x < w; x++ )
33       {
34         float blue = 0.0, green = 0.0, red = 0.0;
35         for ( int fy = 0; fy < filtersize; fy++ )
36         {
37           long iy = y - (filtersize/2) + fy;
38           for ( int fx = 0; fx < filtersize; fx++ )
39           {
40             long ix = x - (filtersize/2) + fx;
41             if ( (iy<0)  || (ix<0) ||
42                 (iy>=h) || (ix>=w) ) continue;
43             blue  += filter[fy][fx] *
44                     (float)imgData[iy * step + ix * ch];
45             green += filter[fy][fx] *
46                     (float)imgData[iy * step + ix * ch + 1];
47             red   += filter[fy][fx] *
48                     (float)imgData[iy * step + ix * ch + 2];
49           }
50         }
51         out[y * step + x * ch]     = 255 - (scale * blue);
52         out[y * step + x * ch + 1 ] = 255 - (scale * green);
53         out[y * step + x * ch + 2 ] = 255 - (scale * red);
54       }
55     }
56 #pragma acc update self(out[starty*step:blocksize*step]) \
57                    async(queue)
58     queue = (queue%3)+1;
59   }
60 #pragma acc wait
61   }
62   }
63 }
```

In line 10 of Listing 10.13, you start by querying the number of available devices and then use that number to spawn an OpenMP parallel region with that number of threads. In line 14, which is run redundantly by all threads in the OpenMP region, you set the device number that will be used by each individual thread, using the thread number to select the device. Notice also that you change from using a simple modulo operator to set the work queue number to having a per-thread counter. This change prevents the modulo from assigning all chunks from a given device to a reduced number of queues when certain device counts are used. The remainder of the code is unchanged, because each device will have its own data region (line 16) and will have its own work queues.

Table 10.2 shows the results of running the code on one, two, and four GPUs (three is skipped because it would not divide the work evenly). Notice that you see a performance improvement with each additional device, but it is not a strict doubling as the number of devices doubles. It is typical to see some performance degradation as more devices are added because of additional overhead brought into the calculation by each device.

Table 10.2 Multiple-device pipeline timings

NUMBER OF DEVICES	TIME (MS)	SPEEDUP
1	20.628	1.00×
2	12.041	1.71×
4	7.769	2.66×

Figure 10.4, presented earlier, shows another screenshot from PGProf, in which you can clearly see overlapping data movement and computation across multiple devices. Note that in the example code it was necessary to run the operation twice so that the first time would absorb the start-up cost of the multiple devices and the second would provide fair timing. In short-running benchmarks like this one, such a step is needed to prevent the start-up time from dominating the performance. In real, long-running applications, this is not necessary because the start-up cost will be hidden by the long runtime.

10.2.2 OPENACC AND MPI

Another common method for managing multiple devices with OpenACC is to use MPI to divide the work among multiple processes, each of which is assigned to work with an individual accelerator. MPI is commonly used in scientific and high-performance computing applications, so many applications already use MPI to divide work among multiple processes.

This approach has several advantages and disadvantages compared with the approach used in the preceding section. For one thing, application developers are forced to consider how to divide the problem domain into discrete chunks, which are assigned to different processors, thereby effectively isolating each GPU from the others to avoid possible race conditions on the same data. Also, because the domain is divided among multiple processes, it is possible that these processes may span multiple nodes in a cluster, and this increases both the available memory and the number of accelerators available. For applications already using MPI to run in parallel, using MPI to manage multiple accelerators often requires fewer code changes compared with managing multiple devices using OpenACC alone. Using existing MPI also has the advantage that non-accelerated parts of the code can still use MPI parallelism to avoid a serialization slowdown due to Amdahl's law. When you're dealing with GPUs and other discrete accelerators, it is common for a system to have more CPU cores than it does discrete accelerators. In these situations, it is common to either share a single accelerator among multiple MPI ranks or to thread within each MPI rank to better utilize all system resources.

When you are using MPI to utilize multiple discrete accelerators, to obtain the best possible performance it is often necessary to understand how the accelerators and host CPUs are connected. For instance, if a system has two multicore CPU sockets and four GPU cards, as shown in Figure 10.6, then it's likely that each CPU socket will be directly connected to two GPUs but will have to communicate with the other two GPUs by way of the other CPU, and this reduces the available bandwidth and increases the latency between the CPU and the GPU.

Furthermore, in some GPU configurations each pair of GPUs may be able to communicate directly with each other, but only indirectly with GPUs on the opposite socket. Best performance is achieved when each rank is assigned to the nearest accelerator, something known as good accelerator **affinity**. Although some MPI job launchers will handle assigning a GPU to each MPI rank, you should not count on this behavior; instead you should use the `acc_set_device_num` function to manually assign a particular accelerator to each MPI rank. By understanding how MPI assigns ranks to CPU cores and how the CPUs and accelerators are configured, you can assign the accelerator affinity so that each rank is communicating with the nearest available accelerator, thereby maximizing host-device bandwidth and minimizing latency. For instance, in Figure 10.6, you would want to assign GPU0 and GPU1 to ranks physically assigned to CPU0 and GPU2, and assign GPU3 to ranks physically assigned to CPU1. This is true whether or not ranks are assigned to the CPUs in a round-robin manner, packed to CPU0 and then CPU1, or in some other order.

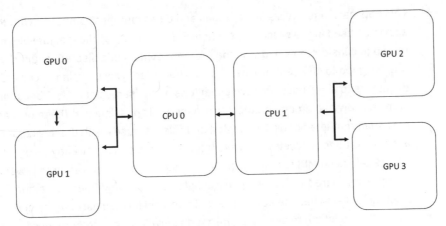

Figure 10.6 System with two multicore CPU sockets and four GPU cards

Many MPI libraries can now communicate directly with accelerator memory, particularly on clusters utilizing NVIDIA GPUs, which support a feature known as GPUDirect RDMA (remote direct memory access). When you are using one of these MPI libraries it's possible to use the host_data directive to pass accelerator memory to the library, as shown in Chapter 9 and discussed next.

MPI Without Direct Memory Access

Let's first consider an OpenACC application using MPI that cannot use an accelerator-aware MPI library. In this case, any call to an MPI routine would require the addition of an update directive before, after, or potentially before and after the library call, depending on how the data are used. Although MPI does support asynchronous sending and receiving of messages, the MPI API does not understand OpenACC's concept of work queues, and therefore either update directives must be synchronous or a wait directive must appear before any MPI function that sends data. Similarly, an OpenACC update directive should not appear directly following an asynchronous MPI function that receives data, but only after synchronous communication or the associated MPI_Wait call; in this way, you ensure that the data in the host buffer are correct before they are updated to the device. Listing 10.14 shows several common communication patterns for interacting between OpenACC and an MPI library that is not accelerator aware.

Listing 10.14 Common patterns for MPI communication with OpenACC updates

```
// When using MPI_Sendrecv or any blocking collective, it is
// necessary to have an update before and after.

#pragma acc update self(u_new[offset_first_row:m-2])
```

```
MPI_Sendrecv(u_new+offset_first_row, m-2, MPI_DOUBLE, t_nb, 0,
             u_new+offset_bottom_boundary, m-2,
             MPI_DOUBLE, b_nb, 0,
             MPI_COMM_WORLD, MPI_STATUS_IGNORE);
#pragma acc update device(u_new[offset_bottom_boundary:m-2])
// When using either MPI_Send or MPI_Isend, an update is
// required before the MPI call
#pragma acc update self(u_new[offset_first_row:m-2])
MPI_Send(u_new+offset_first_row, m-2, MPI_DOUBLE, t_nb, 0, i
         MPI_COMM_WORLD);

// When using a blocking receive, an update may appear
// immediately after the MPI call.

MPI_Recv(u_new+offset_bottom_boundary, m-2, MPI_DOUBLE, b_nb, 0,
         MPI_COMM_WORLD, MPI_STATUS_IGNORE);
#pragma acc update device(u_new[offset_bottom_boundary:m-2])

// When using a nonblocking receives, it is necessary to MPI_Wait
// before using an OpenACC update

MPI_Irecv(u_new+offset_bottom_boundary, m-2, MPI_DOUBLE, b_nb, 0,
          MPI_COMM_WORLD, MPI_STATUS_IGNORE, &request);
MPI_Wait(&request, MPI_STATUS_IGNORE);
#pragma acc update device(u_new[offset_bottom_boundary:m-2])
```

The biggest drawback to this approach is that all interactions between OpenACC and MPI require a copy through host memory. This means that there can never be effective overlapping between MPI and OpenACC and that it may be necessary to communicate the data over the PCIe bus twice as often. If possible, this approach to using MPI with OpenACC should be avoided.

MPI with Direct Memory Access

Having an MPI implementation that is accelerator aware greatly simplifies the mixture of OpenACC and MPI. It is no longer necessary to manually stage data through the host memory using the update directive, but rather the MPI library can directly read from and write to accelerator memory, potentially reducing the bandwidth cost associated with the data transfer and simplifying the code. Just because an MPI library is accelerator aware does not necessarily guarantee that data will be sent directly between the accelerator memories. The library may still choose to stage the data through host memory or perform a variety of optimizations invisibly to the developer. This means that it is the responsibility of the library developer, rather than the application developer, to determine the best way to send the message on a given machine. As discussed in Chapter 9, the OpenACC host_data directive is used for passing device pointers to host libraries. This same directive can be used to pass accelerator memory to an accelerator-aware MPI library.

Note, however, that if the same code is used with a non-accelerator-aware library a program crash will occur. Listing 10.15 demonstrates some common patterns for using `host_data` to pass device arrays into the MPI library. This method has far fewer caveats to highlight than the preceding one.

Listing 10.15 Example using OpenACC host_data directive with accelerator-enabled MPI

```
// By using an accelerator-aware MPI library, host_data may be
// used to pass device memory directly into the library.

#pragma acc host_data use_device(u_new)
{
MPI_Sendrecv(u_new+offset_first_row, m-2, MPI_DOUBLE, t_nb, 0,
             u_new+offset_bottom_boundary, m-2,
             MPI_DOUBLE, b_nb, 0,
             MPI_COMM_WORLD, MPI_STATUS_IGNORE);
}

// Because the Irecv is writing directly to accelerator memory
// only the MPI_Wait is required to ensure the data are current,
// no additional update is required.

#pragma acc host_data use_device(u_new)
{
MPI_Irecv(u_new+offset_bottom_boundary, m-2, MPI_DOUBLE, b_nb, 0,
          MPI_COMM_WORLD, MPI_STATUS_IGNORE, &request);
}
MPI_Wait(&request, MPI_STATUS_IGNORE );
```

One advantage of this approach over the other one comes when you're using asynchronous MPI calls. In the earlier case the update of the device data could not occur until after `MPI_Wait` has completed, because the update may copy stale data to the device. Because the MPI library is interacting with accelerator memory directly, `MPI_Wait` will guarantee that data have been placed in the accelerator buffer, removing the overhead of updating the device after the receive has completed. Additionally, the MPI library can invisibly perform optimizations of the way the messages are transferred, such as pipelining smaller message blocks, a feature that may be more efficient than directly copying the memory or manually staging buffers through host memory, for all the same reasons pipelining was beneficial in the earlier example.

This section has presented two methods for utilizing multiple accelerator devices with OpenACC. The first method uses OpenACC's built-in `acc_set_device_num` function call to direct data and work to specific devices. In particular, OpenMP threads are used to assign a different host thread to each device, although this is not strictly necessary. The second method uses MPI to partition work across multiple processes, each of which utilizes a different accelerator. This approach is often simpler to implement in scientific code, because such code frequently uses MPI partitioning, meaning that non-accelerated code may still run across multiple MPI ranks. Both approaches can take advantage of multiple accelerators in the same node, but only the MPI approach can be used to manage multiple accelerators on different nodes. Which approach will work best depends on the specific needs of the application, and both techniques can be used together in the same application.

The source code in GitHub accompanying this chapter (check the Preface for a link to GitHub) includes the image filter pipeline code used in this chapter and a simple OpenACC + MPI application that can be used as examples.

10.3 Summary

You can exploit advanced techniques using OpenACC asynchronous execution and management of multiple devices. These techniques are designed to maximize application performance by improving the way the application uses all available resources. Asynchronous execution decouples work on the host from work on the accelerator, including data transfers between the two, allowing the application to use the host, accelerator, and any connecting bus concurrently, but only if all data dependencies are properly handled. Multidevice support extends this idea by allowing a program to utilize all available accelerators for maximum performance.

10.4 Exercises

1. The source code for the image-filtering example used in this chapter has been provided at the GitHub site shown in the Preface. You should attempt to build and understand this sample application.

2. You should experiment to determine the best block size for your machine. Does changing the image size affect the result? Does changing the accelerator type change the result?

Chapter 11

Innovative Research Ideas Using OpenACC, Part I

This chapter, along with Chapter 12, is dedicated to examining the directions being taken by new research on the OpenACC programming model. We discuss several innovative ideas, highlighting the feasibility and adaptability of the model to target more hardware platforms than only the conventional ones. In section 11.1, Lin Gan, a researcher from Tsinghua University and the National Supercomputing Center in Wuxi, China, presents the use of OpenACC on the Sunway TaihuLight supercomputer, which ranks first in the Top500 list as of November 2016. The author discusses a few proposed language extensions to the programming model to better support the effective utilization of manycore processors.

Then in Section 11.2, author Daniel Tian, a compiler developer from NVIDIA, discusses an open source OpenACC compiler in an industrial framework (OpenUH as a branch of Open64) and explains the various loop-scheduling reduction strategies for general-purpose GPUs, with the intention to allow researchers to explore advanced compiler techniques.

11.1 Sunway OpenACC

Lin Gan, Tsinghua University/ National Supercomputing Center in Wuxi

The Sunway TaihuLight supercomputer,[1] located at National Supercomputing Center in Wuxi, China, is the world's first computer system that operates at 100 petaflop/s. The entire supercomputer, including the high-performance SW26010 manycore CPU, is a homegrown system that was entirely created, manufactured,

---

1. H. Fu, J. Liao, J. Yang, L. Wang, Z. Song, X. Huang, C. Yang, W. Xue, F. Liu, F. Qiao, and W. Zhao, "The Sunway TaihuLight Supercomputer: System and Applications," *Science China Information Sciences* 59(7) (2016): 072001: 1–16.

and assembled in China using Chinese technology. Since June 2016, at the Top500 Sunway Taihulight has been ranked the top supercomputer in the world. It contains a heterogeneous computing architecture, a network system, a peripheral system, and a maintenance and diagnostic system, as well as power and cooling. The TaihuLight software ecosystem includes basic software, a parallel operating system, and high-performance storage management; in addition, a parallel programming language and compilation environment supports mainstream parallel programming language interfaces such as MPI, OpenMP, OpenACC, and others. This chapter focuses on OpenACC and specifically on the OpenACC version used on the Sunway TaihuLight.

OpenACC provides good support for heterogeneous accelerated programming, and this is why OpenACC has been used to port multiple applications from a variety of fields, including climate, geological prospecting, and shipbuilding.

There are differences between the structures of the SW26010 manycore CPU and current heterogeneous computing platforms consisting of GPUs and MICs. This meant that the Sunway TaihuLight implementation of OpenACC had to provide new functions and some extensions to the OpenACC syntax.[2]

11.1.1 THE SW26010 MANYCORE PROCESSOR

We first describe the structure of the SW26010 manycore CPU so that you can understand how this processor architecture differs from GPUs. Figure 11.1 shows that the SW26010 uses a heterogeneous architecture that contains multiple general CPU cores and many accelerator cores integrated on the same chip.

The SW26010 contains four core groups, and each group contains one management processing element (MPE) and 64 computing processing elements (CPEs). This means that each SW26010 contains 260 CPU cores. The MPE and CPEs share memory within each core group. Each CPE has independent 64KB scratch pad memory (SPM), which can be used to customize data with finer-grained methods and is specifically important for performance. Data between SPM and main memory can be transformed by direct memory access (DMA) initiated by CPEs. The MPE, as the core of the general CPU, can perform operations such as communication, IO, and computation. CPEs in the same core group are used to accelerate computations to boost computation-intensive sections of code.

---

2. In this chapter, we use OpenACC* to distinguish the Sunway TaihuLight OpenACC implementation from the OpenACC version 2.0 standard.

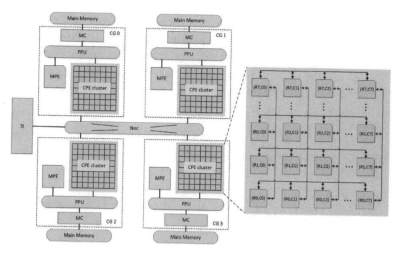

Figure 11.1 Architecture of the SW26010 CPU

Succinctly, each MPE in the SW26010 can be regarded as the core in an x86 plat-form, and 64 CPEs can be regarded as the GPUs that accelerate the computation through parallelism.

11.1.2 THE MEMORY MODEL IN THE SUNWAY TAIHULIGHT

Data is shared between MPE and CPEs, and this means that OpenACC data man-agement (e.g., `copy`, `copyin`, `copyout`, etc.) is not required. The Sunway Taihu-Light exploits the OpenACC 2.5 standard, which states that compilers can leave data in place and are not required to create copies or move data. However, directly accessing the shared memory on accelerator devices can cause performance deg-radation. For this reason, applications make heavy use of local high-speed memory on the CPEs. To assist in this, OpenACC* in the Sunway TaihuLight was extended to help programmers describe the usage of 64KB on-chip high-speed memory (SPM) instead of gigabytes of graphics memory on the GPU. In SW26010, an accelerator thread sees three kinds of memory, as illustrated in Figure 11.2.

1. The main thread data space, located in the main memory, is directly accessible to accelerator threads created by the main thread as well as the main thread. All the variables declared outside the accelerator region are within this space.

2. The private space in the accelerator thread, located in the main memory, is independently owned by each accelerator thread and contains all the variables declared with `private` and `firstprivate`.

217

3. The local space in the accelerator thread, located in the device memory, is independently owned by each accelerator thread and provides the highest performance compared with the other data spaces. Variables declared with `copy`, `local`, and so on are totally or partially stored in local space controlled by the compiler system. Data transfer between the main memory and the local space is controlled by the accelerator thread.

The `cache` directive in OpenACC* is designed to store data at the memory level where the speed of data access is the highest, whereas the `cache` directive in the OpenACC standard is designed to utilize the accelerator's hardware- or software-managed caches. Because the `copy`, `copyin`, and `copyout` directives in OpenACC* can meet the requirements of moving data between SPM and main memory in most circumstances, the `cache` directive in OpenACC* is used mostly when the `copy` clauses do not work, such as when you are copying arrays whose indexes are not fixed.

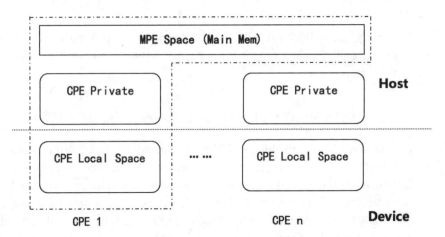

Figure 11.2 The storage model of the Sunway OpenACC

11.1.3 THE EXECUTION MODEL

The OpenACC* execution model is almost the same as that of OpenACC, as Figure 11.3 illuminates.

The program starts on the MPE. It is a serial section of code executed as a main thread or concurrently executed as multiple main threads through the use of programming interfaces such as OpenMP or MPI. The computation-intensive part is loaded onto the CPEs as kernel jobs controlled by the main thread.

The main execution processes of the kernel include the following:

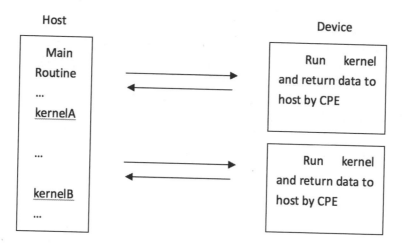

Figure 11.3 Sunway OpenACC execution model

- Allocating needed data space on device memory SPM

- Loading kernel code, including kernel parameters, into the device

- Transferring the needed data from main memory to device memory initiated by the device, and waiting until finish

- The device conducting the computation and returning the results to the main memory

- Releasing the data space on the device

In most cases, each MPE loads a series of kernels and executes them one by one on the accelerator device.

11.1.4 DATA MANAGEMENT

In OpenACC*, programmers are encouraged to store data on the SPM to improve memory-access performance. Some data transfer and usage methods are covered next. The basic concepts and syntax are almost the same as in OpenACC, but OpenACC* provides additional functions and syntax extensions to adapt to the architecture of CPEs on the SW26010 CPU. Because the SPM space for each CPE is only 64KB, the purpose of these extensions is to make better use of SPM and improve the bandwidth of copying data between SPM and main memory. Only the usage difference is discussed here.

Direct Memory Access (DMA)

Data can be directly transferred between main memory and SPM by data components as well as `copy`, `copyin`, and `copyout`, and the space needed by SPM is applied and released by the compiler, as Figure 11.4(b) shows. Figure 11.4(a) shows a code snippet that uses the current OpenACC specification `data` constructs, in which data components are described outside parallel components. In comparison, OpenACC* data components can be used within the dynamic execution region of parallel components.

```
!$acc data copyin(A) copyout(B)
!$acc parallel loop
  do i=1,128
    m = func(i)
    do j=1,128
      B(j, i) = A(j, m)
    enddo
  enddo
!$acc end parallel loop
!$acc end data
```

(a)OpenACC

```
!$acc parallel loop
  do i=1,128
    m = func(i)
      !$acc data copyin(A(*, m)) copyout(B(*, i))
    do j=1,128
      B(j, i) = A(j, m)
    enddo
     !$acc end data
  enddo
  !$acc end parallel loop
```

(b)OpenACC*

Figure 11.4 Code example: Using data to implement data exchange

Data Copy

In OpenACC*, the copy annotation in parallel components has been extended to describe data transfers between main memory and multiple SPMs. In particular, the size of the copied data is controlled by using loop components and tile annotations collectively, as does the Fortran code in Figure 11.5. This is important so that the programmer can make use of SPM space.

The SW26010 execution method in Figure 11.5 is different from that of OpenACC on a standard GPU platform, because the compiler can automatically analyze the mapping relation between the data-access method and the loop division method and determine the data division method based on the loop division method. In particular, the i loop is divided and runs in parallel with a chunk size of 1, whereas the j loop is serially divided, with a chunk size of 2 according to the tile annotation. With this information, the division method for arrays A, B, and C can be determined. In array A, for instance, each computation iteration needs (256, 2, 1) of data. Thus the compiler will apply (256, 2, 1) caches for A, B, and C, respectively, and will automatically generate the control sequence for data transfer.

```
!$acc parallel loop copyin(A, B) copyout(C)
do i = 1, 64
    !$acc loop tile(2)
    do j = 1, 128
        do k = 1, 256
            C(k, j, i) = A(k, j, i)   + B(k, j, i)
        end do
    end do   !end of j-loop
    !$acc end loop
end do   ! end of i-loop
!$acc end parallel loop
```

Figure 11.5 Code example: Data exchange in a loop

Directly Applying for Space by Local Annotation

Local annotation is extended in OpenACC* to directly request space needed by variables in an on-chip high-speed cache. The data properties for local annotation and private annotation are the same, because both are private variables in accelerator threads. The only difference is that the variables described by local annotation will utilize space from the higher-performance cache SPM. We skip the details, because the use of local annotation is similar to that of private annotations.

Data Transfer Control

In addition to using the copy annotation for data transfer as in OpenACC, OpenACC* extends two other optimized data transfer control annotations: swap, swapin, and swapout, and pack, packin, and packout. Both extensions boost data transfer efficiency by data transformation on the Sunway TaihuLight.

Figure 11.6 shows how swap series annotation can be used to transpose the arrays and then perform the data transfer.

Swap annotation is generally used to access the discontinuous array data, because discontinuous data generally lead to poor data transfer performance. Swap annotation gets around this problem by first transposing the arrays and then transferring the data to improve data transfer efficiency.

As Figure 11.7 shows, the access to array B is not continuous. By transposing B to exchange the dimension order, you can guarantee the sequential ordering of the data addresses and ensure transfer efficiency. Sunway TaihuLight supports transposition of arrays having as many as six dimensions.

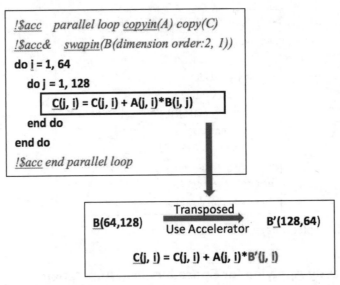

Figure 11.6 Example of the use of swap

Pack series annotation is used to package multiple scattered variables and transfer the packaged data as a sequential whole, as shown in Figure 11.7. Specifically, the compiler packages A, B, and C into a single array for transfer and uses this packaged memory directly in the computation. Pack annotation is used mostly for packaging multiple arrays or scalar data.

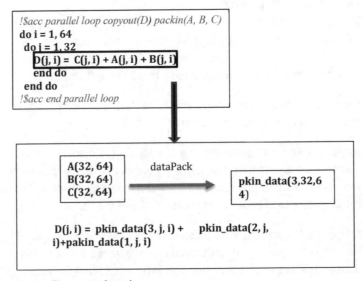

Figure 11.7 Code example: The use of pack

11.1.5 SUMMARY

OpenACC has been used to program more than 20 essential domains, such as climate modeling,[3] material simulation, deep learning, geophysics exploration, life science, and more, on the Sunway TaihuLight supercomputer, the fastest supercomputer in the world as of the November 2016 Top500 list. More than 100 applications have delivered inspiring performance results on the Sunway TaihuLight hardware.

Work is proceeding to scale six important applications so that they can run efficiently on the entire system, which contains more than 10 million computing cores and is capable of delivering tens of petaflops' worth of sustainable performance.

Other notable projects include a fully implicit solver for atmospheric dynamics, which won the 2016 ACM Gordon Bell Prize.[4] Two other 2016 ACM Gordon Bell Finalists are focused on climate modeling[5] and material simulation.[6]

OpenACC* is one of the major parallel programming tools used for application development on the Sunway system. All told, OpenACC has greatly facilitated the programming efforts of users and has played an important role in supporting research covering various applications. In November 2016, the National Supercomputing Center in Wuxi officially became a formal member of the OpenACC Alliance, an international organization that supports cooperation to improve the performance and widespread use of OpenACC. In summary, Sunway OpenACC will continue to be improved based on feedback as well as the international standard.

3. H. Fu, J. Liao, W. Xue, L. Wang, D. Chen, L. Gu, J. Xu, N. Ding, X. Wang, C. He, and S. Xu, "Refactoring and Optimizing the Community Atmosphere Model (CAM) on the Sunway TaihuLight Supercomputer," in *Proceedings of the International Conference for High Performance Computing, Networking, Storage and Analysis* (November 2016): 83.
4. C. Yang, W. Xue, H. Fu, H. You, X. Wang, Y. Ao, F. Liu, L. Gan, P. Xu, L. Wang, and G. Yang, "10M-core Scalable Fully-Implicit Solver for Nonhydrostatic Atmospheric Dynamics," in *Proceedings of the International Conference for High Performance Computing, Networking, Storage and Analysis* (November 2016): 6.
5. F. Qiao, W. Zhao, X. Yin, X. Huang, X. Liu, Q. Shu, G. Wang, Z. Song, X. Li, H. Liu, and G. Yang, "A Highly Effective Global Surface Wave Numerical Simulation with Ultra-High Resolution," in *Proceedings of the International Conference for High Performance Computing, Networking, Storage and Analysis* (November 2016): 5.
6. J. Zhang, C. Zhou, Y. Wang, L. Ju, Q. Du, X. Chi, D. Xu, D. Chen, Y. Liu, and Z. Liu, "Extreme-Scale Phase Field Simulations of Coarsening Dynamics on the Sunway TaihuLight Supercomputer," in *Proceedings of the International Conference for High Performance Computing, Networking, Storage and Analysis* (November 2016): 4.

11.2 Compiler Transformation of Nested Loops for Accelerators

Daniel Tian, University of Houston/NVIDIA

OpenACC lets programmers make use of directives via pragmas to offload computation-intensive nested loops onto massively parallel accelerator devices. Directives are easy to use but are high level and need smart translation to map iterations of loops to the underlying hardware. This is the role of the compiler, which helps users translate annotated loops into kernels to be run on massively parallel architectures. Therefore, the loop-scheduling transformation serves as a basic and mandatory feature in an OpenACC compiler infrastructure.

11.2.1 THE OPENUH COMPILER INFRASTRUCTURE

The creation of an OpenACC compiler requires innovative research solutions[7],[8] to meet the challenges of mapping high-level loop iterations to low-level threading architectures of the hardware. It also requires support from the runtime to handle data movement and scheduling of computation on the accelerators. In this work, we have used OpenUH, a branch of the open source Open64 compiler suite, for our compiler framework.[9] The components of the OpenUH framework are shown in Figure 11.8.

The compiler is composed of several modules, with each module operating on a level of the compiler's multilevel intermediate representation (IR), WHIRL. From the top, each module translates the current level of WHIRL to a lower level.

We have identified the following challenges that must be addressed to create an effective implementation of the OpenACC directives. First, it is important to create an extensible parser and IR system to facilitate the inclusion of new and modified features of the OpenACC standard. Fortunately, the extensibility of the OpenUH framework and the WHIRL IR allowed us to add these extensions without much difficulty. Second, you need to design and implement an effective strategy to distribute the loop nest across the general-purpose computing on graphics processing

---

7. Rengan Xu, "Optimizing the Performance of Directive-based Programming Model for GPGPUs" (PhD Dissertation Thesis, University of Houston, 2016).

8. Xiaonan Tian, "A Compiler Optimization Framework for Directive-based GPU Computing" (PhD Dissertation Thesis, University of Houston, 2016).

9. https://github.com/uhhpctools/openuh.

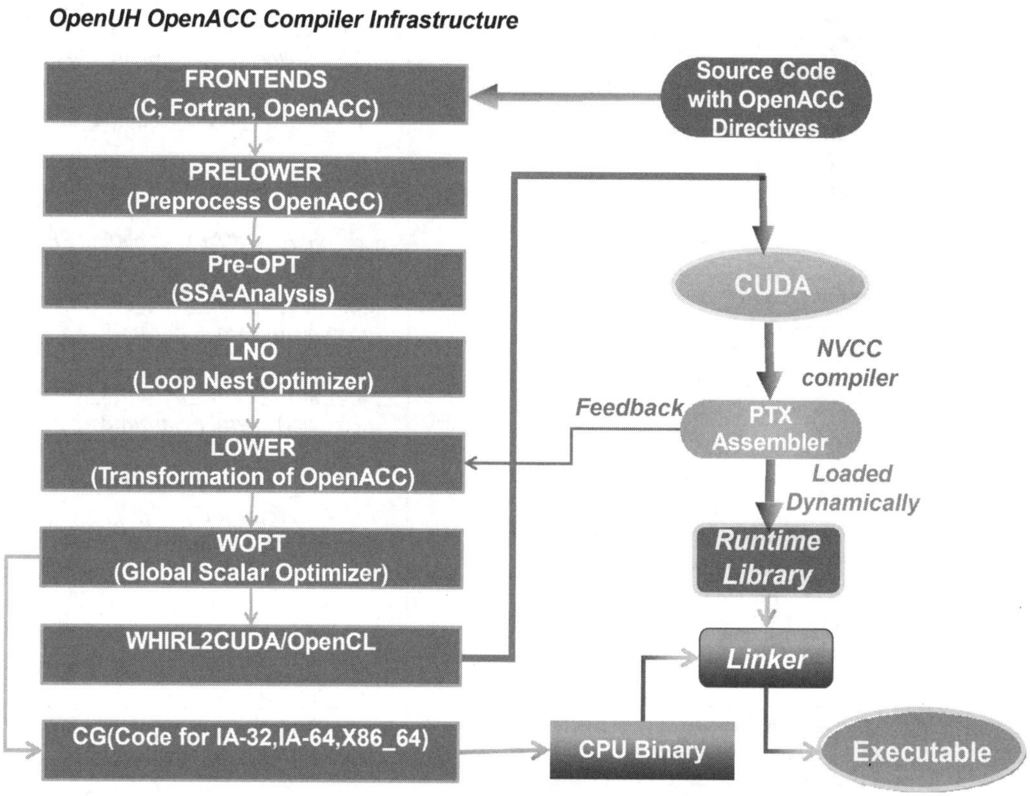

OpenUH OpenACC Compiler Infrastructure

Figure 11.8 OpenUH compiler framework for OpenACC
Note: NVCC is the NVIDIA CUDA compiler; PTX is the pseudo-assembly language used in NVIDIA GPUs.

unit (GPGPU) thread hierarchy. We discuss our solutions in more detail in the next subsection.

As shown in Figure 11.8, we use a source-to-source translation technique to translate the OpenACC offload region into CUDA code. OpenUH directly generates object code for an x86 host CPU. Consider the OpenACC code in Figure 11.9(a) as an example. Figure 11.9(b) and (c) show the translated CUDA kernel and the equivalent host CPU pseudocode. We have created a WHIRL2CUDA module that can produce NVIDIA CUDA kernels after the transformation of offloading code regions. Compared with binary code generation, the source-to-source approach provides much more flexibility to users. It allows users to leverage the advanced optimization features in the back-end compilation step performed by the CUDA compiler nvcc. It also gives users some options to manually optimize the generated CUDA code for further performance improvement.

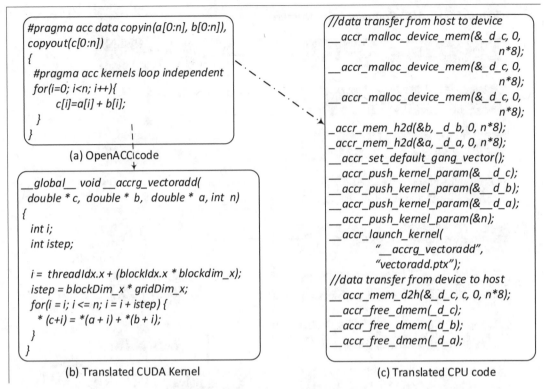

```
#pragma acc data copyin(a[0:n], b[0:n]),
copyout(c[0:n])
{
  #pragma acc kernels loop independent
  for(i=0; i<n; i++){
      c[i]=a[i] + b[i];
  }
}
```

(a) OpenACC code

```
__global__ void __accrg_vectoradd(
 double * c, double * b,  double * a, int  n)
{
  int i;
  int istep;

  i =  threadIdx.x + (blockIdx.x * blockdim_x);
  istep = blockDim_x * gridDim_x;
  for(i = i; i <= n; i = i + istep) {
   * (c+i) = *(a + i) + *(b + i);
  }
}
```

(b) Translated CUDA Kernel

```
//data transfer from host to device
__accr_malloc_device_mem(&_d_c, 0,
                                 n*8);
__accr_malloc_device_mem(&_d_c, 0,
                                 n*8);
__accr_malloc_device_mem(&_d_c, 0,
                                 n*8);
_accr_mem_h2d(&b, _d_b, 0, n*8);
_accr_mem_h2d(&a, _d_a, 0, n*8);
__accr_set_default_gang_vector();
__accr_push_kernel_param(&__d_c);
__accr_push_kernel_param(&__d_b);
__accr_push_kernel_param(&__d_a);
__accr_push_kernel_param(&n);
__accr_launch_kernel(
        "__accrg_vectoradd",
        "vectoradd.ptx");
//data transfer from device to host
__accr_mem_d2h(&_d_c, c, 0, n*8);
__accr_free_dmem(_d_c);
__accr_free_dmem(_d_b);
__accr_free_dmem(_d_a);
```

(c) Translated CPU code

Figure 11.9 OpenACC vector addition example

11.2.2 LOOP-SCHEDULING TRANSFORMATION

Programmers usually offload a computation-intensive nested loop to massive parallel accelerators. One of the major challenges of compiler transformation is to create a uniform loop distribution mechanism that can effectively map nested loop iteration across the GPU parallel system. As an example, NVIDIA GPGPUs have two levels of parallelism: the block level and the thread level. Blocks can be organized as multidimensional in a grid, and threads in a block can also be multidimensional. How to distribute iterations of multilevel nested loops across the multidimensional blocks and threads is a nontrivial problem (see Figure 11.10).

In our design, we propose loop-scheduling strategies for an OpenACC offload region: `parallel` and `kernels` loop scheduling. The use of `parallel` loop scheduling follows the OpenACC specification, but the scheduling methods are quite limited. To fully utilize the GPU resources, we also propose nested gang and vector parallelism as part of the `kernels` loop scheduling. The nested gangs

```
#pragma acc loop
for(i=istart; i<iend; i++){
  ...
}
```

(a)Single Loop

```
#pragma acc loop
for(i=istart; i<iend; i++){
  #pragma acc loop
  for(j=jstart; j<jend; j++){
    ...
  }
}
```

(b)Double Nested Loop

```
#pragma acc loop
for(i=istart; i<iend; i++){
  #pragma acc loop
  for(j=jstart; j<jend; j++){
    #pragma acc loop
    for(k=kstart; k<kend; k++){
      ...
    }
  }
}
```

(c)Triple Nested Loop

Figure 11.10 OpenACC loop without scheduling clauses

and vectors can help create multidimensional thread-block and grid topology, a technique that might help generate enough parallelism and improve performance. We discuss these loop-scheduling methods and our proposed methodologies in the following two subsections.

Note

In the following subsections, p is parallel, k is kernel, g is gang, w is worker, v is vector, and x, y, and z denote the three dimensions.

Parallel Loop Scheduling

In the OpenACC specification, loop scheduling cannot nest a higher-level loop schedule within a lower level; that is, a loop with a gang schedule can contain only inner loops with workers or vectors (or both), and a worker loop can include only vector loops. Loop iterations can be distributed across multiple gangs or in a single gang containing one or more workers, where this gang in turn contains one or more vector lanes. Multiple loop schedules can also be listed on the same loop, in which case the iterations are distributed among one or more levels of parallelism.

The OpenACC specification allows the compiler some flexibility of interpretation and code generation for three levels of parallelism. However, all workers must complete execution of their assigned iterations before any worker proceeds beyond the end of the loop, and all vector lanes will complete execution of their assigned iterations before any vector lane proceeds beyond the end of the loop. Meanwhile, synchronization is supported only inside each thread block. The `gang` can map only to the thread block, whereas `worker` and `vector` may have different interpretations depending on their implementations in the compiler. In our implementation, the `gang` is mapped to thread-block-level parallelism, and `worker` and `vector` are mapped to the thread topology inside the thread block.

Table 11.1 shows the CUDA terminology that we use in our OpenACC implementation. In OpenUH, a `gang` maps to a thread block; a `worker` maps to the y dimension of a thread block; and a `vector` maps to the x dimension of a thread block. Because contiguous iterations tend to access contiguous data, this strategy allows for coalescing accesses to the global memory on the GPU architecture (both AMD and NVIDIA). Based on these definitions, the implementation for the single-loop nest is shown in Figure 11.11. Figure 11.11(a) demonstrates an example in OpenACC, and Figure 11.11(b) demonstrates an example of the loop-scheduling transformation in CUDA. In this example, all the iterations are distributed evenly across gangs, workers, and vector lanes.

Table 11.1 OpenACC and CUDA terminology mapping

LOOP-SCHEDULING CLAUSE	CUDA
`gang`	Thread block
`worker`	y-dimensional threads
`vector`	x-dimensional threads

```
#pragma acc loop gang worker vector
for(i=c; i<iend; i++){

    ...

}
```

(a) Scheduling p-gwv

```
init=blockIdx.x*blockDim.x*blockDim.y +
    threadIdx.y*blockDim.x + threadIdx.x+c;
istep = gridDim.x * blockDim.x*blockDim.y;
for(i=init; i<iend; i+=istep){

    ...

}
```

(b) Scheduling p-gwv in CUDA

Figure 11.11 Single-loop transformation in a parallel region

Kernels Loop Scheduling

From the OpenACC language perspective, the kernels construct is a descriptive approach that allows the compiler to perform loop analysis and generate efficient GPU code without burdening the programmer. We have explored other potential loop-scheduling strategies in the compiler in order to exploit better mapping techniques of given code to the GPU. In the parallel construct, the model can create only one-dimensional grid and two-dimensional thread blocks. To take advantage of multidimensional grid and thread blocks in the NVIDIA and AMD GPUs, we propose kernels loop-scheduling strategies to efficiently distribute loop iterations in an

OpenACC kernels region. In our rules, both `gang` and `vector` can appear only at most one time in the same level of loop. Or users can leave loop-scheduling clauses empty and let the compiler generate suitable loop scheduling for the nested loops.

Table 11.2 lists our six proposed OpenACC clauses and shows how they map to corresponding CUDA descriptions for the `kernels` directive. These new clauses can guide the compiler to create multiple-dimensional thread topologies.[10]

Table 11.2 OpenACC and CUDA terminology mapping in the kernels construct

OPENACC CLAUSE	CUDA DESCRIPTION
gangx	Block in x dimension of grid
gangy	Block in y dimension of grid
gangz	Block in z dimension of grid
vectorx	Threads in x dimension of block
vectory	Threads in y dimension of block
vectorz	Threads in z dimension of block

The example in Figure 11.12(a) shows the loop-scheduling `gangy vectory` for the outer loop, and `gangx vectorx` for the inside of the loop. The translated CUDA version (Figure 11.12(b)) follows Equations 11.1 and 11.2. In this loop scheduling, `gang` and `vector` are two dimensions that the parallel loop scheduling cannot do. After the mapping, the outer loop thread stride is `gridDim.y * blockDim.y`, and the inner loop thread stride is `gridDim.x * blockDim.x`.

$$
init : iinit = \begin{cases} blockIdx.\,x \mid y \mid z + c & gangx \mid y \mid z \\ threadIdx.\,x \mid y \mid z + c & vectorx \mid y \mid z \\ blockIdx.\,x \mid y \mid z * blockDim.x \mid y \mid z \\ \quad + threadIdx.x \mid y \mid z + c & gangx \mid y \mid z \ \ vectorx \mid y \mid z \end{cases}
$$

Equation 11.1

$$
incre : istep = \begin{cases} gridDim.\,x \mid y \mid z & gangx \mid y \mid z \\ blockDim.\,x \mid y \mid z & vectorx \mid y \mid z \\ gridDim.\,x \mid y \mid z * blockDim.x \mid y \mid z & gangx \mid y \mid z \ \ vectorx \mid y \mid z \end{cases}
$$

Equation 11.2

---

10. For a detailed description of Table 11.2 and the mapping strategies, see J. Zhang et al., "Extreme-Scale Phase Field Simulations of Coarsening Dynamics on the Sunway Taihu-Light Supercomputer," cited earlier.

```
#pragma acc loop gangy vectory
for(i=c1; i<iend; i++){
  #pragma acc loop gangx vectorx
  for(j=c2; j<jend; j++){
    ...
  }
}
```

```
iinit = blockIdx.y * blockDim.y+threadIdx.y+c1;
istep = gridDim.y * blockDim.y;
jinit = blockIdx.x * blockDim.x+threadIdx.x+c2;
jstep = gridDim.x * blockDim.x ;
for (i=iinit; i<iend; i+=istep) {
  for (j=jinit; j<jend; j+=jstep ) {
    ......
  }
}
```

(a) Scheduling k-gyvy-gxvx   (b) Scheduling k-gyvy-gxvx in CUDA

Figure 11.12 An example of double-nested loop transformation with new loop-scheduling clauses
Note: (a) Original loop scheduling k-$gyvy$-$gxvx$ with clauses; (b) Generated CUDA version of loop.

Current OpenACC compilers do not offer a variety of loop-scheduling strategies that several real applications may benefit from. The six proposed clauses address this limitation as well as the one discussed earlier in the parallel scheduling section. With the proposed scheduling strategies, either compiler middle-end can provide enough search space to support tuning of performance, or expert users can explicitly specify appropriate loop scheduling for the nested loops in their program.

We have chosen to introduce these six clauses within the kernels construct because this technique allows the compiler to analyze and automatically parallelize loops as well as select the best loop-scheduling strategy. So far, OpenUH requires the user to explicitly specify these loop schedules, but in the future we plan to automate this work in the compiler so that the programmer does not need to worry about the choice of the loop-scheduling strategy. Another issue lies with the barrier operation in kernels computation regions. For example, if the `reduction` is used in the inner loop of scheduling-gv-gv, it would require synchronization across thread blocks, and such synchronization is not supported in the AMD or NVIDIA GPU. In this situation, the work-around is to use parallel loop scheduling.

11.2.3 PERFORMANCE EVALUATION OF LOOP SCHEDULING

The experimental platform we used has an Intel Xeon E5-2698 processor and 256GB main memory. Attached to this machine are the NVIDIA Kepler GPU card (K80) with 12GB global memory, and the Pascal GPU card (P100) with 16GB HBM2 global memory. The CUDA 8.0 SDK is used to compile the generated GPU kernels for OpenUH. OpenUH uses the following flag to compile the given OpenACC program:

```
-fopenacc -nvcc,-arch=sm_35
```

The flags following -nvcc are passed to the CUDA 8.0 `nvcc` compiler. We use `sm_35` for the Kepler architecture. When targeting Pascal P100, `sm_60` is used.

Matrix multiplication (see Figure 11.13 and the stencil-like Laplacian benchmarks in Figure 11.14) is used to demonstrate the performance difference among various loop-scheduling methods. The two benchmarks are simple and easy to understand, with only a single kernel within each benchmark. The matrix size is 8,192×8,192 (see Table 11.3), and its kernel is executed only one time. The Laplacian data size is 256×256×256, and its kernel is iterated more than 20,000 times.

```
01 #pragma acc kernels loop gangy((n+1)/2) vectory(2)
02 for (i = 0; i < n; i++)  {
03    #pragma acc loop gangx((n+127)/128) vectorx(128)
04    for (j = 0; j < n; j++)   {
05       c = 0.0f;
06       for (k = 0; k < n; k++)
07          c += A[i * n + k] * B[k * n + j];
08       C[i * n + j] = c;
09    }
10 }
```

Figure 11.13 Matrix multiplication kernels with double nested loop parallelism

Note: Only the two outer loops are parallelized; the innermost loop is executed sequentially. In this code, the compiler creates a two-dimensional grid as well as a two-dimensional thread block; each thread block has 256 threads in total. Loop-scheduling clauses can be replaced with other combinations.

```
01 #pragma acc kernels loop gangx(ns-2)
02 for (k = 1; k < ns - 1; k++)  {
03    #pragma acc loop gangy(ny-2)
04    for (j = 1; j < ny - 1; j++)   {
05       #pragma acc loop vectorx(256)
06       for (i = 1; i < nx - 1; i++)     {
07          _A(w1, i, j, k) = alpha * _A(w0, i, j, k) + beta * (
08             _A(w0, i+1, j, k) + _A(w0, i-1, j, k) +
09             _A(w0, i, j+1, k) + _A(w0, i, j-1, k) +
10             _A(w0, i, j, k+1) + _A(w0, i, j, k-1));
11       }
12    }
14 }
```

Figure 11.14 Stencil-like Laplacian kernels with triple nested loop parallelism

Note: Loop scheduling is `gy-gx-vx`; A is a macro that defines the array offset calculation; the `alpha` and `beta` variables are constant in this kernel. The i loop is always mapped on x-dimension threads in order to keep memory access coalesced.

Table 11.3 Benchmarks and their data size

BENCHMARKS	DATA SIZE
Matrix multiplication	8,192×8,192
Laplacian	256×256×256

Figure 11.13 shows simple kernel code of **matrix multiplication** (MM). MM has double nested parallelized loops. The B and C arrays accessed from the inner loop j are contiguous memory access, whereas they are noncontiguous when accessed from the outer loop. The inner loop j uses vector parallelism, and this means that the threads executing the inner loop are consecutive with maximal memory access coalesced.

Figure 11.14 gives a Laplacian kernel example, which is a typical stencil application. The Laplacian example shows a triple nested loop, which can support more loop-scheduling combinations. In the Laplacian example, the data accessed in the innermost loop i are consecutive in memory. To achieve better performance, memory access must be coalesced. So the innermost loop i is mapped to vectorx.

In terms of the performance comparison, Figures 11.15 and 11.16 show the following for the NVIDIA K80 architecture.

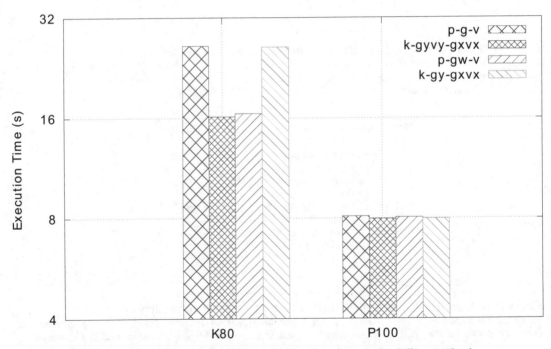

Figure 11.15 Matrix multiplication performance with various loop-scheduling methods
Note: k *means OpenACC kernels region;* p *means OpenACC parallel region;* gx, gy, *and* gz *are short for* gangx, gangy, *and* gangz. *Also note that* vx, vy, *and* vz *are short for* vectorx, vectory, *and* vectorz; *and* g, w, *and* v *represent the* gang, worker, *and* vector *clauses in the OpenACC parallel region.*

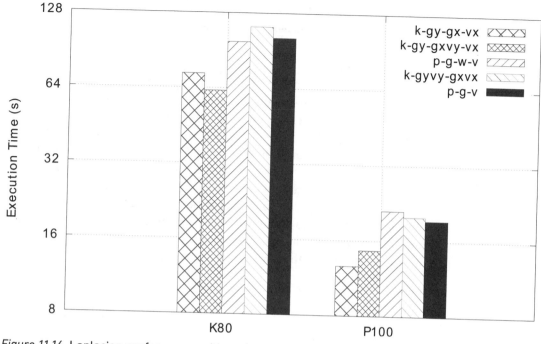

Figure 11.16 Laplacian performance with various loop-scheduling methods

Note: k means OpenACC kernels region; p represents OpenACC parallel region; and k-gx-vy-vx is the same as p-g-w-v. Also, k-gx-vx, which is the same as p-g-v, parallelizes only the loop j and loop i, with loop i running sequentially.

- The extended loop scheduling can help improve performance in our matrix multiplication example.

- The k-gyvy-gxvx loop scheduling demonstrates significant performance improvement compared with the parallel loop scheduling.

- The Laplacian kernel also benefits from k-gy-gx-vx and k-gy-gxvy-vx.

However, for NVIDIA's P100 target,[11] the various loop schedules show little to no difference in the MM example.

To improve performance portability across various GPU generations will require further research. There are many factors affecting performance, with loop scheduling directly impacting how data are accessed and how loop parallelism is exposed to the

---

11. https://images.nvidia.com/content/pdf/tesla/whitepaper/pascal-architecture
-whitepaper.pdf.

hardware. The compiler can build a heuristic cost model in the loop nest optimization phase to help identify the optimal loop scheduling for a particular target.

11.2.4 OTHER RESEARCH TOPICS IN OPENUH

Because it is tedious and time consuming to find an optimal loop-scheduling method for each kernel, especially when you are working with a relatively large application having many kernels, we propose an analytical model-based auto-tuning framework to identify an optimal or suboptimal loop schedule that is better than the default loop schedule chosen by the compiler. The framework model is **locality aware** in that it can predict the cache locality for each loop schedule. The model also predicts the total number of global memory loads, which it uses to ascertain the memory-access cost of each loop schedule. Overall, the framework iterates over all loop-scheduling patterns, launches a configuration space, and picks the loop schedule with the lowest memory-access cost.

We analyzed the proposed framework using multiple benchmarks. The results indicate that memory-access cost modeling has a strong correlation with kernel performance, and the loop schedule picked by the framework can achieve 1.29× speedup over the default loop schedule chosen by the compiler.[12]

Poor locality of memory access leads to inefficient use of processing capabilities. This direct relation is exacerbated when you are faced with deep memory hierarchies in GPUs. We adopt classic data flow analysis to utilize the read-only data cache as well as register file optimization. The compiler may not find optimal solutions; in these cases, the user can use a proposed data clause to identify the read-only data, and the compiler determines from this where the data should

---

12. Xiaonan Tian, "A Compiler Optimization Framework for Directive-based GPU Computing," cited earlier.

be placed.[13,14,15] We extend the scalar replacement algorithm to OpenACC offload regions. The new algorithm combines latency cost model and register information feedback from lower-level vendors' tools to guide the scalar replacement.[16,17]

13. Rengan Xu, Xiaonan Tian, Yonghong Yan, Sunita Chandrasekaran, and Barbara Chapman, "Reduction Operations in Parallel Loops for GPGPUs," in *2014 International Workshop on Programming Models and Applications for Multicores and Manycores (PMAM 2014)*, Orlando, FL (February 2014): 10:10–10:20.

14. Xiaonan Tian, Rengan Xu, Yonghong Yan, Zhifeng Yun, Sunita Chandrasekaran, and Barbara Chapman, "Compiling a High-Level Directive-based Programming Model for Accelerators," in *26th International Workshop on Languages and Compilers for High Performance Computing (LCPC 2013)*, Santa Clara, CA (September 2013): 105–120.

15. Xiaonan Tian, Rengan Xu, Yonghong Yan, Sunita Chandrasekaran, Deepak Eachempati, and Barbara Chapman, "Compiler Transformation of Nested Loops for GPGPUs," in *Concurrency and Computation: Practice and Experience, Special Issue on Programming Models and Applications for Multicores and Manycore* (2015): 537–556.

16. Xiaonan Tian, Dounia Khaldi, Deepak Eachempati, Rengan Xu, and Barbara Chapman, "Optimizing GPU Register Usage: Extensions to OpenACC and Compiler Optimizations," in *Proceedings of 2016 45th International Conference on Parallel Processing (ICPP 2016)*, Philadelphia, PA (August 2016): 572–581.

17. Rengan Xu, Sunita Chandrasekaran, Xiaonan Tian, and Barbara Chapman, "An Analytical Model-based Auto-tuning Framework for Locality-aware Loop Scheduling," in *Proceedings of 2016 International Supercomputing Conference (ISC 2016)*, Frankfurt, Germany (June 2016): 3–20.

Chapter 12

Innovative Research Ideas Using OpenACC, Part II

This chapter serves as Part II of the discussion of innovative research ideas using OpenACC begun in Chapter 11. In Section 12.1, Seeyong Lee, a research scientist from Oak Ridge National Laboratory (ORNL), presents a programming framework based on OpenACC for high-performance computing targeting reconfigurable computing on field-programmable gate arrays.

In Section 12.2, Jinpil Lee, a scientist from Riken, Japan, describes an OpenACC programming interface in the Omni compiler infrastructure to develop applications on accelerator cluster systems.

12.1 A Framework for Directive-Based High-Performance Reconfigurable Computing

Seeyong Lee, Oak Ridge National Laboratory

This section presents a directive-based, high-level programming framework for high-performance reconfigurable computing on field-programmable gate arrays (FPGAs).[1] Our programming framework takes a standard, portable OpenACC

---

1. This material is a modified version of the author's previously published paper: Seyong Lee, Jungwon Kim, and Jeffrey S. Vetter, "OpenACC to FPGA: A Framework for Directive-based High-Performance Reconfigurable Computing," *30th IEEE International Parallel & Distributed Processing Symposium (IPDPS)* (2016).

C-language program as input and generates a hardware configuration file for execution on FPGAs.

The prototype system is built on top of Open Accelerator Research Compiler (OpenARC), an open source OpenACC compiler; it performs source-to-source translation and optimization of the input OpenACC program into OpenCL code, which is further compiled into an FPGA program by the back-end Altera Offline OpenCL compiler.[2]

Internally, the design of OpenARC uses a high-level intermediate representation that separates concerns of program representation from underlying architectures, a design that facilitates portability of OpenARC. In fact, this design allowed creating the OpenACC-to-FPGA translation framework with minimal extensions to the existing system.

In addition, we present some novel OpenACC pragma extensions and an FPGA-specific compiler optimization, which annotates the code so that the compiler can generate more efficient FPGA hardware configuration files.

We demonstrate the benefit of the proposed strategy by porting eight OpenACC benchmarks to an Altera Stratix V FPGA. The portability of OpenACC is also demonstrated as these same benchmarks are compiled to run on other heterogeneous platforms, including NVIDIA GPUs, AMD GPUs, and Intel Xeon Phi processors.

Hopefully, the empirical evidence we present will help you understand the potential of directive-based, high-level programming strategy for performance portability across heterogeneous HPC architectures.

12.1.1 INTRODUCTION

Future exascale supercomputers will need to satisfy numerous criteria: high performance on mission applications, wide flexibility to serve a diverse application workload, efficient power usage, effective reliability, and reasonable cost. Heterogeneous computing with GPUs and Xeon Phis has recently become a popular solution to this challenge. However, the preceding exascale architectural criteria must be balanced against the user-driven goals of portable, productive development of software and applications. Many applications, such as climate model simulations, are being actively developed (e.g., improved) and will execute on dozens of different architectures over their lifetimes. Consequently, many scientists have opted to postpone porting their applications to these heterogeneous architectures until a single portable programming solution exists.

---

2. https://www.altera.com/en_US/pdfs/literature/rn/rn_aocl.pdf.

Reconfigurable computers, such as FPGAs, have had a long history of offering both performance and energy efficiency advantages for specific workloads compared to other heterogeneous systems.

An FPGA is an integrated circuit (IC) that can be reconfigured by a customer multiple times in the field. FPGAs contain an array of programmable logic blocks that can be wired together by a set of reconfigurable interconnects. Logic blocks may also include memory elements such as simple flip-flops or more complex memory blocks.

The FPGA configuration is generally specified using hardware description languages (HDLs) such as VHDL and Verilog. Together, the configured logic blocks perform specific types of computations. FPGA chips, primarily from Xilinx and Altera, are often at the forefront of technology available on the market, and they make use of the latest process feature sizes, highest-performance IO and transceivers, and most effective memory subsystems. Furthermore, manufacturers offer reconfigurable systems, such as the Altera Arria 10, in a wide array of configurations that include the tight integration of the systems' custom reconfigurable logic with hard IP processors (e.g., ARM Cortex-A9) into a system-on-a-chip (SoC).

Nevertheless, FPGAs have traditionally suffered several disadvantages that have limited their deployment in large-scale HPC systems. From our perspective, the most significant challenges are programmability and portability. Many projects have explored the complexity of mapping source-code-level control and data to FPGAs. However, synthesizing the logic and balancing the flexible resources offered by the FPGA with those requested by the application create additional complexity. This often requires an iterative approach, which can lead to long compilation delays and even more complexity.

Aware of this challenge, FPGA vendors have recently introduced the OpenCL programming system for their FPGA platforms. This new level of abstraction hides some complexity while providing a new level of widespread portability not offered by earlier approaches. Still, many users consider the OpenCL programming system as too low a level of abstraction for their large, complex applications. In this regard, this section introduces a preliminary implementation of an OpenACC compiler that compiles and builds applications for the Altera Stratix V FPGA using the Altera OpenCL programming system.

12.1.2 BASELINE TRANSLATION OF OPENACC-TO-FPGA

Let's look at the intermediate language for the mapping process and the translation strategy in this section.

High-Level-Representation-based, Functionally Portable OpenACC Translation

The baseline OpenACC-to-FPGA translation framework is based on OpenARC. OpenARC performs a source-to-source translation of an input OpenACC C program into an output CUDA or OpenCL program, which is further compiled by appropriate back-end compilers. OpenARC uses a high-level, architecture-independent intermediate representation, called HeteroIR, as an intermediate language to map high-level programming models (such as OpenACC) to diverse heterogeneous devices while maintaining functional portability. HeteroIR fills the semantic gap between the OpenACC program and the target architectures by encapsulating the common accelerator operations into high-level function calls. During application execution, these function calls are orchestrated on the target architecture by the runtime system.

HeteroIR constructs can be broadly classified into four distinct categories:

1. Configuration constructs

2. Compute constructs

3. Memory constructs

4. Synchronization constructs

A host CPU will execute these HeteroIR constructs to control a target device. (Note that accelerator kernels are not a part of the HeteroIR.) Listing 12.2 is example HeteroIR code that is translated from the OpenACC code in Listing 12.1. (Listing 12.2 represents only the host code.)

Listing 12.1 Matrix multiplication (MM) in OpenACC

```
 1: #pragma acc kernels loop gang worker (workers) \
 2:                     copyout (C[0:M][0:N] \
 3:                     copyin (A[0:M][0:P], B[0:P][0:N])
 4: for (i=0; i<M; i++) {
 5:     for (j=0; j<N; j++) {
 6:         float sum = 0.0f;
 7:         for (k=0; k<P; k++) { sum += A[i][k] * B[k][j]; }
 8:         C[i][j] = sum;
 9:     }
10: }
```

Listing 12.2 HeteroIR code for MM program in Listing 12.1 (host code only)

```
 1: float *C, *B, *A, *devC, *devB, *devA;
 2: HI_set_device(HI_device_type_default, 0);
 3: HI_init();
 4: . . .
```

```
 5: HI_malloc(C, &devC, M*N*sizeof(float));
 6: HI_malloc(B, &devB, P*N*sizeof(float));
 7: HI_malloc(A, &devA, M*P*sizeof(float));
 8: HI_memcpy(A, devA, M*P*sizeof(float), DEFAULT_QUEUE);
 9: HI_memcpy(B, devB, P*N*sizeof(float), DEFAULT_QUEUE);
10: HI_register_kernel_arg("kernel_0", &devC, 0, sizeof(void*));
11: HI_register_kernel_arg("kernel_0", &devA, 1, sizeof(void*));
12: HI_register_kernel_arg("kernel_0", &devB, 2, sizeof(void*));
13: HI_register_kernel_arg("kernel_0", &M, 3, sizeof(int));
14: HI_register_kernel_arg("kernel_0", &N, 4, sizeof(int));
15: HI_register_kernel_arg("kernel_0", &P, 5, sizeof(int));
16: int dimGrid_kernel_0[3] = {(int)ceil(((float)M)/workers),1, 1};
17: int dimBlock_kernel_0[3] = {workers, 1, 1};
18: HI_kernel_call("kernel_0",dimGrid_kernel_0, dimBlock_kernel_0,\\
19:                DEFAULT_QUEUE);
20: HI_memcpy(devC, C, M*N*sizeof(float), DEFAULT_QUEUE);
21: ...
22: HI_shutdown();
```

Figure 12.1 shows the overall OpenARC system architecture; the OpenARC compiler translates an input OpenACC program into host code that contains HeteroIR constructs and device-specific kernel code. With the help of complementary runtime systems (e.g., CUDA driver for NVIDIA GPUs, OpenCL runtime for AMD GPUs, or Intel Xeon Phis), the host code and related kernel code can be executed on any supported architecture.

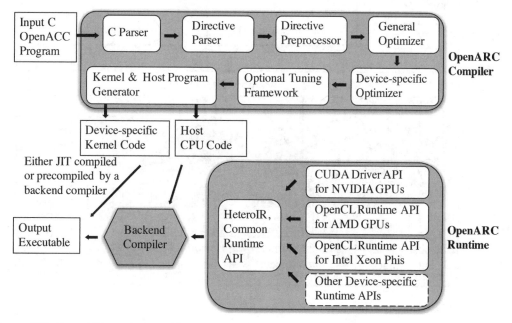

Figure 12.1 OpenARC system architecture

OpenACC-to-FPGA Translation

OpenARC supports both CUDA and OpenCL as output programming models. To port OpenACC to FPGAs, we use OpenCL as the output model, and the Altera Offline compiler (AOC) as its back-end compiler. We use the same HeteroIR runtime system of the existing OpenCL back ends, and most of the compiler passes for the kernel generation are also reused, thanks to their architecture-agnostic behaviors.

OpenCL is architecture independent, and thus the same OpenCL code generated for GPUs can be executed on FPGAs, being functionally portable. However, the unique features of an FPGA architecture necessitate customizing the OpenCL code to achieve performance portability. Figure 12.2 shows the FPGA OpenCL architecture. Each OpenCL kernel function is transformed into dedicated and deeply pipelined hardware circuits. Generated pipeline logics are connected to external memory via a global memory interconnect and to on-chip memory blocks through a specialized interconnect structure.

The key benefit of using FPGAs is that they support heterogeneous and deeply pipelined parallelism customized for an input program. In OpenCL-based,

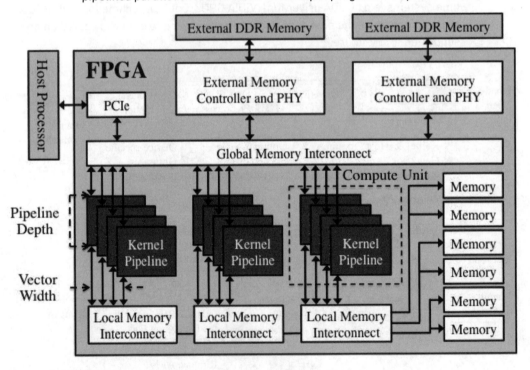

Figure 12.2 FPGA OpenCL architecture

high-level FPGA programming, the underlying OpenCL compiler synthesizes all the hardware logic for the input program, and thus the efficiency of the OpenCL compiler is critical for performance. Therefore, we extended the existing OpenCL generation passes of OpenARC to generate output OpenCL codes customized for the OpenCL compiler.

12.1.3 OPENACC EXTENSIONS AND OPTIMIZATION FOR EFFICIENT FPGA PROGRAMMING

Let's look into some of the extensions proposed to OpenACC to support FPGAs along with kernel pipelining strategies.

OpenACC Extension to Support Architecture-Specific Features

Kernel Configuration Boundary Check Elimination. In the OpenCL model, a kernel represents device code executed by each work item; each work item executes the same code, but the specific execution pathway through the kernel code can vary per work item.

When OpenARC translates an OpenACC compute region into a kernel, each iteration of the worker loop in the compute region is mapped to each work item. If the total number of workers in the region does not match the number of corresponding loop iterations, the kernel body should be conditionally executed so that only the work items with valid mapping can execute the kernel. Listing 12.3 shows such an example of kernel code, which is translated from the OpenACC code in Listing 12.1, with no optimizations enabled. The `if` statement in line 6 enforces the requirement that only the work items whose global ID is less than the upper bound of the outermost loop in Listing 12.1 (line 3 in Listing 12.1) execute the kernel. This approach prevents possible array-index-out-of-bounds errors.

Listing 12.3 Device kernel code for MM program of Listing 12.1 (unoptimized version)

```
 1: __attribute__((reqd_work_group_size(workers,1,1)))
 2: __kernel void kernel_0(__global float * C, __global float * A,
 3:                         __global float * B,
 4:                         int M, int N, int P) {
 5:     int i, j, k; i = get_global_id(0);
 6:     if (i < M) {
 7:         for (j = 0; j < N; j++) {
 8:             float sum = 0.0f;
 9:             for (k = 0; k < P; k++)
10:                 sum += A[i*P+k] * B[k*N+j];
11:             C[i*N+j] = sum;
12:     }
```

Listing 12.3 Device kernel code for MM program of Listing 12.1 (unoptimized version) (*continued*)

```
13:      }
14:      return;
15: }
```

Generally, diverging control paths of work items is less of an issue in FPGA programming compared with GPU programming, because the back-end AOC can eliminate diverging control paths of work items by collapsing simple conditional statements into single bits that indicate when an FPGA functional unit becomes active, resulting in a flat control structure. However, AOC cannot handle complex conditional structures and the work-item-ID-dependent backward branching, which involves looping structure. The kernel code that contains a nonflat control structure can cause significant performance penalty by disabling various compiler optimizations, including the kernel vectorization (explained in the next section).

In the earlier example translation (Listing 12.3), the OpenARC compiler had to add the `if` statement, because the number of iterations is a runtime variable. In this case, only the programmer (or the runtime) can resolve this issue. For this, we added a new directive and command-line option for programmers to inform the compiler whether it is safe to remove the conditional statements for a specific kernel or whole program. If guaranteed by programmers, OpenARC generates kernel code without the guarding statements, allowing opportunities for the underlying OpenCL compiler to perform more aggressive optimizations.

Directive Extension for Loop Unrolling, Kernel Vectorization, and Compute Unit Replication. In FPGA programming, deep pipelining is a primary method to increase throughput, but there exist three other important optimization techniques to maximize the performance of the OpenCL kernel: *loop unrolling, kernel vectorization,* and *compute unit replication.*

Loop unrolling decreases the number of iterations that the Altera back-end compiler executes, at the expense of increased consumption of hardware resources. The compiler expands the pipeline by the number of unroll factors specified, resulting in a deeper pipeline. In addition, the compiler further optimizes the kernel by coalescing the memory operations. To increase the number of parallel operations, the memory bandwidth, and the number of operations per clock cycle, we add a new loop unroll directive for users.

Kernel vectorization allows multiple work items in the same workgroup to execute in a single-instruction multiple-data (SIMD) fashion. The underlying Altera Offline compiler implements this vectorization by replicating the kernel datapaths; this allows SIMD operations to share control logic across each SIMD vector lane, and it might coalesce memory accesses.

Kernel vectorization is usually beneficial, but finding optimal SIMD width may require experimentation, because of its resource contention with other optimizations. The OpenACC `vector` clause provides similar effects, but its behavior is not the same as the kernel vectorization.

In the OpenACC execution model, vector lanes are executed in an SIMD manner only when the kernel is in the vector-partitioned mode. However, in kernel vectorization, the whole kernel is executed in an SIMD mode, and SIMD vector lanes exercise a strict vectorization (vector lanes execute in a lockstep manner), although not all vector lanes in the OpenACC model may execute synchronously. (The vector width in the OpenACC `vector` clause provides a hint for optimal vectorization; the vector lanes may be executed as a set of SIMD operations with a narrower width, if necessary.) Therefore, to enable high-level control over this optimization, we add a new directive to allow users to specify the SIMD width of a specific kernel.

The **compute unit replication** optimization generates multiple compute units for each kernel, and the hardware scheduler in the FPGA dispatches workgroups to additional available compute units. Increasing the number of compute units can achieve higher throughput. However, it will also increase the bandwidth requests to the global memory because of memory-access contention among the compute units. Like kernel vectorization, this optimization also increases hardware resource utilization, and thus you need to balance between these optimizations to achieve optimal performance. For this, we also add a new directive and command-line option to control this optimization.

Kernel-Pipelining Transformation

In the OpenACC model, device kernels can communicate with each other only through the device global memory, and synchronizations between kernels are at the granularity of a kernel execution; no mechanism exists to synchronize actively running kernels in a fine-grained manner. Therefore, for a kernel to communicate with other kernels, the involved kernels should be split into multiple subkernels at each communication point, and the data transfer should be done via the global memory in a sequential manner, as shown in Figure 12.3(a). However, launching or synchronizing kernels requires host involvement, incurring non-negligible overhead, and the limited bandwidth and long latency of the global memory may degrade overall performance significantly.

To address this issue, the underlying AOCL provides a mechanism, called **channels,** for passing data to kernels and synchronizing kernels with high efficiency and low latency. The channels extension allows kernels to directly communicate with each other via a FIFO buffer (Figure 12.3(b)), decoupling the kernel execution from the host.

Listing 12.4(a) is example OpenACC code showing the global memory-access pattern in Figure 12.3(a), where `kernel0` and `kernel1` are executed in sequential order, and array b is used as a temporary buffer to send the output of `kernel0` to `kernel1`. Listing 12.4(c) shows example OpenCL code that utilizes the channel mechanism for `kernel0` to directly transfer its output to `kernel1` without using the global memory, as shown in Figure 12.3(b). In Listing 12.4(c), the channel variable (`pipe_b`) is accessed via special functions (`write_channel_altera()` and `read_channel_altera()`), which are blocking calls, and thus channel calls offer implicit synchronization between a producer kernel (`kernel0`) and a consumer kernel (`kernel1`).

As shown earlier, pipelining kernels using channel variables as FIFO buffers allows you to bypass global memory accesses and fine-grained synchronizations between kernels. To enable this fancy mechanism in OpenACC while maintaining portability, we propose a set of new data clauses: `pipe`, `pipein`, and `pipeout`. A `pipe` clause is used in an OpenACC data construct, which replaces a `create` clause and indicates that the variables in the `pipe` clause are used as temporary device buffers for kernel communications, convertible to AOCL channel variables. `Pipein` and `pipeout` clauses are used in an OpenACC parallel or kernels constructs, which replace `present` clauses and indicate that the variables in the clause are read-only (`pipein`) or write-only (`pipeout`), and they are declared as channel variables in a `pipe` clause of an enclosing data region.

Listing 12.4(b) is a modified version of Listing 12.4(a), where array b is declared as a channel variable (the `pipe` clause in line 1 of Listing 12.4(b)), the first compute region writes the channel data (the `pipeout` clause in line 3), and the second compute region reads the channel data (the `pipein` clause in line 5). When you are targeting Altera FPGAs, OpenARC automatically transforms the code in Listing 12.4(b) into output OpenCL code with channels (Listing 12.4(c)) by converting the temporary buffer array b into a scalar channel variable (`pipe_b` in line 2 of Listing 12.4(c)) and changing the array accesses with special channel calls (lines 5 and 9). To enable concurrent execution of the pipelined kernels, OpenARC also modifies the host code to instantiate multiple command queues and assigns each kernel to separate queues. When targeting other devices without the channel support, OpenARC automatically reverts Listing 12.4(b) back to Listing 12.4(a), preserving functional portability.

Basically, if two or more kernels execute in sequential order and communicate with each other using temporary device buffers, these kernels can be pipelined using the channel variables, as shown in Listing 12.4. More precisely, for the pipelining transformation to preserve the original execution semantics, the following conditions should be met.

1. Kernels have sequential dependencies only in one direction; there are no dependency cycles among kernels.

2. Temporary device buffers used for kernel communications are accessed only by the involved kernels.

3. A kernel can either read or write (but not both) the same temporary buffer only once per loop iteration.

4. A consumer kernel should read a temporary buffer in the same order that the producer kernel writes the buffer.

OpenARC can detect kernels that satisfy these conditions to automate the pipelining transformation, but ensuring the same access order of a temporary buffer can be difficult if a kernel contains complex control flows. In this case, the proposed pipe clauses are used for users to inform the compiler which kernels can be pipelined.

Listing 12.4 Altera OpenCL (AOCL) channel example

```
                    (a) Input OpenACC code
1: #pragma acc data copyout(a[0:N]) create(b[0:N]) copyin(c[0:N])
2: {
3:    #pragma acc kernels loop gang worker present(b, c)
4:    for (i=0; i<N; i++) b[i] = c[i]*c[i];
5:    #pragma acc kernels loop gang worker present(a, b)
6:    for (i=0; i<N; i++) a[i] = b[i];
7: }
            (b) Modified OpenACC code for kernel pipelining
1: #pragma acc data copyout(a[0:N]) pipe(b[0:N]) copyin(c[0:N])
2: {
3: #pragma acc kernels loop gang worker pipeout(b) present(c)
4:     for (i=0; i<N; i++) b[i] = c[i]*c[i];
5: #pragma acc kernels loop gang worker pipein(b) present(a)
6:     for (i=0; i<N; i++) a[i] = b[i];
7: }
                (c) Output OpenCL code with channels
1: #pragma OPENCL EXTENSION cl_altera_channels : enable
2: channel float pipe__b;
3: __kernel void kernel0(__global float * c) {
4:   int i = get_global_id(0);
5:   write_channel_altera(pipe__b, (c[i]*c[i]));
6: }
7: __kernel void kernel1(__global float * a) {
```

Listing 12.4 Altera OpenCL (AOCL) channel example (*continued*)

```
8:    int i = get_global_id(0);
9:    a[i] = read_channel_altera(pipe__b);
10: }
```

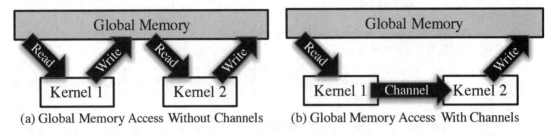

(a) Global Memory Access Without Channels   (b) Global Memory Access With Channels

Figure 12.3 Global memory-access pattern change by channel implementation

12.1.4 EVALUATION

This section presents the results and analysis of OpenACC translation to FPGAs.

Methodology

Target Device. We evaluated the proposed framework on an Altera Stratix V GS D5 FPGA, which consisted of 457K logic elements, 172,600 ALMs, 690K registers, 2,014 M20K memory blocks, and an 8GB DDR3 device memory. We used the Altera SDK for OpenCL 15.0 as its back-end compiler and runtime. For comparative tests, we used the Intel Xeon Phi coprocessor 5110P, the NVIDIA Tesla K40c GPU, and the AMD Radeon R9 290X GPU.

Benchmark Applications. We used eight OpenACC applications: NW, HotSpot, and SRAD from the Rodinia OpenCL benchmark suite; FFT-1D and FFT-2D from the Altera SDK for OpenCL; and Jacobi, MatMul, and SpMul from the OpenARC compiler suite. The OpenACC versions of the Rodina and Altera benchmarks are manually translated from their OpenCL versions.

Results

Worker Size. Figure 12.4 presents the performance effect of different worker sizes (workgroup sizes in OpenCL) on each application. We measured the application performance with worker sizes of 32, 128, and 512 on the Altera Stratix V GS D5 FPGA, the Intel Xeon Phi coprocessor 5110P, and the NVIDIA Tesla K40c GPU. For the AMD Radeon R9 290X GPU, we used a worker size of 256 instead of 512 because of the limit of the underlying AMD OpenCL framework. The figure indicates that the NVIDIA GPU was the most sensitive to the worker size. This is because the worker size in the GPU architecture affects hardware thread scheduling, which implicitly determines the occupancy, latency hiding, register spilling, and resultant multiprocessor utilization. These are the key factors affecting the overall performance of GPU applications.

On the other hand, Figure 12.4(a) shows that FPGA is the least sensitive to the worker size. Unlike GPUs and the Xeon Phi, FPGA transforms each kernel to a custom, deeply pipelined hardware circuit, in which a work item is clocked in on each clock cycle. If the pipeline depth is long enough, multiple workgroups can be present in the pipeline at the same time. In this case, the worker size will not affect overall performance, if no workgroup-related operations such as workgroup barriers exist.

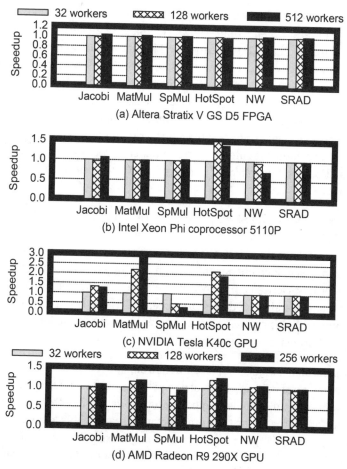

Figure 12.4 Performance variation depending on worker size
Note: The numbers on the y axis show the speedup over 32 workers.

Compute Unit Replication and Kernel Vectorization. Figure 12.5 shows the performance effect of replicating the compute units (CUs) and changing the SIMD width in the kernel vectorization on the tested FPGA.

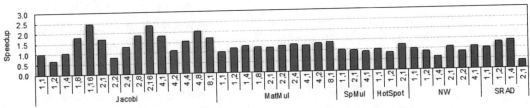

Figure 12.5 Speedup over CU, SIMD (1,1)
The numbers on the x axis represent the number of replicated CUs and SIMD widths (CU, SIMD).

The speedups in the figure are normalized to the performance of each application with 1 CU and 1 SIMD width. The worker sizes of all kernels are set to 128. In the FPGA architecture, CU replication and kernel vectorization achieve higher throughput by, respectively, executing multiple workgroups concurrently on the available CUs and allowing multiple work items to execute in an SIMD fashion. The figure shows that Jacobi and MatMul perform better with increases in CUs and SIMD, although their best configurations differ. They have no work-item-dependent control-flow divergence, and they perform regular memory accesses. These characteristics allow the Altera Offline compiler to vectorize their kernels and replicate CUs, resulting in higher performance than the base version (1 CU and 1 SIMD width).

However, SpMul and SRAD perform more poorly with multiple CUs. This is mainly due to their irregular memory accesses, which incur suboptimal bandwidth utilization and become worse by replicating CUs. On the other hand, HotSpot and NW show performance enhancement with multiple CUs. However, they perform worse with kernel vectorization. HotSpot and NW have many work-item-dependent control-flow divergences and strided memory accesses. These make kernel vectorization and memory coalescing inefficient and complex, incurring lower performance and higher hardware resource consumption.

Loop Unrolling. Figure 12.6(a) demonstrates the performance impact of the loop unrolling on Jacobi and MatMul. We set the unroll factors to 4 and 8, and we compared them with the original, no-unroll version. Both Jacobi and MatMul show better performance as the unroll factor increases. This is because the loop unrolling expands the pipeline, thereby allowing more work items to run at the same time. Moreover, it enables the coalescing memory operations from global memory, resulting in higher bandwidth.

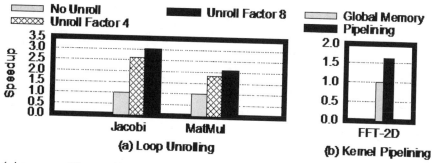

Figure 12.6 Loop unrolling and kernel pipelining

Kernel Pipelining. Figure 12.6(b) shows the speedup of FFT-2D when the kernel pipelining is applied. The baseline version (*Global Memory* in the figure) uses global memory to transfer data between kernels. The optimized version (*Pipelining* in the figure) exploits our kernel pipelining extension. The kernel pipelining increases data transfer efficiency between kernels by communicating directly with FIFO buffers. Moreover, it enables the concurrent multiple kernel execution on the FPGA with fine-grained synchronizations between kernels, bringing higher throughput. The figure shows that the pipelining version achieves about a 60 percent performance improvement over the baseline version.

Overall Performance. Figure 12.7 compares the overall performance of the tested OpenACC benchmarks on each target accelerator.

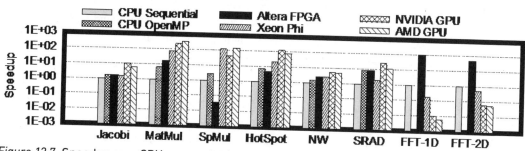

Figure 12.7 Speedup over CPU sequential (CPU: Intel Xeon E5520 octacore)

These results indicate that the performance behavior of FPGAs differs from that of GPUs and Xeon Phi: specifically, GPUs prefer applications with massive parallelism (e.g., Jacobi, MatMul, SpMul, HotSpot, and SRAD), but FPGAs prefer applications with deep execution pipelines (e.g., FFT-1D and FFT-2D). For example, FFT-1D is a sequential program with deeply pipelined instructions. Being sequential, FFT-1D is not suitable for traditional accelerators with massively parallel computational units. However, FPGAs can build deeply pipelined hardware customized to the input program, and thus FFT-1D (and FFT-2D, which is parallel) can perform much better on FPGAs than other accelerators and CPUs.

For traditional HPC applications with abundant parallel floating-point operations, the results imply that it will be difficult for FPGAs to outperform other accelerators such as GPUs, even though FPGAs can be more power efficient. This is because GPUs are equipped with fully optimized hardware units for floating-point operations, running at a higher clock frequency, whereas the tested FPGA (Stratix V) does not contain dedicated floating-point cores. (The performance gaps are more pronounced in the evaluation, because the tested FPGA is a middle-class product whereas other accelerators are high-end versions.) The current and upcoming high-end FPGAs, such as the Altera Stratix 10, are equipped with hardened floating-point units, which will offer much higher floating-point performance than that of the tested FPGAs with synthesized floating-point units. We expect that the performance of high-end FPGAs will be comparable to other accelerators while remaining power efficient.

12.1.5 SUMMARY

A directive-based, high-level programming system for high-performance reconfigurable computing is built on top of an existing OpenACC compiler called OpenARC. OpenARC's high-level abstraction allowed us to easily port the OpenACC programming model to heterogeneous reconfigurable architectures such as FPGAs, with minimal extensions to the existing OpenACC framework. Porting eight OpenACC benchmarks onto four representative accelerator architectures (FPGAs, NVIDIA GPUs, AMD GPUs, and Xeon Phis) demonstrates the functional portability of OpenACC.

Preliminary evaluation of the OpenACC benchmarks on an FPGA and a comparison against GPUs and a Xeon Phi show that the unique capability of an FPGA to generate custom hardware units dedicated to an input program offers a great many performance tuning opportunities. Especially, the reconfigurability of existing hardware resources in FPGAs exposes a new type of tradeoff between the hardware resources versus throughput, such as compute unit replication, kernel vectorization, resource sharing, heterogeneous memory support, loop unrolling, streaming channels, and the like. Utilizing these features to exploit high-performance reconfigurable computing as a possible energy-efficient HPC solution will be an interesting research topic.

12.2 Programming Accelerated Clusters Using XcalableACC

Jinpil Lee, RIKEN

In this section, we introduce **XcalableACC (XACC)**,[3] a parallel programming model to program multiple accelerators in a distributed memory environment. XACC is a part of a research project at the RIKEN Advanced Institute for Computational Science (AICS) and the University of Tsukuba. The directives are implemented in the Omni compiler.[4]

Modern supercomputers consist of multiple compute nodes that have dedicated processing units and memory modules. To build a fast supercomputer, an enormous number of nodes are connected via an interconnection network. To exploit the potential performance of the system, the user should use multiple compute nodes in parallel. MPI is a standard programming model to describe such parallelism. However, because of its library-based programming model, data distribution and transfer between nodes should be done manually.

XcalableMP (XMP)[5] is a programming language to describe parallel processing on supercomputers. It extends the C and Fortran languages with directives. Directives are comments in the base language specifying parallelism in the source code, including data distribution and loop iteration mapping onto nodes. The user can add XMP directives into the serial code to parallelize the code. The compiler will generate the parallel program from the XMP source code. This incremental approach makes parallel programming much easier than writing parallel programs from scratch. Thus, XMP improves the productivity of parallel programming on supercomputers.

---

3. Masahiro Nakao, Hitoshi Murai, Takenori Shimosaka, Akihiro Tabuchi, Toshihiro Hanawa, Yuetsu Kodama, Taisuke Boku, and Mitsuhisa Sato, "XcalableACC: Extension of XcalableMP PGAS Language Using OpenACC for Accelerator Clusters," Workshop on Accelerator Programming Using Directives (WACCPD) (New Orleans, LA, November 2014).
4. Omni XcalableMP Web site, http://www.xcalablemp.org/.
5. Jinpil Lee and Mitsuhisa Sato, "Implementation and Performance Evaluation of XcalableMP: A Parallel Programming Language for Distributed Memory Systems," *39th International Conference on Parallel Processing Workshops* (ICPPW10) (San Diego, CA; September 2010): 413–420.

XMP provides directives to describe internode parallelism on a cluster system. However, because of the lack of language constructs to describe inner-node parallelism, XMP does not exploit manycore accelerators available on modern clusters.

The primary solution is to use OpenACC with XMP. However, the current XMP specification (version 1.2) does not define a behavior when you mix XMP and OpenACC directives in the same code. Thus, we have been designing the new programming model XACC as a hybrid programming model using XMP and OpenACC directives. In addition, XACC extends the XMP directives to improve productivity and performance by integrating internode and inner-node parallelism in the same programming model. Although this section provides sample code written in C, the XACC model also supports Fortran.

12.2.1 INTRODUCTION TO XCALABLEMP

XMP has two programming models to describe parallelism on a distributed memory system. One approach is to use a directive-based programming model, named *global view*; the other approach, *local view*, uses coarrays. Because XACC extends the global view model with new directives, we explain XMP global view directives before we go to XACC. Listing 12.5 shows example code for XMP written in C. Without XMP global view directives, the code is sequential C code so that it can be compiled by any compilers (such as GCC and LLVM), and the binary runs sequentially. The XMP global view model allows incremental parallelism from sequential code. But this is not true when the user uses the local view model, which extends the language syntax in C and Fortran (e.g., coarray and subarray references).

Listing 12.5 XcalableMP example code in C

```
int A[YMAX][XMAX];
#pragma xmp nodes p(XPROCS, YPROCS)
#pragma xmp template t(XMAX,YMAX)
#pragma xmp distribute t(block, block) onto p
#pragma xmp align A[i][j] with t(j, i)

void main(void) {
    int sum = 0;
    #pragma xmp loop (i, j) on t(j, i) reduction (+:sum)
    for (int i = 0; i < YMAX; i++)
        for (int j = 0; j < XMAX; j++)
            sum += calc(A[i][j]);
}
```

The XcalableMP Execution Model

The execution model of XMP is **single-program multiple-data** (SPMD). Figure 12.8 shows the hardware model that XMP assumes. The XMP nodes have dedicated processors and memory and are connected to each other via a network. The nodes directive declares the executing node set. In Listing 12.5, a nodes directive declares a two-dimensional node set p, which has XPROCS×YPROCS nodes.

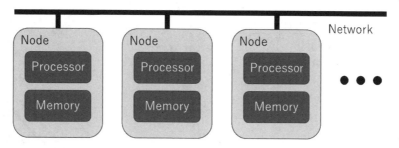

Figure 12.8 XcalableMP hardware model

Each node will execute the same program but modify different parts of the data according to the data parallelism described by the user. Data distribution in XMP is done by using a **template,** which is a virtual array representing global index space among the nodes. The template directive declares the virtual array. Because it is used to distribute array A, template t has the same shape (dimension and size). Template t is duplicated among nodes, and this means that every node in p has the ownership of every index in t.

Data Distribution and Work Mapping

The distribute directive is used to distribute index space among nodes. The data distribution process in XMP is shown in Figure 12.9. In Listing 12.5, the block specifier is used in the distribute directive, which specifies two-dimensional block distribution. As a result, the template is distributed into four chunks among node set p. After distributing the template, it is then used to distribute the data array. The align directive in Listing 12.5 specifies the data distribution. The meaning of the align directive is that each element in array a has the same owner, with its matching index in template t. Because the template is distributed among nodes, array A will be distributed in the same manner.

XMP requires loop work mapping to make a loop statement run in parallel. The loop construct in Listing 12.5 specifies that the following loop will be executed by the owners of template t. Because t is distributed among node p, the iteration

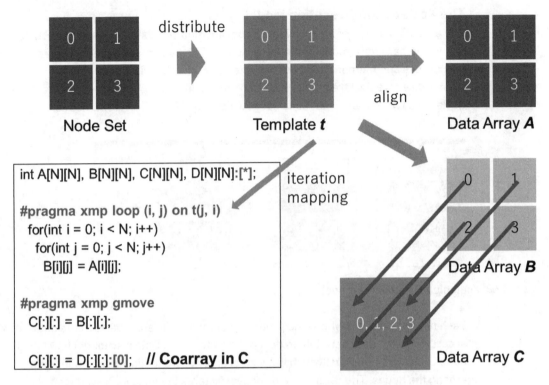

Figure 12.9 Data distribution and work mapping in XcalableMP

space will be distributed and run in parallel. One of the most important features in XMP is that it supports **explicit** parallelism. The compiler does not generate parallel loops or inter-node communication without any user description. All memory access refers to the node local memory. This is why we use a template both in data distribution and in loop work mapping. By using the same template, we can make the data distribution and loop work mapping access the same array index, something that leads to local memory access in a node. Figure 12.10 shows the matching process.

Internode Communication

As mentioned, all memory access in the code refers to the local memory. To access the remote node data, special language constructs should be described. Typical internode communications are provided in directive form. For example, reduction can be done in the `loop` construct by adding the `reduction` clause (Listing 12.5). Other collective communications, such as `broadcast` and `allgather`, are also supported in the global view model.

If a statement refers to a remote array element, the user can add a gmove directive to generate internode communication. Figure 12.8 shows an example. All of the array elements in B are copied to array C. Because array C is duplicated among nodes, it requires internode communication (allgather). The compiler generates allgather communication by using the information from the distribution descriptor of B. Without the gmove directive, the program will fail because it refers to unavailable elements in B.

A more explicit way to describe internode communication is by using a coarray. XMP extends the C language with the coarray dimension (co-dimension), and a statement is available in the Fortran 2008 specification. However, it belongs to the local view model, which is not covered in this section.

12.2.2 XCALABLEACC: XCALABLEMP MEETS OPENACC

OpenACC provides incremental parallelization of a sequential code by using directives. With multithreading programming models (such as OpenMP), OpenACC can be used to program multiple accelerators in a single machine. With MPI, OpenACC can be used to program clusters equipped with accelerators. However, hybrid programming in MPI and OpenACC is not straightforward. XACC provides a seamless interface connecting XMP's partitioned global address space (PGAS) model for cluster computing, and the OpenACC multithreading model for manycore computing.

The XcalableACC Memory Model

Figure 12.10 shows the memory model of XACC as well as the design concept of XACC. The OpenACC data section replicates a specified region on the host memory as well as explicitly controls data transfer between the host and accelerator memory. Because XACC is designed as an extension of OpenACC for distributed computing, all OpenACC directives can be specified in XACC code.

The major difference is that, in XACC, the OpenACC data section replicates a distributed chunk on PGAS memory space.

When a data directive specifies a distributed array (by XMP directives), a distributed chunk—including a communication buffer (e.g., XMP shadow region, illustrated in Figure 12.10 as white boxes)—will be replicated on the accelerator memory. As with XMP, internode communication between host memory will be done by XMP directives or coarray statements. XACC supports direct communication between accelerators by extending XMP communication features.

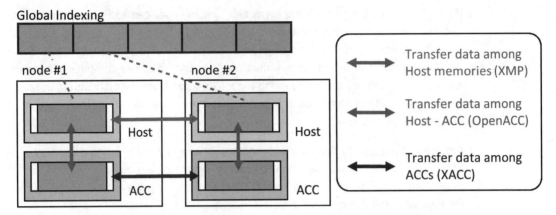

Figure 12.10 XcalableACC memory model

Programming with XcalableACC Directives

Listing 12.6 shows XACC example code written in C. The code is a simple two-dimensional, five-point stencil calculation. The data arrays, u and uu, are distributed by XMP directives. The arrays have *shadow* elements, because they need to access boundary elements that are allocated to other nodes. To get the correct data, an internode data exchange is required. This communication pattern can be specified by using the `reflect` directive.

Before the outermost loop, a `data` construct is specified. It replicates the host memory image on the accelerator memory. Because the arrays are distributed among nodes, the 2D block-distributed chunks (including shadow elements) are allocated on the accelerator memory. Finally, the array data in u and uu are copied from the host to the accelerator. At the end of the data region, the data in u are copied from the accelerator to the host. The data copy includes shadow elements.

OpenACC work-sharing directives can be written with the XMP `loop` directive. In Listing 12.6, a `parallel loop` is specified to a loop, which is already distributed by the XMP loop construct. In the XACC compiler, two directives work together so that loop iterations that are mapped to the node can be parallelized on the accelerator. Without the XMP loop construct, the XACC compiler will try to schedule the entire iteration space for the `parallel loop` construct on the accelerator. It will cause a runtime error on the distributed memory system.

Listing 12.6 XcalableACC example code in C

```
double u[XSIZE][YSIZE], uu[XSIZE][YSIZE];
#pragma xmp nodes p(x, y)
#pragma xmp template t(0:YSIZE-1, 0:XSIZE-1)
#pragma xmp distribute t(block, block) onto p
```

```
#pragma xmp align [j][i] with t(i,j) :: u, uu
#pragma xmp shadow uu[1:1][1:1]
. . .
#pragma acc data copy(u) copyin(uu)
{
   for (k = 0; k < MAX_ITER; k++){
      #pragma xmp loop (y,x) on t(y,x)
      #pragma acc parallel loop collapse(2)
      for (x = 1; x < XSIZE-1; x++)
         for (y = 1; y < YSIZE-1; y++)
            uu[x][y] = u[x][y];

      #pragma xmp reflect (uu) acc

      #pragma xmp loop (y,x) on t(y,x)
      #pragma acc parallel loop collapse(2)
      for(x = 1; x < XSIZE-1; x++)
         for(y = 1; y < YSIZE-1; y++)
            u[x][y] = (uu[x-1][y]+uu[x+1][y]
                       +uu[x][y-1]+uu[x][y+1])/4.0;
   } // end k
} // end data
```

One of the most difficult points in accelerator-based cluster computing is internode communication between accelerators on different nodes via node interconnection. Even if the data are on the accelerator memory, the data should be transferred to host memory so that communication can use the interconnection device connected to the host. If the target platform supports direct communication between accelerators, this data transfer is unnecessary. XACC extends XMP directives so that accelerators can directly communicate with each other. In Listing 12.6, the acc clause is given in reflect directives. This specifies that the shadow element exchange will occur between accelerators.

If the target system provides special hardware features supporting direct communication between accelerators (e.g., GPU direct), the communication will be done on the replicated memory region. If not, the communication will be processed via the host memory, but you should still specify direct communication in the syntax level to improve productivity. The user does not need to care about the hardware feature. All communication directives (such as bcast, reduction, and reflect) can be specified by using the acc clause. Coarray statements are also extended in XACC so that the user can describe one-sided communication within accelerator memory.

Source-to-Source Code Translation

The Omni compiler is a source-to-source compiler. It parses language constructs and translates code at the source level. Figure 12.11 shows the code translation process for data region creation and loop work sharing in XACC.

```
int a[N];
#pragma xmp nodes p(4)
#pragma xmp template t(0:N-1)
#pragma xmp distribute t(block) onto p
#pragma xmp align a[i] with t(i)
 ...
#pragma acc data copy (a)
{
```

```
//
// XMP Global Array is allocated by
// malloc()
//
 ...
int start = ...
int length = ...
#pragma acc data copy (a[start:length])
{
```

```
#pragma xmp loop on t(i)
#pragma acc parallel loop
for(int i=0;i<N;i++){
 ...
```

```
int _XMP_init i, _XMP_cond_i, _XMP_step_i;
// index calculation
#pragma acc parallel loop
for(int i=_XMP_init_i;i<_XMP_cond_i;i+=_XMP_step_i){
```

Figure 12.11 XcalableACC code translation in the Omni compiler

12.2.3 OMNI COMPILER IMPLEMENTATION

Here we explain code transfer and the runtime implementation of XACC in the Omni compiler.

The compiler dynamically allocates a memory region for distributed arrays. In Figure 12.11, for example, `(N/4)*sizeof(int)` bytes will be allocated on each node. As specified in the OpenACC specification, when you are using dynamic memory allocation, you must specify the start index and the length of the array in the `data` construct. Therefore, when you are using a distributed array in the `data` construct, the compiler inserts the start index and the length of the array. For example, the compiler translates `acc data copy(a)` into `acc data copy(a[start:length])`. The `start` and `length` variables are the start index and the length of the distributed array on each node. The compiler also inserts functions to calculate correct values before the `data` construct.

When an XMP `loop` directive and OpenACC `loop` construct is given to the same loop statement, the compiler translates the `loop` statement as specified in the XMP directive. Next, the compiler places the OpenACC directive before the `loop` statement. Figure 12.11 shows the code translation. Note that `_XMP_init_i`, `_XMP_cond_i`, and `_XMP_step_i` are inserted by the compiler for parallel execution among the nodes. Those values are calculated at run time. Along with the `parallel loop` directive, each node calculates its allocated iteration space on the accelerator.

Runtime Implementation

The Omni XMP/XACC runtime library uses MPI for internode communication. CUDA is used to program NVIDIA GPU devices. For better portability, we implement our OpenACC runtime in OpenCL to replace vendor-dependent manycore libraries and languages.[6]

If you are using data transfer among accelerators on distributed systems, data should be copied to the host memory through a PCIe connection (in case of GPUs). To reduce the overhead, some accelerators provide special hardware features. NVIDIA GPUs support GPUDirect. The University of Tsukuba has developed PEACH2[7] based on the PCIe interface to enable direct communication between GPU devices. PEACH2 is used in the HA-PACS/TCA (tightly coupled accelerators) system. Figure 12.12 shows a picture of the HA-PACS system and the PEACH2 interface board.

Figure 12.12 HA-PACS system and PEACH2 network interface board

The Omni XACC runtime is optimized for the HA-PACS/TCA system, which has both GPUDirect over InfiniBand and PEACH2 hardware. It uses the InfiniBand and PEACH2 runtime to improve inter-GPU communication. Figure 12.13 shows the performance of GPUDirect over InfiniBand and PEACH2 on HA-PACS/TCA (PEACH2 provides two communication modes: host and internal). Generally, PEACH provides better latency with small messages. The XACC runtime selects the interconnection according to the size of the data to minimize latency.

---

6. Akihiro Tabuchi, Yasuyuki Kimura, Sunao Torii, Hideo Matsufuru, Tadashi Ishikawa, Taisuke Boku, and Mitsuhisa Sato, "Design and Preliminary Evaluation of Omni OpenACC Compiler for Massive MIMD Processor PEZY-SC," *OpenMP: Memory, Devices, and Tasks: 12th International Workshop on OpenMP, IWOMP* (October 2016): 293–305.
7. https://www.ccs.tsukuba.ac.jp/wp-content/uploads/sites/14/2013/06/01-Taisuke-Boku.pdf.

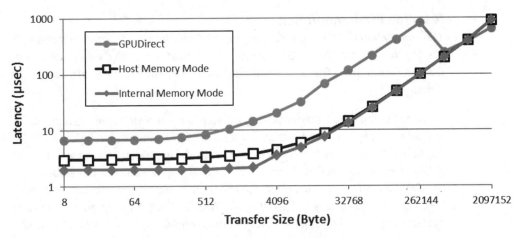

Figure 12.13 Latency of TCA and GPUDirect RDMA over InfiniBand

12.2.4 PERFORMANCE EVALUATION ON HA-PACS

Here, we evaluate two benchmark kernels: the Himeno benchmark[8] and NAS Parallel Benchmarks CG (NPB-CG),[9] written in XACC. The source code was compiled by the Omni XACC compiler. We used the HA-PACS/TCA system from the University of Tsukuba. Table 12.1 shows the evaluation environment.

Table 12.1 HA-PACS/TCA system configuration

ITEM	DESCRIPTION
CPU	Intel Xeon E5 2680v2 2.8GHz (2 sockets)
Accelerator	NVIDIA Tesla K20X, GDDR5 6GB (4 GPUs)
Memory	DDR3 1866MHz (4 channels), 128GB
Network	Mellanox InfiniBand Connect-X3 Dual-port QDR
Compiler	GCC 4.7, CUDA 6.0, Omni XACC (internal development version)
MPI Library	MVAPICH2-GDR 2.0b

Himeno Benchmark

The Himeno benchmark solves the 3D Poisson's equation using the Jacobi iteration method. It is a typical example of stencil computation. We parallelized the serial version of the Himeno kernel using XACC and OpenACC+MPI for our GPU cluster

8. Masahiro Nakao et al., "XcalableACC: Extension of XcalableMP PGAS Language Using OpenACC for Accelerator Clusters," cited earlier.
9. Akihiro Tabuchi, Masahiro Nakao, Hitoshi Murai, Taisuke Boku, and Mitsuhisa Sato. "Implementation and Evaluation of One-sided PGAS Communication in XcalableACC for Accelerated Clusters," *17th IEEE/ACM International Symposium on Cluster, Cloud and Grid Computing (CCGrid 2017)* (Madrid, Spain, May 2017).

system (see Listing 12.7). Because data arrays are distributed among nodes, the XACC runtime updates the distributed memory chunk in the data region at each iteration. Scalar variables such as `gosa` are duplicated on each node. The boundary elements of the arrays are exchanged directly among GPU accelerators at the end of each iteration. To this end, we added the `acc` clause to the `reflect` directive. The runtime switches between GPUDirect over InfiniBand and PEACH2 to minimize communication overhead.

Figure 12.14 shows the performance of the Himeno kernel. In problem sizes S and M using multiple nodes, the performance of XACC using the PEACH2 is as much as 2.7 times as fast as OpenACC+MPI using GPUDirect RDMA over InfiniBand. The performance is faster because the transfer time of boundary elements in the XACC version is smaller than the OpenACC+MPI version, thanks to the lower latency of PEACH2. In problem size L, the performance of XACC is almost the same as OpenACC+MPI, because computation time dominates the total execution time. If we divide only the first dimension in problem size L, the size of the boundary elements is about 520KB, and the latencies for the communication with PEACH2 and GPU-Direct RDMA over InfiniBand are almost the same, as you see in Figure 12.14. In the cases of (4×1×1), (8×1×1), and (16×1×1) with problem size L, the OpenACC+MPI version shows better performance. The reason is that the current implementation of the `reflect` directive requires an MPI barrier after the boundary elements are exchanged (because of the hardware resource limitation of the PEACH2 device). Therefore, the boundary transfer time of XACC is greater than with OpenACC+MPI. When we used a single node in all problem sizes, the performance of XACC is slightly worse than with OpenACC+MPI, because the Omni XACC compiler translates the global memory address among nodes into the local memory address on each node. This address calculation affects the performance of array references.

Listing 12.7 Himeno benchmark in XACC

```
#pragma acc data present(p, bnd, wrk1, wrk2, a, b, c) \
                 create(gosa)
for(n=0 ; n<nn ; ++n){
   gosa = 0.0;
   #pragma acc update device(gosa)

   #pragma xmp loop (k,j,i) on t(k,j,i)
   #pragma acc parallel loop firstprivate(omega) \
                     reduction(+:gosa) \
                     collapse(2) gang vector_length(64) async
   for(i=1 ; i<imax-1 ; ++i)
      for(j=1 ; j<jmax-1 ; ++j)
         #pragma acc loop vector reduction(+:gosa) private(s0, ss)
         for(k=1 ; k<kmax-1 ; ++k){
            s0 = a[0][i][j][k] * p[i+1][j  ][k  ]
               + . . . + wrk1[i][j][k];
```

Listing 12.7 Himeno benchmark in XACC (*continued*)

```
                ss = ( s0 * a[3][i][j][k]
                    p[i][j][k] ) * bnd[i][j][k];
                gosa += ss*ss;
                wrk2[i][j][k] = p[i][j][k] + omega * ss;
            }
#pragma xmp loop (k,j,i) on t(k,j,i)
#pragma acc parallel loop collapse(2) \
                        gang vector_length(64) async
for(i=1 ; i<imax-1 ; ++i)
    for(j=1 ; j<jmax-1 ; ++j)
        #pragma acc loop vector
        for(k=1 ; k<kmax-1 ; ++k)
            p[i][j][k] = wrk2[i][j][k];

#pragma acc wait
#pragma xmp reflect_do (p) acc
#pragma acc update host (gosa)
#pragma xmp reduction(+:gosa)
} /* end n loop */
```

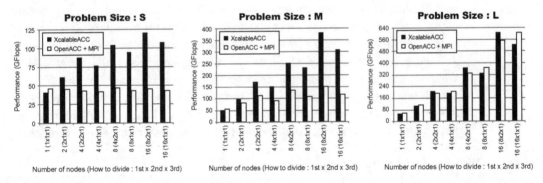

Figure 12.14 Performance of the Himeno kernel

NAS Parallel Benchmarks CG

The NPB-CG kernel finds the smallest eigenvalue of a large sparse symmetric positive-definite matrix by using the conjugate gradient method. Listing 12.8 shows the NPB-CG kernel code written in XACC. The hot spot of NPB-CG is matrix-vector multiplication. The matrix is stored in compressed sparse row (CRS) format, which makes vector access irregular. Because vector p is distributed among GPUs, the elements of the vectors should be collected before the matrix-vector multiplication by using interdevice communication.

Listing 12.9 shows the communication code used for the NPB-CG kernel. We describe the communication in two ways. The first way is to use directives in the global view model, wherein the vectors are distributed by using XMP/XACC directives. The interdevice communication is specified by the `reduction` and `gmove` directives. Therefore, all of the elements are collected on each node. Note that these directives have the `acc` clause. The compiler generates inter-GPU communication for the data exchange.

The second way of communication is to use coarrays in the local view model. In that case, vectors are declared as coarrays. The communication is described as a reference to the co-dimension. First, the coarrays are declared on the host memory. Then its memory images are duplicated by using the `acc declare` directive. Because the `use_device` clause is given for the `host_data` region, coarrays `w` and `q` are manipulated on the GPU memory.

Figure 12.15 shows the performance of NPB-CG in XACC and OpenACC+MPI. We used the problem size class C (the matrix size is 750,000×750,000) and class D (the matrix size is 1,500,000×1,500,000) for the evaluation.

The performance of the XACC local view version (XACC-L) is more than 97 percent of the OpenACC+MPI `send/recv` version (MPI+ACC (s/r)) for class C, and 99 percent for class D. Even though performance is degraded on more processes for class C, the performance is almost the same with the OpenACC+MPI `get` version (MPI+ACC (get)), which uses a similar communication mechanism.

Listing 12.8 NAS parallel benchmarks CG in XACC (computation)

```
#pragma acc data pcopyin(colidx[0:nz], rowstr[0:size_rowstr], \
                         a[0:nz])  pcopyin(w, q, r, p, x, z)
for( it = 1; it <= 1; it++){
   conj_grad( colidx, ...);
}


void conj_grad(int colidx[restrict], . . .) {
   #pragma xmp loop on t(*,j)
   #pragma acc parallel loop gang pcopy(a[0:nz], p[0:size_x], \
                      colidx[0:nz], rowstr[0:size_rowstr], \
                      w[0:size_x])
   for(int j=0; j < na; j++){
      double sum = 0.0;
      int rowstr_j = rowstr[j];
      int rowstr_j1 = rowstr[j+1];
      #pragma acc loop vector reduction(+:sum)
      for(int k=rowstr_j; k < rowstr_j1; k++){
         sum = sum + a[k]*p[colidx[k]];
      }
      w[j] = sum;
}
```

Listing 12.9 NAS parallel benchmarks CG in XACC (communication)

```
// Global view
/* array reduction */
#pragma xmp reduction(+:w) on subproc(:) acc
/* column-distributed array <- row-distributed array */
#pragma xmp gmove acc
q[:] = w[:];

// Local View
double w[na/num_proc_rows+2]:[*];
double q[na/num_proc_rows+2]:[*];
#pragma acc declare create(w,q)
#pragma acc host_data use_device(w, q)
{
    /* array reduction */
    for(i = l2npcols; i >= 1; i--){
        int image = reduce_exch_proc[i-1] + 1;
        int start = reduce_recv_starts[i-1] - 1;
        int length = reduce_recv_lengths[i-1];
        xmp_sync_image(image, NULL);
        q[start:length] = w[start:length]:[image];
        xmp_sync_image(image, NULL);
        #pragma acc parallel loop
        for(j = send_start-1; j < send_start+lengths-1; j++)
            w[j] = w[j] + q[j];
    }
    /* column-distributed array <- row-distributed array */
    if( l2npcols != 0 ) {
        xmp_sync_image(exch_proc+1, NULL);
        q[0:send_len] = w[send_start-1:send_len]:[exch_proc+1];
        xmp_sync_image(exch_proc+1, NULL);
    }else{
        #pragma acc parallel loop
        for(j=0; j < exch_recv_length; j++)
            q[j] = w[j];
    }
}
```

On the other hand, the XACC global view version (XACC-G) shows lower performance than XACC-L in all cases. One reason is the increased time taken by array reductions to collect vector elements. The array reduction in XACC uses the `MPI_Allreduce()` function. Because MVAPICH2 supports GPUDirect, some MPI functions (such as `MPI_Isend/Recv()` and `MPI_Get()`) that are used in XACC-L and MPI+ACC (s/r) work on the GPU memory. However, the current MVAPICH2 implementation uses host memory buffers to calculate array reduction in `MPI_Allreduce()`. The data transfer time between the GPU device and the host, along with the reduction calculation on the host, lowers performance. The second reason is the increased number of elements exchanged in the communication. Whereas XACC-G collects all elements in vectors, the XACC-L and OpenACC+MPI versions collect the minimum number of elements required for the matrix-vector multiplication. This makes the communication size different on the 2×4 and 4×8 node divisions.

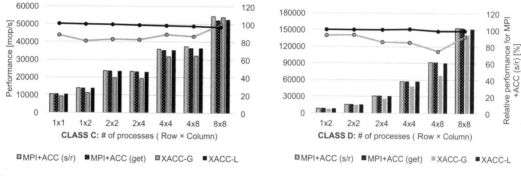

Figure 12.15 Performance of the NPB-CG kernel

12.2.5 SUMMARY

XMP provides an easy and efficient way to exploit parallelism on distributed memory systems, thanks to its directive-based programming model. XACC extends XMP to mix OpenACC and XMP directives. To optimize performance, you can use coarrays on accelerators. The performance evaluation shows that XACC can achieve equivalent performance to the OpenACC+MPI version with small changes from the serial version.

Index

Register Your Product at informit.com/register

Access additional benefits and **save 35%** on your next purchase

- Automatically receive a coupon for 35% off your next purchase, valid for 30 days. Look for your code in your InformIT cart or the Manage Codes section of your account page.
- Download available product updates.
- Access bonus material if available.
- Check the box to hear from us and receive exclusive offers on new editions and related products.

InformIT.com—The Trusted Technology Learning Source

InformIT is the online home of information technology brands at Pearson, the world's foremost education company. At InformIT.com, you can:

- Shop our books, eBooks, software, and video training
- Take advantage of our special offers and promotions (informit.com/promotions)
- Sign up for special offers and content newsletter (informit.com/newsletters)
- Access thousands of free chapters and video lessons

Connect with InformIT—Visit informit.com/community

the trusted technology learning source

Addison-Wesley · Adobe Press · Cisco Press · Microsoft Press · Pearson IT Certification · Prentice Hall · Que · Sams · Peachpit Press

 Pearson